Writing for Broadcast Journalists

...ality ...ngages the reader from ... and the experience and insight of the author occasion-...ly make it difficult to put down, a rare feature of a textbook. I would unreservedly recommend this book not only to those studying journalism, but to students of language and all who use the spoken and written word as the "materials" of their work.'

Barry Turner, *Senior Lecturer, Nottingham Trent University and University of Lincoln*

'Rick Thompson's guidance manual is packed with advice to would-be writers for this medium. He's someone with years of experience at the top level of the national and international profession, and he's smack up to date with his references. The book is aimed at journalists, but anyone with a serious interest in developing their literacy will learn a lot about professional writing skills from what he has to say.'

Roy Johnson, *www.mantex.co.uk*

Writing for Broadcast Journalists guides readers through the significant differences between the written and the spoken versions of journalistic English. It will help broadcast journalists at every stage of their careers to avoid such pitfalls as the use of newspaper-English, common linguistic errors, and Americanised phrases, and gives practical advice on accurate terminology and pronunciation, while encouraging writers to capture the immediacy of the spoken word in their scripts.

Written in a lively and accessible style by an experienced BBC TV and radio editor, *Writing for Broadcast Journalists* is the authoritative guide to the techniques of writing for radio and television. This new edition has a special section about writing online news.

Writing for Broadcast Journalists includes:

- practical tips on how to avoid 'journalese', clichés and jargon
- guidance on tailoring your writing style to suit a particular audience
- advice on converting agency copy into spoken English
- writing to television pictures
- examples of scripts from some of the best in the business
- an appendix of 'dangerous' words and phrases to be avoided in scripts.

Rick Thompson has held senior editorial positions with BBC News at the regional, national and international levels in television and radio. He now trains journalists in central and eastern Europe, and is the Visiting Professor of Broadcast Journalism at Birmingham City University.

Media Skills

SERIES EDITOR: RICHARD KEEBLE, LINCOLN UNIVERSITY

The *Media Skills* series provides a concise and thorough introduction to a rapidly changing media landscape. Each book is written by media and journalism lecturers or experienced professionals and is a key resource for a particular industry. Offering helpful advice and information and using practical examples from print, broadcast and digital media, as well as discussing ethical and regulatory issues, *Media Skills* books are essential guides for students and media professionals.

Also in this series:

English for Journalists, 3rd edition
Wynford Hicks

Writing for Journalists, 2nd edition
Wynford Hicks with Sally Adams, Harriett Gilbert and Tim Holmes

Interviewing for Radio
Jim Beaman

Ethics for Journalists, 2nd edition
Richard Keeble

Interviewing for Journalists, 2nd edition
Sally Adams, with Wynford Hicks

Researching for Television and Radio
Adèle Emm

Reporting for Journalists, 2nd edition
Chris Frost

Subediting for Journalists
Wynford Hicks and Tim Holmes

Designing for Newspapers and Magazines
Chris Frost

Writing for Broadcast Journalists, 2nd edition
Rick Thompson

Freelancing For Television and Radio
Leslie Mitchell

Programme Making for Radio
Jim Beaman

Magazine Production
Jason Whittaker

Production Management for Television
Leslie Mitchell

Feature Writing for Journalists
Sharon Wheeler

Writing for
Broadcast Journalists

SECOND EDITION

Rick Thompson

Routledge
Taylor & Francis Group

LONDON AND NEW YORK

First edition published 2005

This edition published 2010
by Routledge
2 Park Square, Milton Park, Abingdon, OX14 4RN

Simultaneously published in the USA and Canada
by Routledge
270 Madison Ave, New York, NY 10016

Routledge is an imprint of the Taylor & Francis Group, an informa business

© 2005, 2010 Rick Thompson

Typeset in Goudy and ScalaSans by
Florence Production Ltd, Stoodleigh, Devon
Printed and bound in Great Britain by
TJ International Ltd, Padstow, Cornwall

British Library Cataloguing in Publication Data
A catalogue record for this book is available from the British Library

Library of Congress Cataloging in Publication Data
Thompson, Rick, 1947–.
Writing for broadcast journalists/Rick Thompson. – 2nd ed.
        p. cm. – (Media skills)
    Includes bibliographical references and index.
    1. Broadcast journalism – Authorship.   2. Reporters and reporting.
    3. Report writing   I. Title.
    PN4784.B75T48 2010
    808′.06607 – dc22   2010010737

ISBN 13: 978-0-415-58167-7 (hbk)
ISBN 13: 978-0-415-58168-4 (pbk)
ISBN 13: 978-0-203-84577-6 (ebk)

Contents

Acknowledgements

I would like to thank all the journalists whose broadcast scripts or written articles have been used as examples and illustrations of the points made in this book, the various authors of the in-house style guides quoted, and my colleagues in the Broadcast Journalism Department at Birmingham City University for their comments and encouragement.

In particular I would like to express appreciation to those senior practitioners of broadcast news who agreed to be interviewed specifically for this Media Skills guide. Their comments and suggestions have produced an impressive body of advice on the language of broadcast journalism from some of the best in the profession. They include:

The late Brian Barron, for forty years a BBC Foreign Correspondent

Anita Bhalla, former Correspondent and Head of Political and Community Affairs, BBC English Regions

Karen Coleman, former BBC Correspondent, then Presenter and Foreign Editor at Newstalk 106, Dublin

Lyse Doucet, Correspondent and Presenter for BBC World Service radio and World News television

Julie Etchingham, Presenter and Correspondent, Sky News

Steve Herrmann, Editor, BBC News Online

Blair Jenkins, Chair of the Scottish Broadcasting Commission

Bob Jobbins, former Director of News and Current Affairs, BBC World Service and a former foreign correspondent

Rob Kirk, Editorial Development Manager, Sky News

Aminda Leigh, former reporter and BBC local radio News Editor, now an independent website editor

Maxine Mawhinney, presenter, BBC News Channel and BBC World News

Ian Masters, former Controller of Broadcasting at the Thomson Foundation

Clare Morrow, former radio correspondent and Controller of Broadcasting, Yorkshire Television

Sir David Nicholas, former Chairman and Editor in Chief, ITN

Tim Orchard, former Controller, BBC News 24

Richard Sambrook, former Director of the BBC World Service and Director of BBC Global News

Mike Smartt, the first Editor-in-Chief, BBC Online

I am grateful to the authors of previous internal style guides whose work has been used as reference:

Tom Fort, the BBC's *A Pocket Guide to Radio Newswriting*

Sue Owen, *The Heart FM Quick and Dirty Style Guide*

Vin Ray, *The Reporter's Friend* for BBC TV News

The various authors of *The World Service News Programmes Style Guide*

And in particular, the late Peter Elliott, BBC Television News Senior Duty Editor, author of the internal booklet called *A Question of Style*, and an inspiration to many broadcast journalists, including this one.

Thanks are also due to those who helped to find useful examples, check the draft and format the material.

Birth Fox, former secretary, BBC Birmingham

Paul John, Assistant Managing Editor, BBC TV News

Roy Saatchi, Hon. Professor of Broadcast Journalism, John Moores University and Hon. Fellow, Salford University

Gill Thompson, T-Media

Adrian Wells, Foreign Editor, Sky News

1
Introduction

Polonius: 'What do you read my lord?'
Hamlet: 'Words, words, words.'
      (William Shakespeare, *Hamlet*, II.2)

An English style, familiar but not coarse, and elegant but not ostentatious.
      (Dr Samuel Johnson, *Lives of the English Poets*: Addison)

WHAT THIS BOOK COVERS

This is a book about words, words that are usually spoken aloud and received into the brain via the ear, rather than the eye. Specifically, it is about the language and style of broadcast news. It is designed to help journalists working in radio and television to write scripts that will be clear, concise, accurate and elegant. This new edition also has an extended section on writing for online news sites, because many broadcast journalists must do this routinely as the electronic media converge.

There are an estimated ten thousand broadcast journalists working in Britain, with about thirty thousand more studying media or journalism at any one time. Overseas, there are countless thousands more writing in the English language. I have yet to meet one who admits to being a poor writer. But inaccuracies, confusing usage and newspaper-style journalese can be heard on the airwaves every day.

All journalists in broadcasting should aspire to be among the best in their chosen profession, not merely to be competent enough to hold down a job. In any medium, it is impossible to be a great journalist without being a very good writer. So I hope this book will stimulate younger broadcast journalists to become more familiar with the English language, and encourage established reporters and news producers to reassess their own writing style. It should help them to write scripts with more ambition, and I hope it will encourage them to love the language, and enjoy the process of writing.

WHAT THIS BOOK DOES NOT COVER

This book is not about writing for newspapers or magazines, a technique completely different from writing for broadcasting. Nor does it attempt to deal with TV, radio or online production. Many other books and guides cover in detail the various ways news or documentary programmes are planned and assembled, including research, ethics, interviewing techniques, editing sound and pictures, studio design, and the technical aspects of broadcasting such as camerawork, sound recording, satellite newsgathering or studio transmission. For example, other books by Routledge include *Researching for Television and Radio*, *Production Management for Television*, *The Television Handbook*, *The Radio Handbook*, and *Producing for Web 2.0*.

THE APPROACH

Of course, there is no universal writing style. The approach of this book is to recognise the paradox that many writers like to have a set of rules, yet the best writers are individualists, even innovators. Clearly there are generally accepted standards of English. Without a firm footing in those standards, it is much more difficult for a journalist to develop an individual voice that is liked and admired. Clichéd writing is a product of clichéd thinking. So this book tries to give many examples of usages or phrases best avoided. It also gives examples of good technique, but recognises that truly creative writing cannot be copied or even taught.

Style is subjective. In this book, if I wish to express a personal dislike or preference, I try to make it clear that this is my own view. You can judge for yourself whether or not you agree. But I have also included many comments and suggestions taken from interviews with leading professionals with many years' experience, and have referred to in-house style guides from different news organisations (see Further reading). These include the first BBC TV news style book, *A Question of Style*, written in the '70s by the late Peter Elliot; the later *BBC News Styleguide*, compiled by John Allen in 2003; the BBC's internal World Service Radio Guide; and the section on broadcast skills on the BBC College of Journalism website, which became publicly accessible in 2009, as well as house-style booklets from independent radio and television. There are also references to long-established guides to print journalism. So this book is a distillation of the experience and ideas of many others. A key theme is that writers should know precisely what they are doing, using language deliberately and carefully rather than casually and thoughtlessly.

Many of the examples used to illustrate the main points come from BBC News. There are several reasons for this. First, the British Broadcasting Corporation is widely recognised as the benchmark for spoken English. For nearly 90 years, it has developed, studied, considered and debated the best way to write factual scripts for broadcast, and has set a standard of writing practice in the industry. Secondly, with nine TV channels, two of them offering continuous news, about sixty national and local radio stations, the World Service radio network and its big online site, the BBC produces far more electronic and broadcast news than anyone else in Britain, indeed it claims to produce more than any other broadcaster in the world. A third reason is that, during the many years when I worked in the BBC, I was able to collect examples and ideas from the corporation's news programmes. Of course, there are many fine writers working for commercial broadcasting companies, and examples and opinions from independent radio and television news are also included in this book.

The concept of 'BBC English' is not fixed in stone, and the language of newsreaders may seem remote or antiquated to many people who live in the diverse communities of Britain and the English-speaking world. *Writing for Broadcast Journalists* recognises the dynamic nature of the spoken word, and the growing number of different voices on the airwaves. In the age of twittering, blogging and bite-sized news on the move, it tries to give sensible advice to balance the preferences of traditionalists with the rapidly changing usages of younger generations.

2

Good spoken English

The most thorough knowledge of human nature, the happiest delin-
eation of its varieties, the liveliest effusions of wit and humour, are
conveyed to the world in the best chosen language.

(Jane Austen, *Northanger Abbey*)

ARE STANDARDS SLIPPING?

There is a vigorous debate in progress about the standards of English. It is
taking place in the educational establishments, literary and academic circles,
the Palace of Westminster and the columns of almost every national and
regional newspaper. Most commentators attribute the perceived decline in
standards to a less formal English curriculum in schools, reflecting less
formality in society at large. Others blame television. This is not a new subject
of debate.

> Outspoken Prince Charles sparked a storm last night after he blasted
> schools for teaching English bloody badly.
>
> (*Sun*, June 1989)

The Prince of Wales's widely reported contribution indicated a concern
among traditionalists that has grown over the years. In August 2003, David
Hargreaves, a former head of the Qualifications and Curriculum Development
Agency, the body then overseeing exam standards, expressed concern that
children are not being taught to write properly. 'There should be more tradi-
tional grammar and spelling and we should penalise work when it is wrong.
We have to accept that there is a major problem with students writing well'.
(I think he meant 'with students *not* writing well'.)

In the same year, the eminent English scholar Lord Quirk, a former British
Academy president advising the Specialist Schools Trust, deplored the fact
that so few students are now required to read classic literature. 'We are in an

alarming downward spiral towards a culture that values only the contemporary'. He has urged the British people 'to regain pride in using English properly'.

In 2010 The Director of Corporate Affairs at Tesco, Lucy Neville-Rolf, complained bitterly that many of the school-leavers and graduates joining the company 'can't write', and that 'exams are getting easier', a view echoed by Sir Stuart Rose, the Chairman of Marks and Spencer, who said millions of school-leavers are unfit for work because 'They cannot do reading. They cannot do arithmetic. They cannot do writing.'

And if Britain's head teachers are to be believed, many pre-school children are now failing to develop speaking skills during the crucial early learning years. In a survey in England and Wales conducted by the National Literacy Trust and the National Association of Head Teachers in 2002, three out of four respondents said they were concerned about the lack of language ability among three-year-olds. Most blamed the length of time these young children spent in front of a TV screen rather than talking to other members of the family. The trust promptly launched a £2 million campaign to persuade parents to talk and read more to their pre-school children. A year later there had not been much perceived impact. In August 2003, the Chief Inspector of Schools, David Bell, spoke about what he called the lack of basic communication and behavioural skills in some children starting school. 'I am shocked that some 5-year-olds can't even speak properly.' A few months later, the new Primary School National Strategy was announced. It included the requirement that children in their first year at school across England and Wales would be given lessons in speaking skills, a move described by the Department for Education and Skills as the world's first national drive to improve oral communication. In 2007, Communication, Language and Literacy for the under-fives became part of the National Strategy of the Department for Children, Schools and Families.

In the world of literature, too, there is shaking of heads, bafflement and even dismay in some quarters. In his youth, the novelist Martin Amis was regarded by contemporaries as a voice for his generation and something of an innovator in style. But his writing was also widely admired by traditionalists. More recently, he has been regarded as in danger of becoming anachronistic. In his critique on Amis's novel published in 2003, the *Independent* newspaper's columnist, John Walsh, himself a very fine writer, put it this way:

> You might say it's not a crime to write badly, not necessarily a sign of moral bankruptcy. But Oscar Wilde would not agree and nor, I think, would Amis. No writer venerates the creative process more than he, the working of thoughts into prose. And that's one reason why he's parted company with the new literary universe. The generation now in the ascendant – the Zadie Smith generation – don't venerate language in

the same way. They venerate storytelling, personal testimony, plausible characters, understandable endings.

This clearly has a resonance for journalists. 'Storytelling and personal testimony' is our stock-in-trade. So should we be at all concerned that knowledge of grammar, vocabulary and classical models seems to be in decline? And what does this have to do with writing news bulletins?

Standards in broadcast news

Certainly, the use of English is a regular topic of conversation in broadcast newsrooms in Britain. Many senior editors can be heard to bemoan the lack of 'basic standards'. It is not a new concern. For many years, local and regional broadcasters in particular have been accused of accepting standards of scriptwriting that are lower than the general standards in national news and current affairs. In the late '80s, the judges of the Royal Television Society's regional journalism awards declared that they had found 'too much sloppy writing and journalese' in some news magazines. A BBC Local Radio News Editors' Conference in 1990 commissioned a study into the use of language in news bulletins, which concluded, 'There's growing concern that deterioration is creeping in . . . imprecision, Americanisms and newspaper-style writing are too common.' That concern persists into the twenty-first century.

Many experienced broadcasting editors and correspondents have been interviewed for this book. Among the older generation of editors, those recently retired from active service, for example, there seems to be no doubt about declining standards in the use of the language. Sir David Nicholas CBE was the Editor in Chief and Chairman of ITN during its golden years throughout the '70s and '80s, when *News at Ten* was widely regarded as the sharpest and most authoritative news programme on British television.

> I think standards are falling. When you have bad grammar it's like a cracked bell. I'm amazed that some of the loftiest people in the land can produce an ungrammatical sentence . . . The first thing in any writing is to have good English – the basic standards of good grammar. I find that in broadcast news, and in most types of television in Britain these days, there is some appalling, bad grammar! I remember one ITN correspondent said to me once – 'Hey boss, I'd rather go into a combat zone than split an infinitive when you are listening.'

But it's not that simple. Most senior editors, Sir David included, recognise that English usage does not stand still. Bob Jobbins OBE, who for many years was in charge of news and current affairs at the BBC World Service, puts it like this.

Nowadays, people place less emphasis on the prescriptive elements of grammar and the education system. It is quite shocking that young people leave universities with only a flimsy understanding of elementary grammar. On the other hand, the measure I would use to judge the standards of writing are things like imagination, and the ability to surprise and entertain. In that area, I think the writing has got better. If you listen to old bulletins broadcast 20 or 30 years ago, what strikes you is not how well-written they were, but how dull and predictable they were – how unadventurous they were.

Tim Orchard, a leading programme editor at BBC TV News throughout the '80s and '90s, believes that many young people aspiring to be journalists do not know the rules of English very well.

I detect a decline in standards in the use of English. There is so much American media. These phrases wing their way across the Atlantic and soon become common parlance here. But language can't be static. You have got to evolve with it.

Also interviewed for this book was Clare Morrow, who during the same period was Controller of Programmes at ITV's Yorkshire Television, supervising the channel's news and current affairs output. She thinks there is more formulaic and predictable writing these days.

I'm not sure that standards have fallen exactly. But there's now a long-established convention that says – This is the way you do X and this is the way you do Y. That's lazy and sloppy writing. With so many more media outlets, when people can watch news everywhere, we can see a million not-very-good reporters on our screens. There are so many more jobs! There's bound to be less quality than when there were only a few TV reporting jobs. Now there are lots of people who are mediocre. The people who stand out are those who don't write in predictable phrases, and who think carefully about their stories. They make every word count, and they do something slightly different.

I agree with this analysis. There are many brilliant writers working in radio and TV journalism today, who have managed to shake off their inheritance of the stilted and formal broadcasting language of the immediate post-war period without abandoning good grammar. They deploy a wide range of vocabulary with a sensitivity to meaning, cadence and rhythm, which makes them great communicators.

Unfortunately, there are many more who do not achieve this standard. Employed in broadcasting today are hundreds of journalists who are murdering the language. Too many writers are content to deploy sterile phrases and tedious clichés. Blatant inaccuracies are endemic on the airwaves. I hope that readers of this book will be inspired to use English knowingly, correctly and, above all, creatively.

The pressures on broadcast journalists

It is hardly surprising that standards of writing for broadcast seem to be so variable. The pressures on journalists working in the electronic and broadcast media have never been greater. The digital revolution is bringing more and more radio stations and TV channels, all competing for a slice of the audience, and in commercial broadcasting a slice of the advertising revenues. Every year seems to bring further budget cuts and the need for greater productivity. And digital technology has expanded the number of 24-hour news channels. As a member of the team that launched the BBC's first continuous TV news and information channel, BBC World, I remember well the frantic efforts required to keep up the relentless flow of information. It is very different from producing a half-hour flagship news programme on a general channel, where every word is weighed and discussed.

Computer-based technology also allows more multi-skilling. Many BBC journalists are now expected to file their stories for a range of outlets on radio and television; most edit their own radio features; some edit their own TV pictures. Some have been trained to use lightweight cameras, to shoot as well as edit their own TV pictures. ITV regional newsrooms are also deploying more and more of these video-journalists (VJs). And many journalists are now required to provide a version of their story for their station website as soon as it has been broadcast. 'Versioning' is one of the buzzwords of modern multi-media journalism.

There are particular pressures in regional television and local radio, where many graduate entrants or recruits from local newspapers learn their broadcasting skills. Local journalists are often under greater time pressure than their counterparts working for national or international programmes. Each journalist in a local or regional newsroom writes many stories in a day, and seldom has spare moments to redraft, revise or remould a script. There's also a high proportion of young, less-experienced journalists, who have yet to develop a good writing style. And there's less time for analysis and criticism of the output than in national newsrooms, where a reporter or producer is much more likely to be 'roasted' by the editor for using a word out of place.

On the other hand, the desktop or laptop computer with a fast broadband connection has put an amazing research tool at the journalist's fingertips. We can all gather information much more easily, check background facts, and access pictures and sound without having to run up and down stairs all day. We can alter phrases and move whole sentences around as we write, in a way that would have seemed miraculous in the days of the typewriter. We can even allow the computer to correct our spelling for us. So the pressure to produce more news more quickly is partly ameliorated by access to better tools for the job. And pressure is what makes journalism challenging and exciting. As Bob Jobbins of the BBC World Service said, 'If writing were easy, it wouldn't be so much fun.'

WHICH MODEL OF THE SPOKEN WORD?

The currency of broadcasting is the spoken word. But which version of the spoken word is correct? The quest for an authoritative version of the English language goes back hundreds of years, yet the debate about linguistic correctness is as lively today as it has ever been. Before we plunge into the techniques of writing, it is worth reflecting briefly on the evolution of the English language, its continuing growth as the dominant world language, and the special role played in that development by broadcast journalism.

Very many listeners and viewers feel that they know right from wrong in the meaning of words, the use of grammar and punctuation, and the pronunciation of English. In Britain, there is a powerful sense of tradition that is reflected in its political and legal institutions, its architecture and its tourist industry. This sense of continuity is also apparent in attitudes towards our language. Many commentators and writers of newspaper columns assume there is a purity to the language that should be preserved, and that if we don't adhere strictly to the rules, chaos will envelop us! We certainly shouldn't mess around with the language.

In the USA, there seems to be a different view. Language is an instrument on which you can play your own tunes. Inventiveness and individuality are celebrated. So language is used much more flexibly. In America, new words are being invented all the time, and the English language offers countless possibilities for original expression and experiment (sorry, experimentation). In Britain, this attitude is heartily disliked. Correctness is respected. But who decides what is correct?

The Queen's English

One of the reasons for the rise of English as a global language is its unique mix of European source-languages. Celtic, Latin, Anglo-Saxon, Norse, Norman-French, all went into the melting-pot. In the Middle Ages, there were countless dialects. The language of the ruling classes was completely different from those of its subjects. Courtly English was certainly not the national model. (Even today, the English of the Royal Family has a rather peculiar accent, far removed from the everyday speech of the Queen's subjects.) And, of course, language is political. Language is power. Control communication, and you control everything.

In modern times, spin-doctors work behind the scenes to make a good living from this principle. But in the past, the political nature of language was clear to everyone, and for centuries, politics went hand-in-hand with religion.

In his ITV programme *The Adventure of English* in 2002, Melvyn Bragg pointed out that the late medieval period, when modern English was evolving, was a strongly religious time. Attending Catholic church was compulsory for many years. But the priests stood between the people and their God, retaining absolute authority in the process. Only the clergy were allowed to read the word of God – in Latin – and they did so silently. A bell rang to tell the congregation that the priest had reached a significant passage. This clearly produced feelings of frustration among many ordinary Christians.

In 1376, the York Mystery Plays began to enact Biblical stories to popular audiences, and the performances were in English. Around the same time, John Wycliffe was promoting the idea of an English Bible. The church responded by pushing a law through Parliament banning all English bibles, and authorising the arrest of all 'lollards' who toured the country preaching in English. In 1414, long after Wycliffe's death, the Catholic Church felt so threatened by the call for worship in English that it declared him a heretic, dug up his body, and scattered it in the River Avon.

But less than a year later, Henry V was sending letters home from the Agincourt campaign in France, and they were written in English. They were clearly intended to be sent around the country and read aloud in market squares – the first broadcast-news war reports! When Henry had returned from France, he wished to continue these regular newsletters to the people. But which version of English was correct? There were hundreds of dialects and a host of different spellings. He established the 'Chancellry' to produce official and legal documents with uniform spellings and definitions.

The process of standardising English took another leap forward later that century with Caxton's printing press. He complained, 'These days, each man will utter his communication in ways that diverse others will not understand!' He needed a standard, and many of the spellings he chose remain in use today. In the early sixteenth century, the English language Bible finally arrived, courtesy of the remarkable William Tyndale, who translated it from the original Hebrew and Greek, though he had to emigrate and live in Cologne to avoid persecution by the English church, which had convicted him of heresy.

Standardising English

It was Henry VIII's rift with Rome which gave a huge boost to the English language. He ordered that an English Bible be placed in every parish church in the land, in a dramatic reversal of the Catholic Church's policy to deny open access to the word of the Lord. By the end of the sixteenth century, there were many competing versions of the Bible in English. The King James Bible of 1611, largely based on Tyndale's original translation, was the first truly authoritative version of our language. Melvyn Bragg points out that although it was written in a deliberately archaic style, it was written to be read aloud by the clergy. It has rhythm, cadence and poetry. And writers of broadcast news should note that it has short phrases. 'In the beginning was the Word, and the Word was with God, and the Word was God.' So, with most of the population illiterate, the first national model of the English language was written to be heard rather than read.

English still had countless versions and spellings, and in the mid-eighteenth century Dr Samuel Johnson embarked on his great work – his *Dictionary of the English Language*. He hoped it would standardise usage, regularise spelling, define meanings, avoid confusion, and enable the nation to communicate with clarity and certainty. It took him sixteen years. On publication, he found it necessary in his preface to point out that he had found it impossible to fix usage with rules. 'Language is too volatile for legal restraint.' It is almost a confession that he had been wasting his time, because language changes all the time, and no book can stop it.

This notion did not deter the Victorians. With absolute confidence, built no doubt on Britain's extraordinary industrial and military power, they turned to classical models for art, architecture and music, and for language. Books of grammar based on Latin were taught in all schools. My own 'baby-boomer' generation of post-war children were still using school books based on these imposed theories of English. We were told that 'compared with' is correct; 'compared to' is wrong. 'Different from' is correct; 'different to' is wrong, etc. And if the letters to the *Daily Telegraph* from 'Disgusted of Tunbridge Wells' are an indicator, most people of my generation and that of my parents believe these assertions with absolute conviction. The consistency of usage produced by these rules is still the bedrock of modern English. People who had experienced this classical style of English education were the first broadcasters. In Britain and around the world, that meant the voice of BBC Radio.

BBC ENGLISH AND BROADCAST NEWS ENGLISH

As soon as the British Broadcasting Company (later the Corporation) was founded in the 1920s, the notion of 'BBC English' took root. Suddenly there was a national model of the spoken word. It must have had a great impact. Into people's homes across the country, from Aberdeen to Aberystwyth and from Belfast to Brighton, came an educated and authoritative voice, almost as though the Word was coming from the heavens. But these words were coming from London. The speakers were overwhelmingly upper-middle-class, male, mainly public-school-educated, and they came largely from the London area.

The potential impact and influence of BBC Radio on a language that had always been fragmented into regional accents and dialects was soon realised by these broadcasting pioneers. In 1926, a BBC Advisory Committee on Spoken English was established, chaired first by the Poet Laureate Robert Bridges, and then by George Bernard Shaw. The rigid rulings of the Old Etonians on that committee are thankfully things of the past. But many people still regard the BBC as the authority for Good Spoken English, particularly in its news and current affairs output. Every year, hundreds of letters and emails arrive at the corporation's national and regional offices, complaining about sloppy or inaccurate language on the airwaves. In 1979, the language expert Lord Quirk wrote in the *Observer* about the standards of English on BBC Radio.

> No other organisation has such an opportunity or, I believe, such a respon-
> sibility to present a conscious first-rate model of present-day English;
> precise phrasing, well-chosen words, soundly-constructed sentences.

Thirty years later, in 2009, a group of seven Members of Parliament called on the BBC to appoint an 'English Language Standards Tsar', who would sit in Broadcasting House and, by some mysterious process, ensure that all the corporation's factual output would conform to 'correct grammar and usage'. Thankfully this proposition was ignored, and in some quarters ridiculed. But it shows that there is still a view in parts of the establishment that BBC News should be the standard-bearer for spoken English.

Received pronunciation (RP), the widely accepted model of the spoken word, which is relatively classless and, though rooted south of the Trent, is fairly neutral geographically, is, in my view, a product of BBC English. But it is now universal – a voice of the establishment certainly, used by many politicians and lawyers – but also the language of the platform speech to shareholders, or the boardroom presentation. Received pronunciation is by no means the BBC's exclusive preserve.

Nowadays, I believe 'BBC English' has been replaced as an unconscious model by 'Broadcast News English'. It is evidently true that the main British commercial TV channels and the national independent radio stations deliver news with an accent and style very similar to those of the BBC. In a 1994 article marking a Conservative government initiative to improve the teaching of English, the veteran author Anthony Burgess wrote, '... there is nobody to tell us where true English is to be found ... but to most people, *good English* means the language of television newsreaders'. *Guardian* journalist John Mullan believes that BBC English still has a special authority:

> BBC English is often spoken of in jest, as if it were some figment of the '50s. But the official parlance of the Corporation still does have its influence. The use of a word or phrase in, say, a news bulletin can signify its acceptance into standard English.

When he was appointed Director of BBC News, I asked Richard Sambrook whether he welcomed being the arbiter of correct usage.

> Being a guardian of the language is not a responsibility that I want to take upon my shoulders, to be frank with you. I do believe it's right that the BBC should set some standards in the use of English, while being very sensitive to the range of modern usage, the need to be colloquial, and the need to be a part of the audience's world, not remote from it. We have to have good standards. But I do not think it is right for the BBC to carry that responsibility alone.

English as a global language

Overseas, it seems clear that the BBC is still regarded as the model of spoken English. I have conducted journalism training courses in many countries, and everywhere I go, media students and professional journalists say they listen to BBC World Service radio, or watch BBC World News, to help them to learn English, as much as to enjoy the programmes or gain access to independent journalism. Globalisation has brought an unprecedented need for people from many different countries to be able to communicate effectively with one another. For various reasons, English has become the dominant global language.

According to the *Ethnologue* language survey, more than 800 million people speak English as their first language. Almost certainly more people speak Mandarin, but as a second language for international dialogue, English is unrivalled. In an article in the *Sunday Times* in October 2003, the broadcaster Melvyn Bragg wrote, 'English is understood by an estimated 2 billion people. It is the language of international finance, diplomacy, sport and entertainment. The rise and reach of English is a breathtaking adventure.'

Whenever an international language is required, whether for maritime navigation or international air-traffic control, English seems to be chosen. Japanese scientists write many of their papers directly in English. The economic hub of the far east, Singapore, has named English as one of its official languages. About 50 million people in India speak and write English fluently (despite an attempt by Gandhi to ban the language shortly after independence).

As Lord Quirk has written, 'English is just as much big business as the export of manufactured goods.' The spectacular growth of English language schools in China, Japan and the rest of Asia attests to that. *The Economist* reckons that English teaching overseas is now the sixth largest source of invisible earnings, worth over £500 million per year. And after the international boost to the language from American movies, TV programmes and pop music, the internet is now accelerating the demand for English. According to Internet World Stats, English is by far the most popular email language.

Some British writers appear to think that this global dominance is due to an intrinsic superiority in the language. In his book *The English Language*, Robert Burchfield says, 'As a source of intellectual power and entertainment the whole range of prose writing in English is probably unequalled anywhere in the world.' That's quite a claim! I wonder how many other languages Mr Burchfield knows well enough to make a decent comparison. But English is certainly popular. Quite apart from being useful, it seems to be liked. People tell me it sounds quite musical. In his book about the English language, *Mother Tongue*, Bill Bryson says, 'English also has a commendable tendency towards conciseness, in contrast to many other languages.' Overseas students of English tell me they quite like the fact that English does not follow the rules, and that some words have so many different meanings depending on the context. And they even seem to like the nuances available from a wide vocabulary. The *Revised Oxford English Dictionary* lists well over 600,000 words, more than any other European language, and probably more than any language on the planet.

But international English is not the same as the RP we hear on formal occasions in Britain. The global version is hugely influenced by American usage. There's not much point asking a hotel receptionist in Tokyo, Tashkent or Trieste, 'Where's the lift?' – just ask them to show you to the elevator. And international English is a pared-down version of the language. Only when I began working for the World Service did I realise how much metaphor we use in British English. It makes it colourful, but also makes it confusing for foreigners. At the World Service, which broadcasts in over forty languages, there have been many instances of even the expert translators being baffled. On one occasion, the Somali service caused a stir by using a report stating that a neighbouring president had been welcomed at the airport with open arms; this was translated as 'he was welcomed with weapons drawn'.

Popular acceptance

So, whether you are working for a public service broadcaster or for a commercial company, whether for a local, national or international channel, it seems that large parts of the audience expect broadcast news to set a standard of quality in the use of language. This raises the question, where do we find the authority? Who decides what is right and what is wrong?

The philosopher and language expert C.E.M. Joad (1891–1953), a regular contributor to *The Philosopher* magazine, wrote in 1936 about the search for an authority on good English:

> Who should be the arbiters? The lexicographers, philologists, grammarians or schoolmasters? No, *popular acceptance decides*, and rightly so. *We* (writers) must *judge* what our wide audience regards as acceptable.

I think that conclusion holds good today. We must have a very good idea of what our wide audience regards as acceptable, and what offends or distracts some of them. Language is not a branch of logic. If it were, our baffling spellings and silent letters would all have been eliminated long ago. Some preferences about grammar or spelling may not be logical. That is not the point. We want to communicate information to a very wide audience as clearly as possible, with no irritating distractions. The moment listeners become aware of the way language is being used, their concentration on the meaning of the words is lost. So the conclusion for any writer is to adopt a style and tone of voice that the wide audience they are seeking to reach will find acceptable.

Tradition versus changing usage

Seeking a tone of voice that will command wide acceptability is often a question of balancing the traditional with the contemporary. One of the best scriptwriters I have worked with is John Humphrys, for many years a foreign correspondent with the BBC, then a presenter of leading news and current affairs programmes on television and radio. In 2003 he wrote an introduction to *Between You and I: A Little Book of Bad English* by James Cochrane. In this extract, he explains the need for journalists to find this balance and to use the language sensitively and effectively.

> Like any other organism, language changes. It lives in the real world and gets knocked about from time to time. It adapts in order to survive. Look up almost any word in the *Oxford English Dictionary* and you can follow the journey it has taken over the centuries, changing its precise meaning as it twists and turns with the passing of time. Often its present meaning bears little relationship to its original one. It is silly to imagine that this evolution can be halted. It is even sillier to try.
>
> But that is different from hoisting the white flag and surrendering to linguistic anarchy. A degree of discipline is not a constraint; it is a liberation. The more clearly we are able to express ourselves, the less room

there is for ambiguity. The more elaborate and the more precise our vocabulary, the greater the scope for thought and expression. Language is about subtlety and nuance. It is powerful and it is potent. We can woo with words and we can wound. Despots fear the words of the articulate opponent. Successful revolutions are achieved with words as much as with weapons.

This is a typically articulate and heartfelt appeal for writers to harness the power of language by understanding it thoroughly, and to find the acceptable tone of voice by combining 'liberation' with 'discipline'.

It seems clear to me that the great majority of broadcasters respect accuracy, and lean towards conservative correctness rather than rule-breaking. Writing in the *Observer* in January 2010, the comedian and broadcaster David Mitchell mused about his dislike of some coinages that had just appeared in the *Oxford English Dictionary*, such as 'staycation' and 'tweetup'.

> The truth is that I instinctively resent novelty in language . . . when slang becomes correct, mispunctuation is overlooked and American spellings adopted, I feel that I'm a mug for having learned all the rules to start with.

Then, on a more serious note, this articulate broadcaster gets to the heart of why he 'instinctively' prefers to follow the rules.

> They [the rules] need to be there to create a tension between conservatism and innovation. If the innovation continued unchecked . . . then the language would fragment into thousands of mutually incomprehensible dialects. The stickler-advocated rules of spelling, grammar and punctuation slow the speed of change and allow the language to remain united. They're as important to the continued strength of English as the internet's power to coin new usages.

Authority versus accessibility

Finding a tone of voice that combines discipline with liberation is also a question of finding the right balance between the two As of broadcast news – authority and accessibility. For many years, authority has been the key word of broadcast news in all radio and TV stations, from the traditional BBC flagship Radio 4, to local black music stations. It means that the information broadcast as 'news' must be regarded as accurate and credible by the target audience. If the language is sloppy or imprecise, then the journalism will be regarded as untrustworthy. If the newsreader does not seem to know the meaning of words, then why should we believe the information?

In recent years, news organisations have become more concerned with the second A – accessibility – largely as a result of market research and much sharper competition for listeners and viewers. Audience surveys repeatedly show that younger people do not consume very much news (and that 'younger' bracket now includes the advertiser-target groups in their thirties). Quite a high proportion of the under-thirty-fives appear to think news and current affairs programmes are not for them; they are for old people, produced by old people about old people. Some people from ethnic minorities also seem to think that mainstream radio and television in Britain is remote from their own experience, and belongs to others.

Commercial broadcasters want to attract and hold on to a wide audience, but they especially want to attract the younger people who go out and spend. As a publicly funded broadcaster, the BBC has become very concerned about the idea that some licence-payers do not feel the corporation's journalism is relevant to them. Surveys have persistently shown that BBC news scores high on authority and credibility, but rather low on accessibility and friendliness. So the pressure is on to find subjects that will interest these dissatisfied sections of the audience, and to develop more interesting production techniques, particularly on television (such as more imaginative graphics, more live elements, interactive opportunities, and so-called walking–talking sequences, where the reporter speaks to camera and demonstrates things while on the move). The quest for greater accessibility has also included some reassessment of the use of language. Richard Sambrook says the style of writing at BBC News has changed during his career:

> Certainly in the past 20 years it's become more colloquial. That's not necessarily a bad thing. I think we have to use a style of language that the audiences recognise as part of their world. We can't sound aloof, while at the same time being extremely careful not to get into too much slang, which might alienate listeners and viewers, and remaining true to the tenets of good English usage as well as good journalism.

In Britain, the commercial sector in radio and TV has always regarded itself as being less stuffy and more engaging than the BBC. Interviewed for this book when she was Controller of Programmes at Yorkshire Television, Clare Morrow said,

> At ITV we like to think we are more warm and friendly, and we try to be less distant than the BBC. I don't have a problem with a less formal approach to the use of language. But you must be able to recognise the audience you are serving. We serve a very wide audience in terms of age. We must ensure that the language we use doesn't jar with any section of that audience. That's key! Language does change. It's a question of nudging forward. The first rule in broadcasting is – don't alienate your audience. But we have this dilemma in television at the moment. We need to know that the older audience is sticking with us, but we need to attract a younger audience. We mustn't alienate the loyal older age group, but we must become more accessible to people who find us a bit pompous.

The advice in this book is not to confuse a bright, engaging and colloquial style with perceived inaccuracies or slang, which will erode the authority of the channel and very quickly turn off large sections of the audience. Finding an accessible language must not be achieved at the expense of authority. The audience must like you – but they must also respect you. Good Spoken English, as well as being natural and widely accessible, must be elegant and accurate.

3
The language of broadcast news

Write as you would talk. Better still, write as you would hear.
(Peter Elliott, A *Question of Style*, BBC Television,
internal publication, 1979)

WRITING THE SPOKEN WORD

So what principles should guide us as we try to write our bulletins, introductions, voice-pieces or commentaries? The first is that we must try to write scripts that sound natural when spoken aloud. All the broadcasting style guides emphasise this point. 'The script should sound as if the presenter is *talking* to the viewer or listener, not just reading out loud', advised a BBC News Training booklet in the '70s. More than a generation later, the BBC's Director of News was still urging all his journalists to remember this essential guidance:

> The basic principles of writing for broadcast news haven't changed for a long time. They are the same as when I came into the business 25 years ago. You have to write conversationally; you have to write as you would speak to someone . . . it's very different from the written text.

It's notable that, even before the age of broadcasting, many writers believed that the spoken language was the original model and the purest form of communication. Printing it on to a page became the problem. Shakespeare's greatest lines were written to be spoken. William Hazlitt said, 'To write in a genuine, familiar, or truly English style is to write as anyone would speak in common conversation.'

Of course, we don't write exactly 'as anyone would speak in common conversation'. We should not write slang or repeat common grammatical errors. The language of TV news – the version of the language that I have called 'Good Spoken English' – is precise, and will be regarded by listeners and viewers as correct. It will not offend the listener, but it will seem to be natural and conversational.

It is interesting to note that the way scripts are produced in TV and radio newsrooms has changed a great deal in a relatively short time, and in some ways the technology has not encouraged writing for speech. I started as a young journalist in the dark ages before the personal computer. News scripts were typed on stencil sheets, then duplicated on a Gestetner printer, which was wound by a handle. Mistakes were very difficult to change. A red fluid had to be brushed on to the offending letter or word, and after it had dried, a type-over might or might not duplicate successfully. It paid to employ specialist typists, who were fast and very accurate. Some of the newsroom typists at BBC Television in the '70s and '80s could rattle out scripts at dazzling speed. Many journalists dictated their scripts to these typists. Newsrooms were noisy places, with several reporters dictating simultaneously, the typewriters clattering and the duplicating machine making noises like a cement mixer. The appearance of the electronic newsroom system (ENS), based on net-worked computers, was a revolution bringing huge benefits. But journalists stopped dictating their scripts. I strongly recommend any writer to read his or her script out loud before clicking it into the bulletin or programme. Don't be embarrassed to do it. It's good professional practice.

How the audience watches and listens to the news

'Audience focus' is one of the few essential tenets of successful broadcasting. It means knowing the target audiences very well indeed, and developing a service that satisfies their needs, tastes and lifestyles. For the journalist, audi-ence focus means selecting the right stories, but also understanding what kind of language might distract or offend some of the audience. Clare Morrow says,

> The key difference in broadcast news is that you are trying to *tell* a story rather than *write* a story. Picture the person you are speaking to and tell them your story. Then you will use the words you would use if you were telling a friend a story rather than writing something official. When I was a reporter, I always tried to imagine the person I was speaking to. It's a good thing for others to do. It produces more animation in the voice, and it makes you use normal words.

Audience focus also means that we should never forget how broadcast news is consumed most of the time. One of the key differences between newspapers and broadcasting is the way readers or listeners use the various products. Reading a newspaper is, to use a modern word, interactive. Readers can choose which page to read first (it seems that many men start with the back page), and which arti-cle on any page to read. They can browse an article at their own pace. They can stop reading, maybe to pour milk on the breakfast cereal, or sort out the kids' packed lunches, then rejoin the article. And, crucially, they can re-read a sen-tence if it is a little complicated or if they have been distracted.

In television and radio we, the professionals, make all the choices. We decide in which order the audience will receive the news stories, and the pace of the information. Millions have to follow it at exactly the same speed. Our audiences must be able to understand immediately what they hear. Listeners and viewers cannot re-read a difficult paragraph. The internet is much more interactive, and digital technology is delivering more personal selection for TV news. But at the time of writing, most new media observers believe there will be a strong appetite for conventional broadcast news for many years to come, either as constructed bulletins in general channels or on 24-hour news outlets, where the editors decide the running order. And even click-and-play reports on multi-media websites must be written to hold the audience's attention throughout.

When BBC radio first started, news bulletins were read twice, as the presenter explained, 'First at normal speed, then at dictation speed so that listeners can take notes.' During the Second World War, most families in Britain would gather round their bakelite radio to tune in to the BBC's *Nine o'clock News*, and apart from a little determined knitting or fierce pipe-smoking, I imagine all other household activities were suspended. There would have been absolute concentration on the information. Radio is not consumed that way now. It is almost entirely a 'secondary activity'. We listen to the radio while we are doing something else, such as cooking, ironing, having a bath, eating a meal, driving to work, or working – whether it be in the office, in the shop, on the shop floor, in the car, or in the cab of a tractor, taxi or HGV.

Television viewing seems to be following radio with this trend, according to surveys showing that a surprising number of families have their TV set switched on all day and watch television as a kind of moving background. One survey even informed us that nearly 10 per cent of viewers confess to have used the opportunity of the news programme to have sex on the sofa or rug. Of course, TV is more of a primary activity than radio. Nonetheless, many people watch it rather casually. They are certainly not sitting on the edge of their seat taking notes.

So, in broadcasting, we must write our Good Spoken English simply, clearly, accurately, directly and compellingly. The BBC's Tim Orchard says,

> I think the golden rule is that in broadcasting you don't have a second chance. When reading a newspaper or magazine, you can always re-read a paragraph to try to understand it. So the *clarity* of the writing is absolutely the first priority.

Sir David Nicholas, former Editor in Chief, ITN, puts it this way:

> Unlike reading a newspaper, the viewer can't go back over the previous sentence. Each sentence in broadcasting must stand on its own legs with vertical content and thought, with no hanging thoughts or subordinate clauses.

Journalese

So are viewers and listeners treated to this simplicity, clarity, accuracy and style to help them understand the news and to be interested in it? I fear that a lot of the time they are not, because the language of broadcast news is infected by the virus of so-called journalese. It is rampant. There seems to be no known cure.

Over the years, newspaper journalists have developed a style of writing for print that does not transfer to broadcasting. A popular newspaper needs short, dynamic words for headlines that will attract the eye. 'Bid. Probe. Shock. Row. Clash. Blast. Plea.' And print writers may be encouraged to sell their stories with colourful adjectives. 'Dramatic. Angry. Miraculous. Massive. Shocking.' The venerated newspaper columnist Keith Waterhouse identified two versions of this journalese. The first is 'officialese'. It can be found everywhere, in official documents, press releases and corporate literature, and includes convoluted phraseology and pompous adjectives to denote great significance. The second version, which he called 'tabloidese', is characterised by bolted-together monosyllables and sensationalism. Both types of journalese have this in common: people don't speak like that! So journalese can take the form of:

1. The Prime Minister is actively contemplating a fundamental restructuring of Whitehall departments. (*Sunday Times*)

2. A 20-year-old mother of two is making a desperate last-ditch bid to save her tots from the evil clutches of their runaway father. (*Daily Star*)

Unfortunately, many broadcast journalists seem to think that this journalese, or newspaper jargon, is the proper currency of all journalism. It is not. Shoddy English that is riddled with clichés irritates many people. It displays a poverty of original ideas. It is often inaccurate as well. Not every difference of opinion is a 'row' or a 'clash'. Not every medical advance is a 'breakthrough'. We would not say to our colleagues in the office, 'Adverse weather conditions foiled my bid to get to work on time.' But reporters and newsreaders talk to their listeners that way with – dare I say – monotonous regularity.

Here are just a few examples from recent years.

A bid to save stricken telecom giant, Marconi . . . (Saga Radio)

A Birmingham couple are to sue Thomas Cook after their dream wedding on a paradise isle ended in disaster. (BRMB Radio)

British Rail have reduced speed limits amid fears that the rails may buckle . . . (Five News)

Does anyone other than a journalist say 'amid fears that'?

> Police in Paris are questioning a baggage-handler who was arrested at Charles de Gaulle Airport with an arsenal of weapons. (BBC Radio 4)

How many weapons in an arsenal? I don't know, but I think it would be more than the two pistols and four blocks of explosive apparently found in this man's bag. It would have been more natural, and a little more precise, to write '. . . with guns and explosives'.

I do not want to suggest that all newspaper editors are content to print reams of journalese. The campaign against it is being waged in the quality press in Britain almost as vigorously as in broadcasting, and much of the finest writing is to be found in newspapers. The style guide for journalists working at the *Independent on Sunday* acknowledges that headline writers will need very short words, but continues,

> The *Independent on Sunday* is written in ordinary English such as you might encounter in books or conversation. Usages particular to newspapers should be avoided as far as possible. Headline words such as *row* for dispute, *plea* for request and *cash* for money should be kept out of text. *Bid* and *probe*, along with *slam* for attack, are banned even in headlines.

Officialese from the emergency services

All journalists are familiar with the type of officialese used by police officers, members of the emergency services and some spokespeople, when they are choosing their words carefully. We must try to translate this strange patois into normal English without altering the meaning. Here are a few examples. You will be able to think of many more.

> The perpetrators appear to have gained access to the rear of the premises.
> (The thieves got into the back of the shop/house.)
>
> He made good his escape on a motorcycle.
> (He got away on a motorbike.)
>
> The premises are well alight.
> (The building is burning fiercely. Why do fire officers seem to sound so pleased when they say, 'well alight'?)
>
> A young person's pedal cycle has been recovered.
> (A child's bike has been found.)

The driver was fatally injured.
(The driver was killed.)

Adjacent to . . .
(Near)

Approximately . . .
(About)

Accordingly . . .
(So)

He was dead on arrival at hospital.

The frequently-used phrase 'dead on arrival' should hardly ever find its way into a news script. It usually comes from an ambulance service duty officer reading to a journalist the official log, which he/she is required to keep. (Sometimes the ambulance officer will say 'he was DOA' or 'it was a DOA'.) News agencies often include this 'dead on arrival' line. But we are not compelled to broadcast it. Doing so seems to suggest that the victim died on the way to hospital, which may not be true, and it displays a slightly ghoulish interest in the details of the death. In most cases, the main fact will be that the victim was killed in the accident or crime, and that is how we should report it.

The motor vehicle appears to have been in collision with two male persons.

We should not scoff at police officers who use this kind of language. Most have been trained to give witness statements in court in this guarded style. But it sounds preposterous if we repeat it on the air. Better to say that the car, van, bus – try to be specific – hit two men. It's worth noting that the journalistic tradition of 'in collision with', supposedly neutral to avoid any implication of blame, is not supported by many media lawyers when pedestrians are involved. A BBC lawyer, Roy Baker, advised:

> If we report that a bus hit a man, it does not necessarily indicate blame. In common parlance it's a fair description of what happened. Clearly we must not indicate that a driver was being reckless, or report anything else which could be regarded as libelous or prejudicial. But in cases involving two vehicles, there may be an argument about whether they were both moving at the time. So 'a bus hit a car' could be contentious. 'A bus and a car collided' is better.

Even then, 'collided' is not a word used very often in spoken English, and can often be avoided by referring in your script to a crash or serious accident.

In September 2003, the *Independent* reported that two people were injured 'when their van collided with a train at a level crossing'. I think to say 'when their van was hit by a train' would be more natural, and does not indicate blame in any way.

Officialese from politicians

In the United Kingdom, there is a special language that can be heard in the Palace of Westminster, the national assemblies and local government council chambers, and it can spill out along the corridors and into the press rooms. I think it takes quite an effort of will to avoid repeating phrases such as 'The government are contemplating the introduction of a series of measures ...' or 'the party will be bringing forward a set of initiatives to underpin their policy ...'. If you feel you should not change the words used in such phrases, then attribute them to the person who used them.

Political statements quite frequently use the passive tense to conceal individual actions beneath a cloak of collective responsibility. So they might say, 'errors of judgment were made' instead of, 'we made mistakes'. Or 'at the time it was considered necessary ...' rather than, 'at the time I decided ...'. The active tense is better in broadcast scripts.

Even some individual words have the ring of officialese. The columnist Miles Kington campaigned wittily against cliché-journalism for many years. For example, he observed, 'The word *signally*, which I challenge anyone to define, seems only to be used with the word, *fail*. Nobody signally succeeds. Nobody signally promises or delivers anything.'

The BBC News Styleguide (2003) indicates a growing trend to use the word 'raft'. 'The bill has attracted a raft of amendments.' 'The government has unveiled a sweeping raft of proposals.' The guide asks, 'What is a sweeping raft? When was the last time you heard someone in the pub say "I must get home. I've got a raft of ironing to do"?' Another word much loved by politicians, diplomats and journalists is 'broker'. Again, do you hear people saying 'We have brokered a good price for our house'? They would be much more likely to say 'negotiated', or 'agreed', or even 'got'.

In 2008, the Centre for Policy Studies published a 'Lexicon of Contemporary Newspeak' pointing out that 'what George Orwell described as *euphemism, question-begging and sheer cloudy vagueness* now dominates political discourse'. The director of the think tank, Jill Kirby, was scathing about this 'often impenetrable vocabulary'.

Replete with sustainable aspirations and ambitious targets, they promise to use key performance indicators to address the issue, bring about step-change and implement a progressive consensus, to raise awareness and streamline joined-up delivery in order to fast-track transformation. But how many problems have they really succeeded in solving?

Jill Kirby believes that 'the corruption of language has infected all political parties, is endemic in public service, and is rapidly spreading into the media'. I think this is a serious point. All good broadcast journalists not only must avoid this kind of political jargon and stick to everyday spoken English, they should also point out to their audiences, through direct quotes or attribution, that their elected leaders are deploying this kind of obfuscation.

For example, it was interesting that after the start of allied bombing in the first Gulf War, the Pentagon declared that the Iraqi Air Force had been 'decimated'. Many people would take this to mean that most of the aircraft had been destroyed; but technically it meant that one in ten had been destroyed. It emerged later that most of the Iraqi pilots had flown themselves and their planes to safety in neighbouring countries. I think that 'decimated' is a rather unusual word for a Pentagon statement, and guess it had been chosen carefully to suggest more that it actually meant. The way to report such an announcement is with the exact words of the statement, and perhaps to raise the question – what exactly does it mean?

JARGON

Politics and diplomacy are not the only spheres that have a special vocabulary. All professions, industries, services and hobbies have their own jargon, which can be very clubby for those in the know, but which excludes everyone else. The military is well practised at developing its own terminology. So is broadcasting. But I feel sure that radio, television and online journalists should learn to recognise jargon and avoid it as much as possible. There will be occasions when there is a narrow focus on a specialist target audience and jargon is deemed acceptable. The financial TV channels CNBC and Bloomberg TV may feel confident that all their viewers are inside the jargon bubble. But for mainstream channels, I think that even the financial news should be accessible to a wide general audience, and that means the language should be jargon-free.

Many senior news editors feel very strongly about this subject. Bob Jobbins, for many years Director of News at the BBC World Service, says with some feeling that one of his main hates is the use of jargon by correspondents. He believes that it says to the listener, 'Hey, I'm on the inside. You may not be quite sure what this means, but I do!'

Business news jargon

Daniel Dodd, for ten years the Head of the BBC News Business and Economic Unit, acknowledges that the financial world is particularly prone to exclusive words and phrases: 'I dislike all the jargon connected with business. We try to avoid the language of *like for like sales*, or *the numbers*, or *M&A activity*.' On the other hand, it may be impractical to explain a financial term such as a 'rights issue' every time you use it. As ever, a sharp focus on the audience of a particular programme or channel should help the writer decide how much explanation is required. A short financial slot in a breakfast television programme or in a local radio drive-time sequence should tell the story in plain English, with plenty of explanation.

In general terms, I believe that broadcast-correspondents who specialise in financial news overestimate how much most listeners will know about their particular subject area. I wonder how many contestants on *The Weakest Link* would know the difference between a bear market and a bull market? And it gets much more complicated than this. A recent Barclays report explained to shareholders, 'We continue to seek out value-creating non-organic opportunities in selected European markets.' This is the opposite of clear spoken English. It is often designed to be vague. Richard Teffler, when Professor of Accounting and Finance at Cranfield School of Management, commented on a new website designed to detect jargon, 'Jargon is used primarily to obfuscate and mislead. It is a way of denying what's going on.'

Here are a few of the fashionable words and phrases used in business, but which do not figure very often in Good Spoken English.

> synergy . . . scenario . . . leading edge . . . overarching . . . underpinning . . . downsizing . . . human resources . . . brand ascendancy . . . added value . . . meaningful . . . step-change . . . pivotal . . . exponential . . . throughput . . . blue-sky thinking . . . pushing the envelope . . . take on board

On this subject, *The BBC News Styleguide* adds, 'In your haste to use *blueprint, escalation, ceiling* and *target*, do not forget the plainer alternatives, *plan, growth, limit* and *objective*.'

Financial Times correspondent Lucy Kellaway has been campaigning for many years against what she calls brainlessly upbeat office-speak, with regular contributions to her column from a fictional manager called Martin Lukes, who 'talked the talk, or rather he added value by reaching out and sharing his blue-sky thinking'. In 2008, she spotted the rapid growth of 'going forward', meaning 'in the future'. She hates it. So do I, mainly because it is part of the insincere optimism, enthusiasm and caring that businesses think they must exude to succeed. (Lucy Kellaway pointed to an advertisement from one of the big banks that was seeking 'passionate banking representatives to uphold our values'. 'This is a lie' she says. 'It wants competent people to follow instructions.') But when she heard a man from the National Farmers' Union on BBC Radio's *Farming Today* uttering three 'going forwards' in less than 30 seconds, she admitted, 'This most horrid phrase is with us on a going forward basis, like it or not.'

Business jargon has a general tendency to leak into mainstream reporting. In September 2009, *BBC Breakfast* reported that 'there's been a big spike in the number of people taking canal holidays'. Ouch.

Use of Latin phrases in business reporting can be particularly irritating. To some listeners, they will indicate the language of a public school elite, who may have complained about doing their Latin prep, but now in their well paid jobs in the city like to flash their classical knowledge by using *per capita*, *per annum*, *ad hoc* and similar phrases *ad nauseam*.

At its worst, financial news can turn into a sort of meaningless babble, which has the sound and texture of news, but which is really something I call 'newsak' – the journalism equivalent of the music played on aircraft before take-off, designed to numb the brain rather than stimulate it. I once heard a business reporter on CNN telling the anchor, 'These are not particularly good figures. Most people were expecting them to be pretty much in line with expectations.'

Specialist reporting

Financial journalism is just one of many specialist areas of expertise that have expanded in broadcast journalism in recent times. Not so many years ago, specialist correspondents were mainly to be found working for broadsheet newspapers and magazines. Apart from the journalists devoted to politics, international affairs, business and sport, there were very few specialist correspondents working for radio or television news. Now the bigger broadcasters all have experienced reporters who specialise in a much wider range of subjects – subjects that interest viewers and listeners because of their direct relevance to their daily lives – such as health, education, transport, crime, the environment and consumer affairs.

But there can be a tension between the correspondent's desire to demonstrate expertise and the medium's need for simplicity. The more you know about the background to a story, the more difficult it can be to pare it down to the essential facts. If you know a great deal about a subject, you must remember not to try to show off. Expertise should be used to give the general audience a special insight and clear understanding of difficult issues. It should be used to explain complex matters in a clear and concise way.

Sick as a parrot: reporting sport

The area of specialism that takes the gold medal for the greatest displays of jargon, the largest number of clichés per minute, and the highest scoring rate for journalese is – of course – sport reporting. It's a significant part of journalism. Very many viewers and listeners tune in to their preferred news programme or news channel to find out what has happened to their favourite team or favourite sport star. They may be much more interested in a World Cup qualifier than the speeches at the party conference. Sport can be magnificent, a liberating contrast with a boring week at work, a community bond, a drama or a ballet – with more spectators than any conventional drama or ballet. It can be exciting, spectacular, emotional, breathtaking, beautiful, frustrating, ugly, unifying, divisive or completely pointless, depending on your point of view.

I have absolutely no sympathy with any young aspiring journalist who says, 'Oh I don't know anything about sport. I really hated it at school.' Any trainee journalist who tells the editor, 'I don't know a single thing about cricket! And football is really not me, you know?' is signing his or her career-termination warrant. News editors are loath to let loose in their newsroom anyone who hasn't a clue about sport. The credibility of the radio station or TV channel can be blown away by a writer who may have a double first in literature and linguistics, but who doesn't know the difference between a birdie and a bogie, doesn't know the name of the manager of Manchester United, or doesn't know what LBW means. (Incidentally, I was editing a national TV news programme when the newsreader said that England's opening batsman had been dismissed 'one-B-W'. She was rapped on the pads later.)

Sport reporters, particularly when describing the world's most popular sport, football, have developed a jargon of their own. Here come some highlights from the second half:

> after the break . . . making his debut . . . elected to shoot . . . always going wide . . . spared his blushes . . . the jeers turned to cheers . . . was on hand to head home . . . a wicked deflection . . . back on terms . . . upended in the box . . . marching orders . . . early bath . . . made no mistake from the spot . . . gave the keeper no chance

I particularly dislike 'flatters to deceive'. Apparently, it means the player looked good, but didn't actually deliver the incisive passes or goals that would help get a result. But how many people would use this phrase in normal conversation? How many don't understand it? Another hateful expression in football reporting is 'turned provider'. It means that a player who had scored a goal earlier gave a pass to a team mate so that he could score. It is hateful not because it is concise, which it is, but because it is an expression exclusive to a small club of football anoraks, and it is not the way we speak! Can you imagine someone in a pub telling you about the game, and saying, 'Then Torres turned provider . . .'? I think not. You might say 'The goal-scorer then laid on the second for Gerard', or 'Torres tormented the centre-backs, scoring the first and making the second.'

Some in-house news guides seem resigned to the idea that football jargon is here to stay. Some sport journalists defend it confidently. They argue that this kind of language is a convenient shorthand, which all soccer fans understand and accept. And they point out that there is no perceptible tide of complaint to the TV and radio stations every Saturday night, condemning the use of sport clichés. I find these to be very poor arguments.

The best football reporters on radio and television do not resort to a pathetic string of clichés. There are an infinite number of colourful and original ways of describing football action in Good Spoken English. I write with some feeling on this point, because one of my first tasks with the BBC was to be a regional sport reporter, doing some live radio commentary (frightening), but mainly presenting scripted sport news on TV and radio. I promised myself to avoid all sport clichés. It was difficult. These handy and clubby phrases are embedded in our brains. I urge broadcast journalists to write scripts in the natural spoken tongue, not in the sterile jargon of the newspaper back pages. We should not accept that tabloidese is the right way to broadcast sport stories.

News agency copy

When trying to avoid jargon and journalese, writers of broadcast scripts should be wary of copy from news agencies. Readers of this book who work in regional, national or international news agencies will probably be tut-tutting and claiming they all write beautifully. In my experience, that is not quite true. Some agency copy is very stylish. But a lot of it seems to be written in a kind of Lego-language, with sentences composed of easily snapped-together stock phrases. The main difficulty for broadcast journalists is that agency copy is not usually written for the ear, it is written for newspapers. And it is raw material. The agency writers know it is going to be rewritten most of the time.

The newsroom computer system makes it tantalisingly easy to drag-and-drop chunks of agency copy. I think this temptation should be firmly resisted. In November 2002, BBC News 24 reported on the Italian Fiat company's plans to cut over 12,000 jobs. The report began, 'Management and unions began crisis talks Monday ...'. This is fairly standard agency style, but will not do when we are telling the news to viewers in a natural way. International agencies use 'Monday' rather than 'today' to avoid confusion in different time zones, and to be clear for newspapers that will be read 'tomorrow'. In broadcasting, at the very least the sentence should be changed to 'The management and the unions began crisis talks today', or 'Fiat's management and unions ...' but it would be even better to use the present tense (the talks are clearly in progress), and the company name can indicate the management without the need to use the word. 'Fiat are in urgent talks with union leaders this morning, trying to head off an all-out strike. ...' Just write it as you would tell someone.

CLICHÉS

> By using stale metaphors, similes and idioms, you save much mental effort, at the cost of leaving your meaning vague, not only for your reader but for yourself.
>
> (George Orwell, *Politics and the English Language*)

The most blatant, the most disliked and the most derided form of journalese is the cliché, defined in the *Concise Oxford Dictionary* as 'a hackneyed phrase', which implies that it plods along like a tired or overworked horse. (Clichés are certainly used by the hack, which the same dictionary defines as, 'a dull, uninspired writer'.) Clichéd writing reveals clichéd thinking. In interviews for this book, Richard Sambrook, then the BBC's Director of News, says, 'A cliché is a phrase whose power has gone through over-familiarity, and is used unthinkingly', and Rob Kirk, Editorial Development Manager at Sky News, sums it up neatly:

> Clichés are annoying because they're lazy and insulting; lazy because they indicate that the correspondent hasn't the wit or energy to think of a more creative word, and insulting because they patronise the audience. Real people don't stay *tight-lipped* about what they might want for breakfast, *comb* the house for a lost mobile, or *leave no stone unturned* in their search for a magazine.

But can we all agree which clichés annoy because they are lazy, vague and patronizing? Richard Sambrook says,

> It's sometimes the most difficult thing to avoid writing clichés. They are all over the place. And some phrases that start off as innovative, interesting pieces of writing become clichés very quickly.

When the Queen first brushed aside security guards and walked up to the crowds in Australia, I remember being impressed when a reporter used the phrase, 'went walkabout'. It was witty and memorable. Now, when handshakes with the crowd are part of the routine for the royals, the phrase is in danger of being a tedious cliché. When a correspondent described the discrepancy in Enron's accounts as a 'black hole', it indicated the huge scale of the missing funds and the way the uncontrollable debt was sucking in more victims. But when, in December 2002, Saga FM News attributed a relatively minor suspension of share dealing to 'a black hole in the accounts', the phrase had entered cliché-land.

I would not want younger writers to confuse the journalistic cliché with the many colourful figures of speech that make English such a vigorous and picturesque language. Time-honoured phrases such as 'flat as a pancake', 'hale and hearty' or 'as right as rain' will always have their appropriate place in the spoken language, though in broadcasting they are probably more comfortable in the live, ad-libbed report than in the tightly written script. No, the clichés to banish from your mind are the wearisome expressions that journalists wheel out all too readily, but which people would not think of using if they were relating something interesting to a member of their family.

You would be unlikely to say, 'Did you hear that there was a blaze at the nursery school this afternoon, following a blast in an adjacent boiler room? Fleets of ambulances attended the scene and ferried the injured to nearby hospitals. One toddler is fighting for her life . . .'

You will have your own pet hates. Here are a few of mine. There are many more in the list of 'dangerous words' at the end of this book.

ahead of (meaning before or in advance of)	catch-22 situation
	calm but tense
amid tight security	cocktail of drugs
amid fears that	crackdown
angry clashes	death toll
bid (meaning attempt)	famine-stricken (especially when
blueprint	the whole continent of Africa
brutal reminder	is thus described)

fighting for his/her life (very ill)
glaring omission
going forward (in future)
gunned down
gunshot wounds (bullet wounds
    or shotgun wounds?)
helping police with their
    enquiries
ironically
major boost

massive heart attack
meanwhile
quantum leap
riot of colour
sniffer dogs
sweeping changes
the situation remains confused
war-torn
walked free from court
wreak havoc

It may be an old joke, but it is worth remembering to 'avoid clichés like the plague'.

THE DEFINITE ARTICLE

The small word 'the' gets its own small section in this book, because one of the most common examples of journalese used in broadcasting is when the definite article is dropped. 'The' is clearly in danger from scores of unfeeling hacks.

The use of the definite article is central to the main theme of this guide – that broadcasters should write stories as they would speak them. Far too many bulletin writers, in search of a brisk style and a pacey read, copy the newspapers and agencies by dropping the 'the' before titles. So we hear:

Chairman of Leicester Social Services, David Smith says . . .

. . . accused of murdering Leeds teenager Sharon Bailey.

Spokesman for Severn Trent Water John Williams denied . . .

This is not how people speak. 'The spokesman for Severn Trent . . .' takes a fraction of a second longer to say, but it is fluent and natural.

Let's get technical about this for a moment. One of the reasons why dropping the definite article sounds awkward is the effect it has on the grammar of the sentence. 'The England Captain, Andrew Strauss . . .' has as the grammatical subject of the sentence, 'The England Captain' with captain as the primary noun. 'Andrew Strauss' is in parentheses. If the 'the' is dropped, the grammar is altered. 'England Captain Andrew Strauss . . .' has turned the first two words into a bolted-together adjective, describing Andrew Strauss. It's all right in print. And broadcast journalists may well feel, even subconsciously, that they want the name Andrew Strauss to be the main subject of the sentence. But the fact remains that no-one would speak like this in normal conversation. I am aware that dropping the definite article in this way is very widespread in news summaries. I also know that many senior editors dislike it on the air.

The main point is that dropping the definite article makes newsreaders sound as though they are reading newspaper cuttings, rather than telling the audience what's going on in Good Spoken English. I urge all aspiring writers to drop this habit of dropping the 'the'. Listen carefully to the news, and you will hear that the most successful and respected correspondents on radio and television never do it!

AMERICANISMS

> We have really everything in common with America nowadays, except, of course, language.
>
> (Oscar Wilde, *The Canterville Ghost*)

> You say *to-may-to* and I say *to-mah-to* ... Let's call the whole thing off.
>
> (Ira Gershwin, sung by Fred Astaire and Ginger Rogers in *Shall We Dance*)

In addition to the dangers of journalese, jargon and clichéd phrases, writers in Britain must avoid a further linguistic pitfall. As I indicated earlier, anything regarded as American English is disliked by large sections of the British audience. Journalists reading this book in the United States, or Canada, or Australia, or other parts of the English-speaking world, may find it difficult to grasp the strength of feeling this subject uncovers back in the UK.

I should emphasise that the main principles that are developed in this book – those of accuracy, conciseness, the use of a natural spoken form of language, sensitivity, clarity, and style – apply equally well to English-language writers of broadcast news anywhere in the world. But in the British Isles, the preferred version of the language does not have much room for – or perhaps I should say does not have much truck with – American usage.

The differences were brought home in the Second World War, when Britain was flooded with GIs. Winston Churchill is said to have remarked that Britain and America were 'one nation divided only by the language'. And the subsequent influence of American pop music, films (sorry, movies), and television programmes (sorry programs) has been enormous. Now Bill Gates is teaching the world US-style grammar and spelling with Microsoft's little red and green lines. There are countless differences in vocabulary and pronunciation. Here's a short American story.

> Chuck, a realtor who was going to check out a nearby duplex, picked up his garbage can from the yard, stowed it in the trunk of his compact, and drove to the dumpsters at the lot out back of the gas-station mini-mart.
>
> Charlie, an estate agent who was going to inspect a nearby semi-detached house, picked up his dustbin from the garden, put it in the boot of his family car, and drove to the bins in the car park behind the garage shop.

Bill Bryson, an American writer who has made his home in England, reckons that in common speech about 4000 words are used differently between the USA and the UK. 'That's a very large number indeed', says Bryson in his book *Mother Tongue*. 'Some are well known on both sides of the Atlantic: lift/elevator, dustbin/garbage-can, biscuit/cookie; but many hundreds of others are still liable to befuddle the hapless traveller.' He points out that a tramp in Britain is a bum in America, while a bum in Britain is a fanny in America, and a fanny in Britain is something else again. In Britain, to 'table a motion' means to put it forward for discussion, whereas in the USA it means to set it aside. 'Presently' means 'now' in America; in Britain it means 'in a little while'. (But it's interesting that the American meaning is the original, which we in Britain are now re-importing.) Quite a few so-called American words are preserved eighteenth-century usages that have changed in the homeland. Most are more recent inventions, some of which seem to me to be better than their English equivalents. Surely 'thumb-tack' is more descriptive than 'drawing pin' and is slightly easier to say. Is it not better to describe a baby's 'dummy' as a 'pacifier'?

American imports

It is worth noting how quickly some useful American words or phrases become widely accepted in Britain. Not so many years ago, commuters, teenagers, gatecrashers and babysitters could be found only in the USA. When I started writing news stories and traffic reports for BBC radio, 'tail-back' was unacceptable. In the UK, cars formed queues. These days they also tail-back. I remember a news editor warning me against any temptation to call a large vehicle a 'truck'. 'Trucks run on rails; lorries run on roads', he explained. Not so many years later, trucks, it seems, are jumping the rails.

Logically, we should not resist these imports into a language composed of imports. But our attitude to language is not logical. The letters of complaint to broadcasters indicate that many British people loathe 'Americanisms'. They seem to believe that American usage is sloppy, ignorant and imprecise.

The BBC News Styleguide says,

> Our listeners and viewers must not be offended or have their attention diverted by the words we use. American speech patterns drive some people to distraction. Adding unnecessary prepositions to verbs is guaranteed to cause apoplexy in some households. Problems which were once *faced* are now *faced up to* . . . British people *keep* a promise rather than *deliver on* it. Expressions such as *deliver on, head up, check out, free up, consult with, win out, divide up* and *outside of* are not yet standard English.

And they all take more time to say. In Ireland, too, there's growing concern about American influence on the language. Karen Coleman, for several years the Foreign Affairs Editor of the Dublin Radio Station Newstalk 106, is worried about less precision and a shrinking vocabulary.

> When I was lecturing in journalism for a year, I was appalled at the careless use of language by educated young people. Younger Irish students, and those entering the news industry, use a lot of American slang and what I call '*Friends*-speak'. The language of the TV sitcom *Friends* is creeping into their scripts. It shows how we are all subject to the neocolonial powers of American Television! As an Irish person who has lived outside my country for a long time, I've come back to a country with a rich language and a rich tradition of great writing, and I find it depressing that kids are using more uniform language, and losing all the subtleties and idiosyncrasies.

Increasing use of Americanisms

In Britain, I have certainly noticed many more American words and phrases in news reports than a generation ago. I suppose that's inevitable. In 1993, BBC Radio 4 reported on the Waco siege, 'David Koresh, who was wounded in the original shooting incident, is thought to be too sick to talk to negotiators.' I wrote in my notebook – No, in English he was too ill. But now the American usage is everywhere. 'Relatives of the executed man had told the Chinese authorities he was sick', reported BBC Five Live in December 2009, referring to a man with mental illness. Let me emphasise that this changing usage is not to be condemned. After all, 'administering to the sick' and 'in sickness and in health' are long-established phrases in formal English. But the sensitive scriptwriter will know that many people in the audience much prefer 'ill' to 'sick', and will not want them to feel either with a perceived Americanism.

In 2002, a BBC TV report on a night-time search for two missing schoolgirls said how the police had used 'flashlights'. Most British people would have said 'torches'. In August 2003, a GMTV presenter said, 'He dove into the swimming pool'. A BBC programme about novice clergymen was called *Rookie Reverends*(!). In 2008, the ITV *News at Ten* was reporting 'the idea is that people will be able to drop by their local surgery'.

In November 2003, a BBC health correspondent told us that super-bugs in hospitals were 'getting smarter'. I don't think he was referring to their dress-sense. By 2007, *BBC Breakfast* was reporting that 'breast-feeding your children makes then smarter'. With smart bombs and smart electricity meters, and the Sky TV quiz show *Are You Smarter than a 10-year-old?*, the American meaning has firmly taken root. But many older listeners and viewers will not have accepted it yet.

In June 2009, a distinguished presenter of BBC Radio 4's *Today* programme described a newspaper picture as showing 'a bloodstained Iranian protester sprawled across the hood of a car'. A BBC reporter in Port au Prince, in January 2010, said, 'I can see the airplanes coming in' (he wasn't American).

My advice to all young journalists working in the UK is to become aware of which words and usages are regarded as being from America, and to avoid them until they have been truly adopted into the mainstream of the language. Traditional English will annoy no-one and please many.

So don't stretch words needlessly. Transport not transportation. Instruments not instrumentation. And watch out for the American tendency to turn nouns and adjectives into verbs: to hospitalise; to trash; to author a book; to debut; to guest (on a talk programme); to fast-track; even, recently, to euthanise. When a main road in Warwickshire was downgraded, the council announced that it had been de-trunked. This was because the bypass had been dualled. And how about, 'This car is alarmed'! In 2002, Google's Senior Vice-President talked about the possibility of charging for the use of the search engine: 'We may experiment with ways of monetising . . .'. The American runner Michael Johnson, commenting on the 2003 World Athletics Championships on the BBC, said, 'She did well. She medaled.' Despite the fact that we British have accepted many of these coinages in the past, such as finalise, publicise or editorialise, the newer versions irritate British listeners and viewers very much.

Some American usages gain acceptance quite rapidly because they have a particular meaning, and are concise. Some correspondents have adopted 'to meet with' instead of 'to have a meeting with' because it is shorter, and they probably think it indicates a formal occasion, whereas 'to meet' could sound like a chance encounter. 'The President met with his Defence Secretary . . .';

'The Prime Minister met with senior party officials this evening . . .'; 'The Somali Prime Minister has met with relatives of the couple feared kidnapped by pirates . . .' (*BBC Breakfast*, October 2009), Personally, I dislike 'met with'. Surely 'met' will be perfectly clear, and will keep the purists happy.

Other American usages that annoy many Brits are those which drop the word 'against', as in: 'Germany decides to appeal EU's tobacco advertising ban' (Euractiv European News Agency); or 'Thousands turned out to protest the ban' (CNN). These shorter usages are starting to enter the mainstream in UK broadcasting. 'Amanda Knox's parents intend to appeal the verdict' (BBC TV News, 2009). 'Eighty MPs are appealing these judgments' said a BBC political correspondent in December 2009. I think most viewers and listeners would not use this phraseology themselves, so broadcasters should avoid it.

A date in the USA

An American usage that has been gaining ground in Britain quite recently is the shortened way of saying dates. I first noticed this on a television trailer for a forthcoming programme in 1997: 'Starting Monday October 6th . . .'. Surely, I mused, it should be 'Starting on Monday October the 6th'? These days, this kind of usage is the routine for programme trails and commercials, presumably because it saves a fraction of a second, and is more punchy and arresting. Sometimes you will even hear 'Starting Monday October six . . .'.

And this American style of saying dates is starting to creep into some news scripts: 'When the Pope arrives here Monday . . .'; 'The Polish referendum on June seventh . . .' It's a fair bet that a lot of listeners and viewers will regard this as an unwelcome American habit. Even 'Nine-Eleven', as the short way of referring to the 2001 attacks on New York and Washington, is not used by many people in Britain, and I would advise writers in the UK to stick to the longer version, 'September the eleventh'.

In fact, since the end of the 1900s, there has been some confusion about how we should say the number of each year. Most people have been saying 'two thousand and one; two thousand and two'. But in two thousand and three, *BBC Breakfast* told us that a company was expected to be in profit by 'two thousand seven'. This shortening will be widely regarded as American usage, unrelated to normal spoken English in the UK, and will be disliked. My personal view is that the 'two thousand and . . .' form will give way to 'twenty . . .'. This is partly because the novelty of the year two thousand is wearing off, but mainly because it is one syllable shorter and faster to say 'the London

Olympics in twenty-twelve' rather than 'two thousand and twelve'. This form has emerged in the past. The Battle of Waterloo was in 'eighteen-fifteen'. And more pertinently, the Battle of Hastings was in 'ten-sixty-six', not 'one thousand and sixty-six'. As they say in so many pieces to camera, only time will tell.

American pronunciation

In broadcasting, unlike print, differences in pronunciation are just as noticeable as differences in vocabulary or grammar. For example, English retains a tendency to stress the first syllable of the word, which dates back to Anglo-Saxon roots. The epic poem *Beowulf* (part of the oral tradition of story-telling, which broadcasters might like to bear in mind) has strong stresses at the beginning of each word and phrase, and the rhymes in each line are 'front-rhymes' or alliterations, which pre-date the French tendency to stress the end of the word, with rhymes at the end of each poetic line. So the traditional English pronunciation of 'harass' and 'harassment' puts the stress on the first syllable. But these traditions are not cast in stone, and pronunciations are changing all the time. As suggested earlier, good broadcasters are aware of these shifts, and try to judge what will not upset any significant section of their audience.

A classic example of a changing pronunciation is 'schedule' as 'skedule'. Very many young people now say it this way. This American pronunciation will take over eventually because it is slightly easier to say, and because the only other common word in the language which begins with 'sch' is school. So the new pronunciation of 'skedule' seems to be falling into line. But 'skedule' hasn't taken over yet, and is disliked by many people. I urge younger news presenters and reporters to stick to saying 'shedule', which is widely regarded as correct English.

In 1906, the brothers H.W. and F.G. Fowler wrote in their authoritative book *The King's English* as follows: 'The English and the American language and literature are both good things; but they are better apart than mixed.' A century later, few news editors would disagree.

4
Writing broadcast news scripts

People think I can teach them style. What stuff it all is! Have something to say and say it as clearly as you can. That is the only secret to style.

(Matthew Arnold, *Collections and Recollections*)

The life of a journalist is poor, nasty and brutish. So is his style.

(Stella Gibbons, Foreword to *Cold Comfort Farm*)

THE PRINCIPLES

Having established that broadcast journalists should aim to write as they would speak to an individual member of the audience, using a clear and accurate version of the spoken language, and avoiding journalese, the question then arises whether it is possible to learn techniques for writing against the clock, or whether good writing comes naturally. Some editors seem to believe that journalists have their talent genetically embedded somewhere in the anatomy – maybe in the blood, maybe in the nose: 'He has a nose for a story, that one'; maybe in the bladder: 'I have a feelin-in-me-water about this one'; or in the abdomen, home of the gut feeling. Many more distinguished editors believe no such thing.

We can all teach ourselves to write better. Techniques can be developed by younger journalists to subdue the panic induced by a close deadline, and to ensure a comprehensible story. And the best experienced writers are always working on their technique and seeking new ways of telling their stories. Of course, there are a million ways to write any script, and there is no universal formula. But there are principles and practices that give any writer a rock-bed of certainty on which to build his or her personal style.

Clarity, simplicity and conciseness

> In writing, hence in style, the primary consideration is comprehensibility – therefore, clarity.
>
> (Eric Partridge, 'Style', in *Usage and Abusage: A Guide to Good English*)

> Simplicity is the key to happiness in the modern world.
>
> (The fourteenth Dalai Lama, *Happiness, Karma and Mind*, 1969)

The first and overriding principle is that we want our scripts to be understood easily by the audience. Bob Jobbins who was in charge of the journalism at the BBC World Service for many years, says, 'If I were to give one word of advice to a young journalist, it would be *clarity*.' And it is clear that, for most editors, this clarity is coupled with simplicity and conciseness. Broadcast journalism is very much the art of précis; it is the technique of paring down the information to its essentials. A typical television news report may be only ninety seconds long, of which only forty seconds might be the reporter's own voice. That's the equivalent of about four column-inches in a broadsheet newspaper. A local radio report may be even shorter than that. Seconds are precious and cannot be wasted. So no word must be a waste of time. Richard Sambrook, who for several years was the BBC's Director of Global News and before that a lead writer on the main BBC TV news programmes, emphasises the need for scripts to be crisp and concise.

> You have to write as you would speak to someone, but you also have to pare it down. Less is more. Take out the superfluous words. Take out the unnecessary adjectives. At the same time keep it conversational to engage people. It's very different from the written text.

Sir David Nicholas, former Editor in Chief at ITN, created a style that was known for its clarity. He summarises it like this:

> Writing for broadcast news should be composed of short sentences, it should be direct, and it should be tightly, tightly edited. No excess baggage – like an airliner! Be absolutely tough. Go over the script if you have the chance and see what you can expunge without losing any meaning.

Sir David relates that he would practise his own scriptwriting by taking a column in the *New York Times*, and trying to reduce it to half its length without losing any facts.

In schools of journalism in the USA, you will hear tutors urging their students to 'Kiss! Remember to kiss!'. This refers to the now well established advice from a veteran editor to a junior journalist wanting to know how to treat a story: 'Keep it simple, stupid!' In Britain, where we like to think we are a little more polite and sympathetic, KISS is said to stand for 'keep it simple and straightforward'.

Short sentences work better

> A sentence is more likely to be clear if it is a short sentence communicating one thought, or a closely connected range of ideas.
>
> (Harold Evans, *Essential English*)

In broadcasting, writing simply and straightforwardly usually means writing sentences that are not too long. You do not want to have to take a breath in the middle of a sentence when broadcasting live or recording a report. Spoken English is generally composed of short sentences. In fact, when talking to each other, we sometimes use phrases that are not complete sentences. (Writing this way is certainly acceptable for some TV news commentaries, but is much less acceptable on radio, as will be explored in later chapters on the differences between the two broadcast media.) Over three decades, ITN's main news presenter, Sir Alastair Burnet, made short sentences his trade mark. Spare words were cut. Those left carried more emphasis. His scripts were orderly. They were easy to follow. But there's no need to be that rigid. There will be times when a more rounded, flowing sentence is appropriate to the subject matter, lending variety to the rhythm and permitting more expression in the voice. Either style will become monotonous without the other. But as a general rule, short sentences work better.

I would recommend any young broadcast writer to become comfortable with the shorter-sentence style. It makes it easier to write the story when you feel under pressure, and it will always work on the air. Clearly, it should not degenerate into a sequence of unrelated, staccato statements. But when it becomes second nature to write crisply and simply, it is easier to break out into a flowing sentence when the occasion arises. For example, the following sentence has 43 words, so would be difficult to read without having to take a breath.

> The online search engine Google is turning up the pressure on its main internet rivals Microsoft and Yahoo, by launching a free email service called Gmail, which it says will block spam and will have five hundred times more storage capacity than Hotmail. (43 words)

It's easy to break up the sentence. And it should not make it longer to read.

> The online search engine Google is turning up the pressure on its internet rivals Microsoft and Yahoo. Today it launches a free email service called Gmail. Google says Gmail will block spam – and has five hundred times the storage capacity of Hotmail. (42 words)

If you listen carefully to broadcast news, you will notice that many of the most experienced and most respected correspondents use short sentences, especially when they want to convey a sense of tension or expectation. Here is a section of television commentary by the BBC's John Simpson, as he prepared to spend the night with a Belgrade family in their air-raid shelter during the NATO bombing in 1999.

> This is a city Tito built. New Belgrade. A dormitory suburb for the post-communist middle class. On a day like this everyone likes to get out into the sun. It's only at night that clear skies mean heavy bombing. Each part of New Belgrade has its air-raid shelter. Tito thought they might be needed against attacks from Russia. Never conceivably from NATO.

A similar style was deployed when Simpson reported on the fall of Kabul in November 2001. Presumably it was written under some pressure.

> It was just before dawn that the wild dash for Kabul developed. Thousands of soldiers intent on capturing the capital. It seemed to take no time at all to cover the twelve or so miles. As we drew nearer to Kabul, the grim evidence of battle. These were former members of the Northern Alliance who switched sides and joined the Taliban. No mercy for them. Then we saw they had captured another man. The presence of our camera probably saved his life. He was paralysed with terror. By now there were no Taliban left to resist. Then came the critical moment. Would the Northern Alliance simply race on and pour into Kabul itself, even though they'd undertaken not to? The commander in charge was determined not to let it happen. He ordered the armoured vehicles to block the way. The great advance was stopped in its tracks. But Kabul lay temptingly close below us now. The small BBC team decided to head on.

Of course, on air it was not at all as staccato as it looks on paper. Simpson's delivery included pauses for the natural sound, and the pictures provided a flowing continuum of the military advance.

The most striking difference between reporting for broadcast news and reporting for newspapers is the use of very short and simple sentences or phrases.

> Say all you have to say in the fewest possible words . . . and in the plainest possible words.
>
> (John Ruskin, *Essays*)

WHAT'S THE STORY?

> Obscurity of expression generally springs from confusion of ideas.
> (Thomas Babington Macaulay, *English Essays*)

Unfortunately, simplicity isn't all that simple! Clear writing will be possible only if you have a clear idea of the essentials of your story. Good writing is not a display of dexterity, like calligraphy or accurate typing. It happens in the mind. So it is worth reflecting for a moment on what we mean by a 'story'.

In Britain, we tend to take for granted the idea that our journalism is composed of a series of these so-called stories. The question, 'What's the story?' is asked scores of times every day in every newsroom. But in many other countries, the concept is far from clear. After the collapse of the Soviet Union, I organised training courses for producers and reporters in many former Communist countries, where for two or three generations there had been very little independent or enquiring journalism. So-called journalists had simply been reprocessing official information. I soon discovered that, in the new climate of a free press, some writers found it difficult to identify 'stories' because this required a process of analysis and decision-making that was un-familiar to them. Many would confuse events with stories. 'My story is that there is a meeting of the Baltic Environmental Alliance, with representatives of all the countries bordering the Baltic who are discussing how to clean it up.' But what's the *story*? It may be that the clean-up will cost 10 billion euros and will take fifty years. It may be that a Polish chemical factory is defying the agreements and poisoning Sweden's fisheries. Very often, stories emerge from events, but they should not be confused with the event itself. The opening of an art exhibition (still a favourite subject for TV news magazines in former Soviet states) is a story only if there is something about it that is novel and interesting to the viewers.

It seems that in other languages, there is no precise equivalent of the English word 'story' meaning a piece of journalism, which is probably why so many journalists working in other languages use the word. The French *histoire* does not mean quite the same thing. To some students of journalism from overseas, 'story' seems an odd choice of word, suggesting fiction or fairy story. A jour-nalist's story is rooted in fact and related with accuracy. But it is still a narra-tive, and the word indicates quite neatly the idea that the reader will want to know what happens next or how it concludes. Journalism in the free world has developed as a series of short stories because it works. People want to read sto-ries. Stories sell newspapers. In broadcasting, the listeners and viewers certainly want to hear or watch stories. 'Please will you read this document' is a much less appealing invitation than, 'Listen, I'm going to tell you a story'.

Subjects and events are not necessarily stories

But even in Britain, where there is a long tradition of enquiring journalism presented in narrative form, it is still possible to hear scripts that put the event at the beginning, and leave it to the listeners to find for themselves the main point of interest – the story. You, the journalist, should make the decision about what the story is. That is the essence of journalism. Your employer pays you to make those decisions. If you have a host of facts and a number of possible implications that you would like to report, sit back for a moment and consider which will be the one point to attract the attention of the audience and encapsulate the subject of the piece.

In my view, newspaper journalists are better at doing this than broadcasters. Perhaps that is because of the unforgiving discipline of writing the newspaper headline. Once committed to the presses, a boring headline is banged out in black and white perhaps millions of times, seeming more and more boring each time – certainly to the hapless sub who wrote it. So newspaper head-line writers are extremely unlikely to decide that the story is, 'David Hockney opens new exhibition', or 'Hillary Clinton arrives in Jordan on the latest stage of her Middle East shuttle', or 'Tory Party Conference opens in Brighton'. But broadcasters quite regularly use such headlines. They are diary items, not news.

In his book *The Television News Handbook*, the former Director of the BBC College of Journalism, Vin Ray, says,

> Think how you would tell a friend what the story is in one sentence and bear that in mind as you put the piece together. Too much information will make your writing style tortuous and cramped . . . Bear in mind the difference between the subject of a story and your treatment of it.

Story-focus in the treatment of subjects

Even experienced correspondents sometimes write like this:

> The engine, an RB-211C Whisperjet, designed for the new short-range European Airbus commuter-liner, and said to be twenty per cent quieter than equivalent engines, is to be built at Rolls Royce factories in Derby and Coventry.

It's the kind of script that has plenty of facts, probably lifted from a company press release, but no story-focus. The most interesting aspect of the story may well be that this is to be the quietest airliner of its size, and the story would then develop by mentioning new, tougher noise limits being imposed by the EU. It might go on to explain that new carbon-fibre blades in the engines reduce friction and are therefore quieter. That's why Rolls Royce have called the engine the 'Whisperjet'. If the story was being written for a regional service in the midlands, or a local radio station in Derby, the focus would be on the number of local jobs created or secured. For example:

> Five thousand workers at the Rolls Royce aero-engine factories in Derby and Coventry have been told their jobs are safe for at least six years, because of an order to supply engines for the new European Airbus. The company says one of the reasons they won the contract was because the engine, the RB-211C, operates well below the EU's tough new noise limits for short-range aircraft. They've called the new engine 'The Whisperjet', because it's said to be twenty per cent quieter than its rivals. The works convenor at the Derby factory, Daniel Black, said the Airbus contract was 'great news for all the people at Rolls Royce who've worked so hard to turn the company round'.

And whatever the story-focus, as a general rule, the information will be taken in more easily in shorter sentences. Trying to cram too many pieces of information into the same sentence is one of the main faults in broadcast scripts. If you hurl out too many facts and figures, the people listening at home, or on the motorway, simply can't follow the narrative, or remember much of it a few seconds later. Writers are strongly advised to keep to the essential facts that support the key point of the story, and to deliver them one at a time.

Writing the key point of the story first

As another general rule, when writing a bulletin story or the introduction to a full report, try to put the key point of the story first, preferably in the top line.

> At a news conference this afternoon, the Chief Constable of the West Midlands Police, David Jones, announced that . . . '

is much less effective than:

> A new police unit is being set up to fight the spread of crack cocaine in the West Midlands. Announcing the move at a news conference this afternoon, the Chief Constable, David Jones, said . . . '

We should not confuse the peg with the most interesting point of the story. As most readers of this book will know, the 'peg' is journalists' slang for the topical development on which we hang our story about an interesting issue. It is the reason for doing the story today. The peg may be a conference, or the publication of a report, or the start of a hearing, or no more than an anniversary. It should certainly be mentioned early in the story, but not necessarily in the opening phrase. The *Sky News* presenter Julie Etchingham says,

My real pet hates are any links which begin 'A report out today . . .' or 'According to latest figures . . .'. They're dreadful in any news bulletin, but are particularly inappropriate for 24-hour news, which is supposed to be constantly fresh and appealing.

Sometimes there can be several stories in the same news programme stemming from various government initiatives, and the effect can be make your output sound like the official pronouncements of a state broadcaster: 'The Prime Minister has announced that . . .; The Department of Health is to . . .; The Foreign Secretary has arrived in . . .'. Putting the story first avoids this rather dull and formal approach, and will interest your viewers and listeners much more.

In regional television and local radio, where on some days quite a number of bulletin stories can originate from the police calls, the danger is that too many stories can begin with 'Police in . . .': 'Police in Stirling . . .; Police in Dumbarton . . .'. It's much more interesting to put the key subject of your story in the first line. And, incidentally, it should be *The* police in . . . (see 'The definite article', Chapter 3).

There will be occasions when you want to build up to the story, either to make sure the significance or context of the latest development is clearly understood, or simply to attract the listener's attention. The section on writing studio introductions will develop the idea that an inviting opening line is extremely important. Sometimes this will be in the form of a question directed at the listener or viewer. 'Should schoolchildren be forced to wear uniforms?' (Radio Four, *Today*). This introduction then went on to the new angle, which was a report from a head teachers' association.

But introductions that are obviously teasing should be used sparingly, and usually on less serious stories. The formula 'Jane Williams thought it was just another quiet Sunday when she took her Yorkshire terrier, Lucky, for his morning walk . . .' can very easily become a stroll into cliché-land. In general terms, it is good practice to get into the habit of identifying the key point of interest in your story, and putting it first. Teachers of journalism often summarise this advice as, 'First sentence must interest, second sentence must inform.'

THE DIRECT STYLE

Not too many subordinate clauses

It is not very good practice to start with a subordinate clause. 'Following his pledge at last week's party conference to reduce taxes for poorer families, the Chancellor has . . .'. By definition, people expect the news to be new. To attract their interest, it's usually best to put the new development in a running story first: 'A new tax credit for low-income families is likely to be a key part of next month's budget . . .'.

In fact subordinate clauses should be used sparingly throughout broadcast news scripts. The crisp, tight, simple style that avoids long sentences, which is advocated by all leading editors, has little room for hanging ideas, of the 'Following . . . After . . . Due to . . .' variety. You would be unlikely to say, 'Needing some milk, I went to the corner shop.'

Here is a typical paragraph from a quality newspaper. *The Times* is reporting Toyota's apology to its customers for the way they had been treated over the recall of cars in 2010: 'The apology from the commercial director Jon Williams, the highest ranking Briton among Toyota's UK executives, came as the company conceded that the recall of 180,000 cars in Britain – one in nine of the Toyotas on the roads – with potentially defective accelerator pedals, was likely to last for weeks.'

It's perfectly clear in print. But this single sentence, with more than fifty words and some numbers to remember, would be difficult to read on the air without running out of breath or losing the audience's attention. We seldom talk to each other that way; and remember that many people in your audience may be listening a little casually. Presenting them with one idea at a time makes it much easier to follow the news. So if you find yourself writing, as in the above example, . . . from . . . as . . . with . . . in the same sentence, try dropping in a couple of full stops.

The active voice

In a similar way, the simple, direct style of spoken English is much more comfortable with the use of the active voice rather than the passive. So we tend to say, 'Dad bought the paper', rather than 'the paper was bought by Dad', even when replying to a question about who had bought the paper. The active voice suits broadcast news. It is usually a more logical line of thought, it is a more direct and muscular style, and it is more in line with normal speech.

The passive will be more appropriate when the point of the story that you want to emphasise is someone or something on the receiving end of an action. For example, you would probably write that 'fifteen thousand patients were taken to hospital by taxis in London last year, an increase of fifty per cent . . .', rather than 'taxis took fifteen thousand patients . . .'. You would report that a wild kangaroo attacked a British tourist. But if the tourist happened to be Prince Harry, you'd almost certainly write that 'Prince Harry was mauled by a deranged kangaroo . . .'. As ever, there are no firm rules. But there is a strong tendency for the clearest, crispest writing to use the active tenses. The direct style also expunges all redundant words, and has surprisingly few adjectives and adverbs.

Redundant words

> No word should be encumbered by a parasite, consuming space and debasing the language.
>
> (Harold Evans, *Essential English*)

Using redundant words, or tautology, is a serious crime for broadcast journalists, who are allotted just a few seconds to get their story across. Every word uses up precious time. The need for clarity, as well as brevity, requires a ruthless approach. Redundant words must go.

Here are just a few examples. In most cases, the words in italics can be deleted with no loss of meaning, and in many cases the deletion gains the advantage of greater impact from greater precision.

absolute perfection	last *of all*
all-time record	made *out* of
appear *on the scene;* appear *to be*	*more* preferable
as compared with	*mutual* cooperation
best *ever;* first *ever*	never *at any time*
brand new	*new* creation, recruits, record
collaborate *together*	*original* source
complete monopoly	outside *of*
consensus *of opinion*	paying *off* the debt
crisis *situation*	*passing* phase
dates *back* from	*past* history
during *the course of* the day	*patently* obvious
end result/product	reduce *down*
essential condition	resigned *his/her position* as
ever since	*self-*confessed
final completion	short *space of* time
followed *after*	spent his *whole* life
for *a period of* three years	*still* continues/persists
future prospects	*surrounding* circumstances
gainfully employed	*temporary* reprieve
hurry *up*	*total* extinction
inter-personal relationship	*totally* destroyed
in *the world of/in the sphere of*	*usual* custom
business/politics/media	*very* first time
join *together*	*violent* explosion
joint cooperation	worst *ever*

There are many more of these tautological usages, which waste time by saying something twice. A precise style saves valuable seconds, carries more impact, and has a pleasing precision and simple elegance. Be taut rather than tautological.

Adjectives and adverbs

> As to the adjective, when in doubt, strike it out!
>
> (Mark Twain, *Pudd'nhead Wilson*)

One of the biggest differences between writing for print and writing for broad-casting is the number of descriptive or qualifying words deployed. Most print journalism is packed with adjectives, either to sell the paper hard with sensa-tionalist language – massive, miraculous, desperate, tragic, explicit, steamy – or to describe the general mood, context or political climate as concisely as possible – troubled, controversial, bitter, conciliatory, desperate, beleaguered. In spoken English, these adjectives and similar adverbs almost always sound like over-sell, and many are pure journalese. Talking to your listeners and viewers in hyped-up language sounds unnatural and can sound ridiculous. '3G phones are incredibly vital to the entire industry', said an excitable *BBC Breakfast* presenter in 2003. And a political correspondent more recently exclaimed, 'The Department of Education is facing total meltdown!'.

All the senior editors I have spoken to about good broadcast journalism agree that there are too many adjectives and adverbs in too many scripts. Instead of strengthening the effect of the story, these descriptive words can have the opposite effect, reducing the impact of the information. Words such as total, major, huge, massive are becoming meaningless. Why are debts invariably crippling? When is a fire huge? The 2009 bush fires in Australia were certainly huge, and so was the firework factory explosion in the Netherlands, which reduced scores of houses to rubble. So should a factory fire on an industrial estate in Swindon be described as huge just because there was a lot of smoke, and 'ten appliances attended the scene'? Do politicians ever deliver a minor speech? Simple, unadorned nouns or verbs can deliver more punch than when they are weighed down by qualifying words.

I remember being in the BBC's newsroom in Belfast one evening during the worst of the troubles in the '70s, when the Head of News, Robin Walsh appeared. He was a formidable editor of sharp mind and strict standards. Leafing through the script for the midnight news, he asked the duty journalist softly, 'What's the difference between an enquiry and a special enquiry?' The adjective was promptly deleted.

Facts have much more power than vague adjectives inserted to try to make the story seem bigger than it is. Say how many buildings have been flooded, how many destroyed by the earthquake, how many vehicles are involved in the pile-up, and adjectives such as devastating, disastrous or massive become superfluous. And on television, the pictures will often speak for themselves.

Here is an extract from a 2002 television news report on the Queen Mother's funeral, by the BBC's Jennie Bond. It was an emotional occasion for many. But there are no emotive words, few descriptive words. There are no references to grieving crowds or ashen-faced relatives. The elegance of the report is in its simplicity.

> Tonight, within the precincts of Windsor Castle, the Queen Mother has been laid to rest beside her husband George VI. It was a private service attended only by her close family. In contrast, her funeral this morning was a choreographed chapter of history that drew some 400,000 people to central London. It was a day of sorrow, a day of ceremony. As the coffin was born from Westminster Hall, the crowds fell silent. Forming up to escort her once again, her son-in-law and the grandchildren and great-grandchildren she loved – William and Harry, who said she had inspired them. . . . It was a procession marked by the order and dignity which were at the core of her life. The gun-carriage, the same that was used at her husband's funeral 50 years ago.

The report also has a simple symmetry, beginning and ending with a reminder the Queen Mother had been a widow for half a century.

Adjectives and value-judgements

Another difficulty in the over-use of adjectives and adverbs is that very often they can imply value-judgements. Tim Orchard, for many years a programme editor with BBC TV news, particularly dislikes reporters describing something we can see, or worse, describing someone we can see.

> If you can see someone speaking on TV, let that clip of actuality be judged by the audience. If the reporter's commentary introduces it with something like . . . an angry Prime Minister then said . . . how can we be sure that the adjective is fair? Perhaps he was grimly determined, or weary, or resolute, or mildly irritated!

It's a more difficult issue for radio journalists. Good radio should sometimes describe the scene, or give listeners an impression of the mood. I think the best advice is simply to take care, and avoid overstatement or sensationalism. It may be tempting to say that 'the talks went on into the night, with the management desperately trying to head off a second damaging strike . . .', but in reality they may be negotiating confidently, wearily, cunningly or resignedly.

The reporter probably doesn't know. The BBC's Director of News says pointedly (or should that be grimly, or significantly, or cryptically?), 'The choice of descriptive adjectives and adverbs on radio is definitely an issue.'

ACCURACY

Accuracy is also 'definitely an issue' for any aspiring broadcast journalist. It is the number one issue. Readers of newspapers, listeners to radio, and viewers of television all expect the news to be trustworthy. They expect it to be true. Opinion surveys, such as those conducted on behalf of the Eurobarometer or the World Economic Forum, tend to show that broadcast news enjoys a higher level of trust and credibility than the printed press. This seems to be because most newspapers have a recognised position in the political spectrum, or a known stance on important issues. The tradition of broadcasting in Britain is one of impartiality. It is enshrined in the BBC Charter, and in the laws and codes of practice that regulate commercial broadcasting.

Every news and current affairs programme, from a flagship national nightly news to a short summary on a local radio station, shares the same requirement for accuracy. It takes years for a TV or radio channel to establish its credibility, and it can take a couple of seconds for that credibility to be lost through a serious error. It may also lead to a damaging and expensive lawsuit. It is hardly surprising, then, that news editors demand that their journalists get it right. In broadcasting, where the risks of making a mistake are far higher than in the world of print, because the journalism is a continuous process with much of the journalism transmitted live, in-house guides repeatedly urge their staff along these lines:

> We want to be first and we want to be right. But we want to be right first.

No-one that I know lost his or her job because they weren't first with a story. I know several whose careers were damaged by being wrong. So it is of prime importance not to include anything in your script that is not certain or verified. If in doubt, leave it out – better still, find out.

Accuracy in language

> Words are grown so false I am loath to prove reason with them.
> (William Shakespeare, *Twelfth Night*)

Other books on journalism give advice on good research and ways of verifying information. This book is about the *language* of broadcast news. And the accuracy of the language can be as important as the verification of your story. If a bulletin contains inaccurate usage, can the listener trust the facts? If the language is sloppy, does it not indicate a sloppy mind and sloppy journalism? Consistently accurate and stylish use of English brings a strong sense of respect and credibility to your broadcasting. But there are pitfalls. There are many possibilities in the English language for ambiguity or imprecision.

The meaning of words

'When I use a word,' Humpty Dumpty said in rather a scornful tone, 'it means just what I choose it to mean – neither more nor less.'
'The question is,' said Alice, 'whether you *can* make words mean different things.'

(Lewis Carroll, *Through the Looking-Glass*)

As Lewis Carroll was indicating, philosophers like to analyse the meaning of words and the meaning of meaning. Words certainly can mean different things to different people. The meaning of some words is in a constant process of change. The difficulty for journalists is whether to accept the meaning that most of the audience believes is correct, or stick to the meaning in the dictionary, which is the 'traditional' definition of a word, usually related to its root or origin. Better-educated listeners and viewers, who are certainly not all retired colonels living in Tunbridge Wells, are disappointed (if not actually disgusted) when they hear a newsreader or a reporter mistaking the technical meaning of a word. Here are some examples of words used regularly by journalists who clearly do not know what they technically mean.

Anticipate: to take action to prevent something, or to forestall. 'The goalkeeper saved the penalty because he anticipated where the ball would go.' But these days, most people use the word as a synonym for 'expect'.

Apogee: 'The process of European integration, which is reaching its apogee in the joint constitution . . .' (*The Times*). We should avoid using the word in this way, as a synonym for 'peak' or 'climax', for two reasons. First, it really means the point in a planet's orbit when it is furthest from the Earth; secondly, hardly anyone uses the word in normal speech.

Biannual: occurring twice a year; not once every two years, like the Ryder Cup, which is a biennial event. Incidentally, according to the *Concise Oxford Dictionary*, bimonthly can mean either twice a month or once every two months. So it's a word to avoid.

Disinterested: unbiased by personal interest. Uninterested means not interested.

Enormity: does not simply convey the idea of size. It means extreme wickedness. It is not a word to be used lightly. In 2009, BBC Radio 4 was reporting on British Airways staff being called out on a 10-day strike at Christmas: 'Cabin crews seemed stunned by the enormity of what had been decided.' I think that is a mistake. But when Radio 4 reported on 11th September 2001, 'President Bush was in Florida when the attacks began. He made a statement at a time when the scale and the enormity of the deeds was far from realised', the word was used precisely and accurately.

Evacuate: technically, to empty something. So if people are being evacuated, it can suggest that they are undergoing an uncomfortable medical procedure. It will please the purists to say 'houses were evacuated' or 'people were moved from nearby houses'. Nonetheless, 'people/residents/patients were evacuated' is now used so widely that the BBC's *A Pocket Guide to Radio Newswriting* concedes 'Let the people be evacuated', and some dictionaries now include the definition 'remove to safety'.

Forensic: do you know what it means? For several years I have been asking classes of postgraduate students of journalism, and no-one has got it right yet. They tend to think it means 'scientific'. So the meaning of this word is now seriously in doubt. The dictionary will tell you that forensic means 'relating to courts of law'. Forensic medicine is the application of medical science to legal problems. A forensic examination means not a scientific test, but an enquiry carried out as thoroughly as a cross-examination in court. We should write 'forensic scientists' or even 'police scientists' rather than 'forensic experts' or 'forensic teams'. I realise these new usages are very widely accepted; but people working in forensic science, and many police officers listening to your news, will know that you don't know what the word really means.

Fulsome: does not mean generous, it means over-generous, excessive or gushing. So to report that the Prime Minister gave fulsome praise to his retiring press secretary would be rather unflattering to both of them.

Infer: to deduce something. It does not mean 'imply'. A speaker implies what a hearer might infer.

Refute: to prove that something is wrong; it should not be confused with 'deny' or 'disagree'.

Surrogate: substitute. So it's the mother who is a surrogate, not the baby.

There are many more examples in the list of dangerous words at the back of this book. And you will have your own pet hates of words that are often used incorrectly. The celebrated columnist Miles Kington campaigned against sloppy language throughout his career. He once wrote that he saw a listing in *Radio Times* for a programme in which someone would be 'trolling through the archives'. Kington was scathing. 'Anyone who can't tell the difference between *troll* and *trawl* shouldn't be allowed to edit magazines without a grown-up in attendance.'

There are many words in the English language that can be confused with another quite easily. And in broadcasting, where different spellings are irrelevant, words that sound very similar can mean very different things. In *The BBC News Styleguide*, John Allen calls these pairs of similar words 'confusables'. He quotes an example from a story on Radio Four:

> A boy of twelve is in intensive care in hospital after a group of teenagers doused him in inflammatory liquid and then threw a lighted match at him.

The writer meant to use the word *inflammable*, capable of being set on fire, not *inflammatory*, tending to stir up trouble. Here are some of John Allen's list of confusables.

affect/effect
alternate/alternative
appraise/apprise
dependent/dependant
distinctive/distinguished
flounder/founder
inflammable/inflammatory

loath/loathe/loth
militate/mitigate
peddle/pedal
practical/practicable
regretful/regrettable
resistent/resiliant

If you are not sure about any of these, look them up in the dictionary! It really is unforgivable for a professional journalist to mix up words with different meanings. And all who aspire to be excellent writers must have a very good knowledge of the traditional meanings of all the words they use in their news scripts. Only when you know the technical meaning of a word that is in transition can you make a deliberate and informed choice about whether to use it in the modern way. Most editors advise journalists not to pre-empt any changes of meaning. Using words in a precise and fairly traditional way upsets no-one, and will bring greater respect from some in the audience.

Ambiguity

> Language is as capable of obscuring the truth as it is of revealing it.
> (Tom Stoppard, *Professional Foul*,
> television play, 1977)

If we want our scripts to be clear and easily understood, it is important to avoid all risk of ambiguity. I'm sure most readers will know some of Fleet Street's legendary headline ambiguities.

Councillors To Act on Strip Shows

Women Who Smoke Have Lighter Children

and the wartime classics:

Eisenhower Flies Back To Front

Eighth Army Push Bottles Up Germans

Try not to join this hall of fame. In broadcasting, it's surprisingly easy to write something on paper that seems to mean something else when read out loud. A BBC radio headline spoke of '. . . a promise of money to rescue the Scottish steel industry from the recently formed Lanarkshire Development Agency'. An embarrassed TV presenter made it on to YouTube in 2009 with his head-line, 'This is BBC World News. I'm Jonathan Charles. Kept hidden for almost two decades and forced to bear children . . .'. The risk of ambiguity is another reason to read your script aloud before it gets to air-time. Usually any danger of misunderstanding will be avoided by a very precise use of phrases and sentence construction.

Precision

Accurate reporting in a crisp, concise style leaves no room for imprecision. Facts are golden, and we should ensure that every script we write has plenty of key facts. But quite frequently we are not sure whether a fact is a fact. 'Eighty thousand people marched through central London today . . .' Did you count them? Organisers of marches tend to exaggerate the numbers. It is always a good idea to attribute such so-called facts. 'The organisers say that eighty thousand joined the march. The police put the figure at fifty thousand. Certainly it was a strong show of opposition to the bill, and sent a clear message to Downing Street . . .' Attributing information to the source is good journalism. It may take a few seconds longer, but it will mean that your script carries complete credibility with all who hear it, including those who were on that march.

Sometimes our routine use of journalistic phrases can blur or even distort the facts. For example, when we are told that something 'had to be' done, it is not necessarily so. 'The area was evacuated' is fact. 'The area had to be evac-uated' is an assumption. And if we report, 'The police had to open fire to quell the rioters', it is highly contentious.

The river burst its banks.

Did it? The river probably 'overflowed its banks'.

The police are stepping up their search for the missing schoolgirls.

Have they brought in more officers overnight, or are they really 'continuing' the search?

Coming up next, all the business news from around the world.

All of it? Really?

This may seem like nit-picking, but most experienced editors in news and current affairs want their journalists to be able to write extremely precisely, avoiding ambiguities, exaggerations, generalisations and vague pieces of journalese.

Questions of attribution

It is a firm principle of objective journalism that the source of any piece of information or assertion should be made clear if there could be any doubt about it. 'According to witnesses three men burst into the pub ...' 'The Department of Health says that hospital waiting lists are down for the third month running ... '

In print journalism, the information or assertion tends to come first, with the attribution afterwards. 'Hospital waiting lists are down for the third month running, according to figures released by the Department of Health.' In broadcasting, we should normally identify the source of the assertion before making it, for two reasons. First, the spoken assertion from a trusted news presenter carries great conviction. The immediate impression will be that this is unquestionably true, even though the viewers or listeners are in no position to make a judgement on the validity of the assertion until they know where it comes from. We should not write, 'HRT is the modern equivalent of thalidomide, and could be causing 20,000 deaths from breast cancer in Britain every year, according to a medical safety expert in Germany.'

The second reason for putting the source first is that we usually speak that way. You would be unlikely to say, 'I am a lazy good-for-nothing who can't write for toffee, and who should be working in a post room, not a newsroom. That's the view of my little sister.' It's much more natural to say, 'My little sister thinks I'm useless, etc.'

This is particularly important when you are quoting someone directly. Newspapers regularly put the quote first: 'I believe that force can be justified on humanitarian grounds, as it was in the Balkans, or in other places that have been scarred by war. Inaction tears at our conscience and can lead to more costly intervention later', said President Obama in his Nobel Peace Prize acceptance speech. In broadcasting, it just doesn't work. Listeners must know who was saying something before they hear what was said.

Sometimes even the vocabulary we use has to have some form of attribution. Elsewhere in this book, there is advice on the need to attribute words such as 'terrorist' or 'racist'. It is inadvisable for a scriptwriter to put into the mouth of the newsreader a contentious phrase such as 'the war against terror' without either attributing it, for example, '. . . to what Mrs Clinton called "the war against terror"', or at the very least '. . . the so-called war against terror"'.

ACCURATE NAMES

Accuracy in the way names and titles are written is paramount if you don't want the credibility of your service to be eroded. It's not too difficult to avoid irritating errors once you are aware of the main pitfalls. But there are quite a few traps for the unwary.

Names and titles: the establishment

The higher levels of the British establishment tend to be the danger zones, with the church, the military, the aristocracy and the judiciary insisting on the preservation of traditional usages. Here are a few examples.

The judiciary

- Law Lords: Lord Brown
- Appeal Court Judges: Lord Justice Brown
- High Court Judges: Mr Justice Brown (even though they are normally Knights or Dames)
- Circuit Judges: Judge Brown (sitting in either the Crown Court or County Court); when two judges have the same surname, the forename of the junior is given: Judge Brown and Judge Jane Brown

Note that Stipendiary Magistrates are now called District Judges, just like the County Court District Judges, who used to be called Registrars.

There is full guidance on this on the Ministry of Justice website: www.judiciary.gov.uk/about_judiciary/forms_of_address/index.htm

Juries return a verdict; the Coroner records a verdict. In civil cases, the parties are the claimant (formally the plaintiff) and the defendant. But note that the legal system in Scotland is quite separate, and has a host of different names (see page 70).

The church

When using 'Reverend', we should use 'The' and a Christian name: The Reverend John Smith or The Reverend Jane Smith, rather than Reverend Smith or The Reverend Smith. After the first mention, they can be called Mr Smith or Miss/Mrs Smith (see note on 'Ms' in spoken English, below). Or in the Roman Catholic Church, Father Smith. Personally, I think 'Reverend Smith' is so widely used that it does not cause much offence, but I know others disagree. Certainly it is satisfying to get it precisely right. If in doubt, you can refer to *Crockford's Clerical Dictionary*.

The military

Members of the armed forces are rightly annoyed when we get regimental titles wrong. For example, The Royal Fusiliers (now incorrect) was one of five regiments amalgamated to form The Royal Regiment of Fusiliers, which is what we must say.

The Last Post is sounded, not played. The RAF does not have planes, it has aircraft. And in the Royal Navy, submarines are not ships; they are boats.

Gongs

Medals are conferred on, or awarded to, members of the military; not given to them. Civilians are not given a Knighthood or a Peerage, they receive it, or they are made a Peer or a Knight, or a Dame. (As far as I know, there is no such thing as receiving a Damehood.) People do not get a CBE, OBE or MBE, they are appointed.

Lords and Ladies

Titles of nobility are, in descending order, Duke, Marquess, Earl, Viscount and Baron. It makes life a great deal simpler if we call all peers Lord and all peeresses Lady. This means we do not have to worry whether they are a viscount or a marquess, or if their wife is a baroness or countess (wives of earls). 'Lady Thatcher' and 'Baroness Thatcher' are equally acceptable. *The Times Guide to*

English Style and Usage takes the view that the full title is used first, with Lord or Lady used thereafter, which is a quite widely followed policy in the press, and would work in broadcasting. Perhaps it's best to use 'Lord' if we are reporting something relating to the person's position in the upper house, and 'Marquess' (or whatever) if we are reporting trouble with the upkeep of their country estate. This does not apply to Dukes and Duchesses, whose titles do not change; for example, the Duke of Westminster is not called Lord Westminster.

Names and titles: lesser mortals

But it is also very important to give consistently accurate titles to lesser mortals. Every radio station, TV news service or online site should have a guide to house style, which establishes an agreed format for such things as the use of titles. Most broadcasters in Britain follow the BBC style of *Joseph Bloggs* for the first use, and *Mr Bloggs* thereafter. (It's not so many years ago that Radio Four was using Mr Joseph Bloggs, but that sounds pretty old-fashioned now.) With women, it has become a little trickier in recent years, with more women using the title Ms, which some people don't actually say because they don't know how to pronounce it, and which some women dislike. Normally you will know if it is Mrs Bloggs or Miss Bloggs. If you don't, try to avoid the 'Ms' usage, which is not widely used in spoken English and is difficult to say clearly, by using the full name; or find out!

Another relatively recent change in broadcasting has been the use of titles with the names of people charged with crimes or appearing in court. This follows guidelines issued to judges and magistrates. These pointed out that, 'Stand up Bloggs!' is rude, reeks of a past class structure, and also seems to imply guilt, when the defendant is innocent until proved guilty. Even today, some journalists seem uncomfortable with the use of titles in serious cases. But I am certain that it is right to say, 'Mr Huntley appeared in court . . .' or 'Mr Shipman's solicitor . . .' until the defendant has been proved guilty, at which point they lose their courtesy title as well as their liberty. I think this even applies to sport personalities, who by tradition are known by their surname. If a footballer is charged with assault outside a bar, for example, I think he should be termed 'Mr Woodgate', with a proper title just like any other defendant.

Again, it is a matter of house style whether you use foreign titles with foreign names: Señor Barroso; Monsieur Sarkozy. The BBC style is to use the English version: Mr Zapatero; Mr Burlusconi, usually after first using their full name. Most other broadcasters do the same, though some rather inconsistently.

On first-name terms?

In broadcasting, journalists sometimes have to write an introduction to a live interview, or conduct interviews themselves. The convention for news and current affairs programmes is one of courteous formality, when title and surname are used.

> Joining me now is Clare Turner from Amnesty – Good morning Miss Turner.

Only children are normally addressed by their first name in serious factual programmes. But the recent move towards more accessible and less formal news has led to more use of first names.

> Louise Christian is the detainee's solicitor. Good morning Louise . . .' (*BBC Breakfast*).

> 'Joining me now is Dr Hanan Ashrawi, the Palestinian legislator and human rights activist. Hanan, what's your reaction . . . ?' (*Larry King Live*, CNN).

I dislike this usage in mainstream news programmes. It can sound patronising, especially when it is usually women who receive the first-name treatment. It certainly sounds as though the interviewer and interviewee are old friends, which can easily damage a channel's reputation for impartiality. Some programmes may deliberately adopt a friendlier style, but it should be done consistently. For most news programmes, the formal styles of address are better.

Names of organisations

As for names of organisations or offices, it's just a question of noticing what is right and taking care. Here are a few that are sometimes used inaccurately:

- St John Ambulance Brigade, not St John's.
- Register office, not registry office.
- Scouts and Guides, not Boy Scouts or Girl Guides. (In the USA there are also Girl Scouts.) Cub Scouts have replaced Wolf Cubs. Scout Leaders have replaced Scoutmasters.
- Trooping the Colour, not Trooping of the Colour.
- An Ambassador *to* a country, but *in* a capital: the British Ambassador *to* the United States; the British Ambassador *in* Washington.
- The United Kingdom does not have ambassadors in Commonwealth countries, it has High Commissioners, who work in High Commissions.
- The Anglican Church has different branches: the Church *of* England; the Church *of* Ireland; but the Episcopal Church *in* Scotland; the Church *in* Wales.

- Unfair dismissal cases used to be heard in industrial tribunals; now they are employment tribunals.
- The British Athletics Association became the British Athletic Association, then simply British Athletics.

Abbreviated names

Abbreviations and acronyms should be used with care. If you are not sure that a very high proportion of listeners will identify the organisation immediately, you should use an explanatory phrase. Some initials are universally well known. The great majority of listeners and viewers in Britain will probably know NATO, NASA, the CIA, the TUC, the BBC and ITV.

But very many more acronyms are not well known. It is easy for journalists who write about many organisations each day to forget that consumers have to dredge up these initials from memory and work them out instantly if they are going to understand the story. I guess that not everyone immediately knows the MOD (Ministry of Defence), or the CBI (Confederation of British Industry), or the BAA (British Airports Authority). They are certainly going to struggle with Nacro (originally the National Association for the Care and Resettlement of Offenders, NACRO). If your story is about a Nacro report, you must use an explanatory phrase such as 'the charity that helps ex-offenders resettle' or 'the charity that works with individuals at risk of getting involved in crime', depending on the subject of the story.

It is worth noting that ACAS is not the *government's* Advisory, Conciliation and Arbitration Service, as it is sometimes described. It is independent, and guards that independent status jealously.

As a general rule, it is poor writing to clutter a script with abbreviations or acronyms, and if there's any doubt about instant recognition of the organisation, take a couple of seconds to explain what it is.

Registered names

It is quite common in conversation to hear a trade name being used to mean a general type of product. It is not good journalistic practice to reproduce this on the air. Many people might say, 'I've just hoovered the hall and landing', and the verb 'to hoover' is in the dictionary; but all the people who make or sell Dyson, Panasonic, Electrolux or the countless other types of vacuum cleaner may be rather miffed to hear their rival, Hoover, being plugged in this way on the news: for example, 'Forensic teams have been hoovering up every scrap of evidence . . .' (Signal Radio). There is also the occasional risk of legal action in using registered names inaccurately. A story about someone being electrocuted while hoovering the landing might land you in court if it turned out not that no Hoover was involved.

Here are a few commonly used registered names, which we should try to avoid using in an imprecise way.

Cellophane	Kleenex
Fibreglass (Fiberglas)	Outward Bound
Google	Sellotape
Hoover	Teflon
Jacuzzi	Valium
Jiffy Bag	

Outward Bound is an interesting example. It is the name of a long-established company that runs adventure excursions. On several occasions, it has successfully sued broadcasters and newspapers for using the Outward Bound name incorrectly in reports about accidents happening during outdoor-pursuits events run by other organisations.

ACCURATE GEOGRAPHY

One subject that provokes a large number of complaints to broadcasters every year is the inaccurate use of place names, and insensitivity to the audience's sense of place or nationality. Inaccurate geography seriously erodes a news organisation's authority; it also makes the broadcaster seem remote to the listener or viewer. And often the newsroom is indeed remote from many of its target audience. In Britain, most national news programmes come from London, and are written by people who live in and around London. Some of these journalists have never lived anywhere else. If you are listening away from the capital, in Towcester, for example, and you hear your home town pronounced 'teow-sester' (as has happened on BBC radio), you will be contemptuous and unforgiving.

It is very important for journalists to have a decent grasp of the geography of their own country, and at the very least, a basic knowledge of the world. Audiences in different parts of the UK see their country from different perspectives. Their lives have been shaped by different cultural backgrounds, and different civic or political institutions. Political devolution to the Parliament in Scotland, and to the Assemblies in Wales and Northern Ireland, has increased diversity.

If you are going to work for an international channel or agency, such as the BBC World Service, BBC World News, CNN International, CNBC, Bloomberg TV, Reuters TV, APTN, Euronews, Al-Jazeera Europe or Sky News, you should get a good, up-to-date atlas, such as *The Times Concise Atlas of the World*, and study it!

My country – right or wrong?

There are complexities in both the geographical and geopolitical landscapes of the British Isles. Journalists working in Britain should not be baffled by their own country. Here are a few pointers.

• The British Isles is a geographical term describing the group of islands off the north-west coast of mainland Europe. It comprises the United Kingdom and the Republic of Ireland, plus the Isle of Man and the Channel Islands.

• Britain, or Great Britain, is England, Scotland, Wales and the Channel Islands.

• The United Kingdom is Britain and Northern Ireland, and for this reason is becoming more widely preferred to Great Britain. Most editors in broadcasting advise scriptwriters to use the full 'United Kingdom' rather than 'the UK'. After all, we would not start a story with, 'The President of the US ...' but with 'The President of the United States ...' 'UK-wide' is hardly the way we speak. Better to say, 'across the country'. Better still to say 'across the United Kingdom', because words such as country, nation and capital mean different things in different places.

• The word Briton for a person who comes from Britain is not in general use – unless you are talking about the Ancient Britons – and is to be avoided. 'Two people from Britain are thought to be among those injured in the explosion ...' is much better than the marginally shorter 'Two Britons ...'. If the information is available, it is always best to be as precise as possible: 'Two men, one from the London area and one from Wales ...'.

And it is worth remembering that our society is multi-ethnic, and extremely mobile. Many people do not live in the nation of their birth. People residing in England are not necessarily 'English'. There are believed to be about 750,000 Scots people and 550,000 Welsh people living in England. One in twelve people living in Scotland is English-born. In Wales, the figure is one in five. So we should be careful not to make sweeping statements in our writing. It is more accurate to say 'People in Scotland are voting today . . .' rather than 'The Scots are voting today . . .'.

A sense of place

In general terms, journalists writing for a British audience should always remember that each listener and viewer has a sense of place, and views the UK from their own perspective. When the government introduced devolution just before the turn of the twenty-first century, the BBC issued its journalists with a forty-page guide called *The Changing UK*, which listed the powers and structures of the new political bodies, but also took the opportunity to address the lingering and irritating problem of insensitive writing that ignores the differences in sense-of-place. Here is an extract from the guidance.

> Our audience will be deeply interested in any item on a programme about the place where they live. However they will be offended by any sloppiness in how we describe where it is. We must be accurate and consistent. Few people have a perfect geographical knowledge of the UK. For most of our audience, the further away a place is from where they live, the less likely they are to know where it is. We must strike a balance between informing part of our audience while not patronising another section.
>
> We would never say 'Plymouth in England', because England is a large place and that is too imprecise. By the same standard we should never refer to Inverness as 'Inverness in Scotland'. If necessary, say which area a place is in, and if it is remote or little-known, place it as 'near' the closest well-known town. But again, be consistent. If we would never say 'Halifax near Leeds', we should never say 'Hamilton near Glasgow'.

This problem of locating a town is brought into sharp focus when broadcasters have a house style that uses pay-offs at the end of each report, as the BBC and ITN have done for many years. There has been a tendency to use very specific locations when reporting from London, and very general ones when reporting from other parts of the country.

Jane Smith, *BBC News*, Chiswick Magistrates Court

Jane Smith, *BBC News*, Scotland

It would be better and more consistent to say:

Jane Smith, *BBC News*, Chiswick Magistrates Court in west London

Jane Smith, *BBC News*, the High Court in Edinburgh

On television, the use of a simple map in the introduction can help to locate a town or city without the script having to remind us, for example, where exactly Lockerbie is. A few years ago, television news programmes used maps much more than they do now. I don't know why maps have fallen out of fashion – perhaps laziness or lack of time. Or perhaps it is because using a map of a fairly well known place can appear to be stupid or patronising to those who live in that area, so it is easier not to take that risk. Personally, I am sure that simple maps help many viewers who aren't sure about precise locations.

Different organisations in the UK

Journalists working in England should remember that many familiar organisations do not operate across the whole of the UK. If the story is in Scotland, Wales or Northern Ireland, check that you have the correct name of the organisation.

For example, the Football Association (FA) is not called the English Football Association, but it is separate from the Scottish and Welsh Football Associations, while Northern Ireland has the Irish Football Association. (The Republic of Ireland has the Football Association of Ireland.) Depending on the story, it might be worth adding a line to clarify that the FA runs football in England.

Do not assume that a group that has 'National' in its name has a remit across the UK. The National Society for the Prevention of Cruelty to Children (NSPCC) has a sister organisation in Scotland called Children First. The National Union of Teachers (NUT) is the biggest teaching union in England and Wales, but it has no remit in Scotland, where the largest teaching union is the Educational Institute of Scotland. In Northern Ireland, the biggest teaching union is the NAS/UWT.

Even the 'national curriculum' in schools isn't really national. It doesn't apply at all in Scotland, and the Welsh version is slightly different because the Welsh language is included. It's best to talk about the English National Curriculum or the Welsh National Curriculum.

Different social trends and patterns

We should take care when writing stories about trends. 'House prices leapt by nearly twenty per cent in the past six months . . .' is a pretty misleading start to a story if you are hearing it in Scotland, and discover in the fourth sentence that prices in London and the south-east are soaring while in Scotland they are hardly moving. Trends often have wide variations across the country, so we should try to report them as precisely as possible.

School holidays are often taken at different times in various parts of Britain. So beware of the generalised introduction, 'As our children prepare to go back to school next week . . .'. In Scotland, where they tend to have summer holidays earlier, they may have been back for a fortnight already. And sometimes bank holidays are different, a point that can be missed in travel reports.

The Chair of the Scottish Broadcasting Commission, Blair Jenkins, was previously BBC Scotland's Head of News and Current Affairs, and Scottish Television's Director of Broadcasting within ITV. He thinks reporting of the UK has improved a great deal.

> When I worked in London 25 years ago, BBC journalists just didn't understand the need to distinguish between 'British' and 'English'. Editors would be puzzled when, after some trouble at England football matches abroad was attributed to British fans, the switchboard would be jammed with complaints from other countries in the UK. They just didn't get it.
>
> I remember as senior duty editor on the *Nine o'clock News* one night, a sub-editor had written a story about job losses in Dundee and was using a map to show viewers where the city was. I asked him if he would have used a map for Brighton. 'No', he said, 'because everyone knows where Brighton is . . .'.
>
> Nowadays a great deal of thought is given to getting not just the facts right but also the tone. We do still run into problems when things are described as 'national', or happening 'all over the country', when in fact they're not. People in Scotland feel slightly dislocated when Yorkshire or Lancashire are referred to as 'the north' in a UK broadcast. They're certainly in the north of England, but to someone in Inverness, places like Manchester and Bradford are definitely in the south!
>
> The main advice, as always, is to think about the audience you are serving. If it is a UK-wide audience, you have to report from a UK perspective.

The nations of the UK

The structures of government in the United Kingdom have changed significantly with devolution. And the devolved authorities have different powers in the 'nations' of the UK. The Scottish Parliament and the Northern Ireland Assembly can make their own laws. In 2006, the Welsh Assembly gained more legislative powers, but Westminster approval is required in some key areas. The Scottish Parliament can raise taxes; Wales cannot.

When writing stories for a domestic audience, it's wise to keep in mind how it will sound to audiences in the different nations, and whether or not your story is accurate across the UK. Never assume that an issue affects everyone in the same way. Health, education, transport, agriculture, fisheries, environment, planning, economic development, social services and sport are just some of the areas of life that are organised differently in each nation.

So we should make clear who is affected by a story or an issue, normally in the first sentence, and even in headlines.

> Teachers in England and Wales are to be balloted on industrial action . . .
>
> NHS consultants in Scotland are being offered a new kind of contract . . .
>
> University students in England and Wales could face higher tuition fees . . .

Scotland

Some journalists working in England still don't seem to have grasped that they do things rather differently in Scotland, such as running their own legal system, as well as most of the public services (in many people's opinion more efficiently than in England), with wide powers devolved to the Scottish Parliament. Forgetting these differences can infuriate the Scots. So if a story is about water authorities in England and Wales, don't change it to 'Britain's water authorities'.

Devolution has drawn more attention to these differences, but it is not a new problem for writers south of the border. A few years ago, when the first English councils started setting their poll-tax levels, Radio and TV in England regularly ignored the fact that Scotland had gone through it all a year before. 'Derbyshire has become the first council in the country to set its community charge rate above the government limit' (BBC Radio Four). No, it was the first in England.

There is some confusion about these UK terms. The 'country' or the 'nation' can mean either the whole of the United Kingdom, or one of its constituent nations. After devolution, the BBC renamed its Regional Directorate 'Nations and Regions', because there is now a clear difference between an English region, such as the West Midlands, and a nation such as Scotland. My advice to scriptwriters is to be aware of this possible confusion, and try to be specific. For example, 'Sterling is the first Council in Britain/Scotland to ban smoking in restaurants'.

As Blair Jenkins has indicated, a particular irritant for viewers and listeners in Scotland, and indeed in Wales and Northern Ireland, is the habit of confusing national sport teams, or not to give proper credit to the individual nations. During one Commonwealth Games, headlines on *BBC Radio News* proudly announced that England had won another gold and two more bronze medals, ignoring a silver won by Scotland. And if scriptwriters are foolish enough to describe hooligan England football supporters as British fans, they are likely to be thrown over Hadrian's Wall to explain in person to the outraged five million Scots who seem to email or phone the broadcasters whenever it happens. They are England fans, or followers of England.

When locating a story in Scotland, we should be precise. We would be unlikely to write 'Worcester in England', or 'Leeds in England', so should avoid 'Perth in Scotland' or 'East Kilbride in Scotland'. Try to indicate the county or region. 'Central Scotland' is still acceptable, despite the scrapping of the Central administrative region.

Scottish politics

The Scottish Parliament in Edinburgh doesn't have a Prime Minister, it has a First Minister. The different ministers should be referred to as, for example, 'The Minister for Health in Scotland' or 'Scotland's Health Minister', to distinguish clearly from their counterparts at Westminster. The initials MSP, for Members of the Scottish Parliament, are still not very familiar south of the border, so using the full title is advisable in broadcasts outside Scotland.

It's also a good idea to use the full title of The Secretary of State for Scotland, rather than 'The Scottish Secretary', to ensure that the Westminster base and cabinet role are immediately clear to the audience.

The political spectrum in Scotland is very different from that in the rest of the UK. At the time of writing, following the creation of a Conservative-led coalition at Westminster, there is only one Conservative MP in Scotland. So it is particularly important to make sure audiences know what is meant by the ruling party and the opposition when reporting politics in Scotland.

Scottish courts

A major difference between Scotland and the other nations is its separate legal system. As we all know, crime and courts play a big part in journalism, so news writers in the UK should have a broad understanding of the main differences in the Scottish legal system. Here are just a few pointers.

- There are no Magistrates' Courts or Crown Courts in Scotland. The lowest Scottish criminal court is the District Court. Most criminal cases are dealt with in the Sheriff Court (note that it is called Sheriff Court, not Sheriff's Court).

- Don't talk about barristers. Lawyers appearing in higher Scottish courts are called advocates.

- Don't talk about a defendant in a criminal case. He or she is the accused. In a civil case, they are the defender (and the plaintiff is the pursuer).

- A jury in Scotland can choose to return a verdict of not proven, which is the equivalent of an acquittal. In a criminal case, the jury is normally composed of fifteen people.

- There is no Crown Prosecution Service in Scotland. The Procurator Fiscal, or his or her Fiscal Depute, is the prosecutor in a Sheriff Court. The Procurator Fiscal also investigates complaints against the police; there is no Police Complaints Authority.

- There is no injunction in Scotland. The equivalent is an interdict.

- There are no inquests in Scotland; instead there will be a fatal accident enquiry.

- There is no offence of arson; it is called wilful fire-raising.

See www.copfs.gov.uk for more information on the Scottish justice system.

Scottish education

In England, Wales and Northern Ireland, there are GCSE exams, normally taken in the fifth year of secondary school when pupils are 16; and A-levels, taken when they are 17 or 18. In Scotland, the equivalents were Standard Grades and Intermediates, normally taken at 16; Higher Grades or Highers, taken at 17; and Advanced Highers, taken at 18. But the Scottish government has announced that from 2014 there will be a new national exam to replace Standard Grades and Intermediates, with compulsory tests in numeracy and literacy. Highers are to remain.

Most university degrees in Scotland require a four-year course, rather than the three-year standard course found elsewhere in the UK. And they have a completely different policy on tuition fees.

Wales

People living in Wales will scoff if they hear, 'Camarthen in Wales' or Port Talbot in Wales'. Use the four principal regions, North Wales, Mid Wales, West Wales and South Wales, if the town isn't big enough to be easily recognised. Or use the names of the twenty-two unitary authorities, which appeared in the last local government reorganisation. (Note that Clwyd, Dyfed and Gwent no longer exist as authorities, though they are still widely used as names of regions. For example, the *South Wales Argus* still uses in headlines, 'Gwent Man Injured' or 'Gwent House Prices Falling').

Welsh politics

The full title of the assembly in Cardiff is The National Assembly for Wales, though it is usually called The Welsh Assembly. It has a First Secretary rather than a First Minister, and the equivalents of the Ministers in Scotland are called Secretaries, as in 'The Welsh Assembly Secretary for Health'. The elected representatives are called Welsh Assembly Members.

When talking about the Secretary of State for Wales at Westminster, we should beware of the possible confusion between 'Welsh Secretary' and 'First Secretary for Wales', so the full title of the Secretary of State for Wales is preferable.

Incidentally, hardly anyone calls Wales 'The Principality' in normal speech.

Northern Ireland

Reporting events in Northern Ireland places particular demands on journalists. People in Northern Ireland are understandably sensitive to ill-chosen language, and offended by inaccuracies. To some ears, certain words and expressions suggest a political point of view. It is important for broadcasters to use terms that are factual and neutral.

Northern Ireland is part of the United Kingdom, it is not part of Great Britain. Some people in Northern Ireland regard themselves as British; others regard themselves as Irish.

It is widely acceptable to call it The Province as a second reference, though historically, Ulster was one of four provinces of Ireland, and in that context Ulster includes three counties in the Republic, as well as the six counties that make up Northern Ireland. For this reason, it is unwise to use 'Ulster' as a synonym, even if some interviewees do so. 'The Six Counties' is used at times by nationalists and republicans to emphasise the historical separation of Northern Ireland from the rest of the island. The phrase represents a political viewpoint, so impartial journalists should not use it. The best advice is to stick to 'Northern Ireland', with 'The Province' possible as a subsequent reference.

The North of Ireland is a description sometimes used by nationalists in preference to Northern Ireland; again, this makes a political point, and should be avoided by journalists. But it is widely acceptable to talk about 'the North' when referring to Northern Ireland, and 'the South' when referring to the Republic of Ireland. The Republic of Ireland can be referred to as The Irish Republic, or even The Republic, where the context is clear. But if you are writing in English as opposed to Irish, don't call it Eire.

The name of Londonderry/Derry is probably the best known example of terminology that can divide the communities. Broadly speaking, nationalists call the city Derry while unionists call it Londonderry. The BBC practice, which has been followed by most other broadcasters for many years, is to call the city Londonderry on the first use, and Derry thereafter. But note that the local authority is called Derry City Council.

The political landscape in Northern Ireland

Journalists must understand the main points of the political scene in Northern Ireland, and get the terminology right in their scripts. When it is not suspended, the Northern Ireland Assembly sits at Stormont in Belfast, and is run by an Executive Committee headed by a First Minister. Elections are every four years and use the single transferable vote system. Those elected become Members of the Northern Ireland Assembly, or Northern Ireland Assembly Members. Ministers are referred to as 'The Health Minister in the Northern Ireland Assembly' or, more usually, 'The Northern Ireland Health Minister'.

It is important to describe a person's political position accurately, and according to the codes that have gained acceptance in recent years. But journalists should not refer to someone's religion unless it is strictly relevant to the story. The Northern Ireland community is broadly split into two groups, defined by their political affiliations and religious beliefs. But it would be a mistake to characterise the political divisions simply as a conflict between Catholics and Protestants. It is more complicated than that. There are significant sections of the population who do not regard themselves as having an affiliation to either community. And some will regard themselves as nationalists or unionists, but will not espouse any particular religious beliefs. Always try to establish how each person in a political story would like be described.

Here are some suggestions on terminology that might help you write stories about Northern Ireland.

*   *Unionists*: This is used to describe people who want to maintain Northern Ireland's position within the United Kingdom. Unionists are predominantly, though not exclusively, Protestant, usually from one of three main denominations, Presbyterian, Church of Ireland (Anglican), or Methodist. The DUP and the UUP are the main Unionist parties.

*   *Loyalist*: the term comes from those who are loyal to the Crown, and tends to refer to people with very strongly held views, some of whom operate outside the electoral system. The Orange Order is a legitimate loyalist organisation. But 'loyalist' has also been used over the years to describe paramilitary organisations such as the Ulster Defence Association, the Ulster Freedom Fighters and the Ulster Volunteer Force, so the word is weighted towards the more extreme unionist organisations.

*   *Nationalist*: describes those who want a united Ireland. Nationalists are likely to be Catholics, but you shouldn't assume this. For many years, the largest nationalist party was the Social Democratic and Labour Party (SDLP), who consistently rejected violent methods. After the Good Friday Agreement in 1998, Sinn Féin gained considerable support in the nationalist community, and in 2003 became the largest nationalist party.

*   *Republican*: this term has come to mean those who also want to see a united Ireland, but not always through exclusively democratic means. They are generally regarded as more hard-line in their approach, but this doesn't mean that all people who call themselves Republican condone violence. Sinn Féin is described as a Republican party. Historically it had close links with the IRA, but independent journalists should never refer to the party as 'Sinn Féin–IRA', even though some Unionist politicians still do so. The IRA is an illegal organisation. Sinn Féin has many elected representatives. Take care when talking about people living in the Republic of Ireland, most of whom regard themselves as Republicans but do not condone violence. It's best to reserve the word for Republicans in Northern Ireland.

Since the IRA put its weapons 'beyond use' in 2005, the loyalist paramilitary organisations decommissioned their weapons in 2009, and the Irish National Liberation Army (INLA) followed suit in 2010, there has been a continuing threat of violence from relatively small groups known as 'dissident republicans'

– such as the 'Real IRA' and 'Continuity IRA'. We should always ensure viewers and listeners know these are self-appointed titles; for example, 'the police suspect that dissident republicans from the so-called Real IRA are behind the shooting'.

England

Listeners and viewers in parts of England can also be sensitive about their sense of place, particularly if they hear the kind of 'up north', 'in the sticks', or 'out in the provinces' expressions occasionally used by self-styled London sophisticates or home counties types. Journalists working in London and writing news for national channels should always remember that most of the audience does not live in London. To write, 'The Prime Minister will be on his way up to Leeds tomorrow . . .' or 'The Home Secretary is coming back from Blackpool today . . .' makes sense only for listeners in the capital.

In general terms, scripts for national or international news bulletins should talk about 'the west of England' or 'the north of England', rather than 'the west' or 'the north'. It's helpful to be aware of changes to the unitary authorities. For example, Avon, Cleveland, Humberside, and Hereford and Worcester have been abolished. In my view, there is such widespread confusion about the structure of local government that there is no real problem in using the names of regions that people recognise, but that have no technical existence, such as the West Midlands, Greater Manchester, or Humberside.

Europe

More than thirty-five years after the United Kingdom joined the European Community, I am dismayed that some broadcast journalists still seem to think that the UK is not part of Europe. Radio and television scripts frequently compare British healthcare, crime figures or social habits with those 'in Europe'. This is sloppy scripting. It should be 'in the rest of Europe', or maybe 'in mainland Europe', or 'on the Continent'.

Some Europhiles seem to think this sloppiness is evidence of a grand anti-Europe conspiracy in the media. I think phraseology suggesting that Britain is outside Europe is much more likely to have been picked up subconsciously from the attitudes and vocabularies we read every day in the overwhelmingly anti-European British press. The *Sun, Daily Mail, Daily Telegraph, The Times, Daily Express, London Evening Standard* and many more national and regional newspapers regularly use language indicating that we Brits are not part of Europe (though I don't think the little-Englander terminology is quite as blatant as it was in the time of the famous headline in *The Times*, 'Fog in Channel: Continent Isolated'). It may be quite tempting for broadcast journalists to repeat this kind of phraseology, but I think they should resist the temptation. We should use language which is correct and neutral, not weighted with either pro-EU or anti-EU sentiment.

So broadcast journalists should not talk about 'going to Europe for our holidays'. Say 'taking holidays in Europe', or be more specific depending on the story. 'Britain's trade with Europe' should be 'Britain's trade with the rest of Europe'. And talk of 'the Europeans' should certainly be avoided. Usually it is meaningless. Do we mean the Germans or the Greeks, the Portuguese or the Poles? The use of the word Brussels to mean the European Union is particularly vague, and is irritating to many people, especially when we hear that 'Brussels believes . . .' or 'Brussels has issued a directive . . .', with the phrase sometimes followed by an exaggerated claim of bureaucratic lunacy, written by a journalist who clearly does not know how the EU works.

And the word Europe should not be used too often as a short version of 'the European Union'. Europe is a continent, which includes several countries that are not members of the EU, such as Norway and Switzerland.

The EU – getting it right

When the UK was about to hold the presidency of the EU Council of Ministers, the British media magazine *Press Gazette* asked me to conduct a survey of senior broadcast news editors and producers, to establish how much, or how little, they knew about the EU. The results were, to quote the magazine, 'shocking'. No-one could name the President of the European Parliament, few could name the member states of the EU, and fewer still could spot the odd one out among The Council of Ministers, The Council of Europe, and The European Council. (In case you are wondering, The Council of Europe is the odd one out; it is a completely separate body from the EU, older and larger, based in Strasbourg, and concerned with the promotion of human rights, democracy and European cultural values.)

Over the years, many journalists have found it difficult to write about the European Union. It can seem to be a boring story, with no good pictures for television, with complicated procedures which take a long time to produce results, and with few dramatic moments of decision or confrontation. It has been easier for political correspondents to report the EU through the prism of British politics, as a subject that splits parties and brings down prime ministers, rather than an important subject in its own right.

Nowadays, there seems to be a growing recognition that journalist must understand the EU better. Some writers openly admit that 'Europe' has not been reported well since the United Kingdom joined the EEC in 1973. Many commentators argue that the Union has become one of the great projects in European history, driving the economic revival of the continent after the devastation of the Second World War, and making the idea of war between the nations of Europe unthinkable for the first time in history. Yet they remain ill-informed about the way it operates.

In the twenty-first century, a growing number of issues are being addressed at the European level, including the attempts to revive economies after the world recession of 2008–10, globalised business and leisure, action against climate change, anti-terrorism measures, mass migration, a changing relationship with the USA and China, and the need to reform agriculture and fisheries. Many European laws already have primacy over national laws, and with the ratification if the Lisbon Treaty in 2009, there will be more in the future. The EU is a divisive issue. Is it a threat to national sovereignty? Is it hugely wasteful? All young journalists entering the profession should try to understand the EU well. At the very least, they should use accurate language when reporting it. Here are a few reminders.

- There is a triangle of power centres running the EU: the Council, the Commission, and the Parliament.

- Council meetings are the occasions when the member states get together to agree policies. The Council of Ministers is the name of the ministerial-level meetings, held usually in Brussels but sometimes in Strasbourg or Luxembourg. For example, Britain's Chancellor of the Exchequer attends the regular meetings of the Council of Economic and Finance Ministers (known in EU circles as the Ecofin meeting, but never to be described that way on air!). The 'Council of Ministers' may be an unfamiliar title to many people, so it is best to write 'European Farm Ministers meeting in Brussels . . .' or . . . 'A meeting of European Union Environment Ministers . . .'. When the heads of government meet (usually four times a year), it is a meeting of The European Council, which is generally described as a European Summit.

- The European Commission is often described as the civil service of the EU. It certainly is the administration, but it has more political influence than the Whitehall civil service, which carries out the policies of the UK government of the day. The Commission, based in Brussels, oversees the enforcement of EU laws and proposes new ones, attempting to negotiate directives that will be acceptable to all member states. EU

Commissioners hold portfolios that broadly match the ministries in the member states, and attend their Council meetings to try to push through agreements. On appointment, EU Commissioners and the Commission President pledge not to represent their home country, but to work for the general good of the club of European nations.

- The European Parliament meets in plenary session in Strasbourg (in French Alsace, near the border with Germany), nearly every month, and holds five or six so-called mini-sessions in Brussels each year. In the past, the Parliament has been regarded as a talking shop with little real power. But successive treaties have given the directly elected body more powers. Now, following the implementation of the Lisbon Treaty, a wide range of policy areas are subject to 'co-decision' between the Council of Ministers and the Parliament, in effect giving MEPs the right to veto some proposed legislation, as well as the annual EU budget and applications for EU membership. Also, the Parliament's specialist committees have gained more influence in helping to formulate policies before the Commission puts forward proposed directives. Journalists should understand that the European Parliament does not have a government and an opposition like the British House of Commons. The horseshoe-shaped hemicycles in Strasbourg and Brussels group the conservative parties and the socialists in blocks, but the political spectrum is much more complex than the rather simplified despatch-box spats we are used to in Britain.

There are now three presidents within the EU – the President of the Commission, the President of the Parliament, and at the end of 2009 Herman Van Rompuy became the first President of the European Council. So it is important to give their full titles. No-one is 'EU President'. The Lisbon Treaty also saw the first 'High Representative of the Union for Foreign Affairs and Security Policy', Baroness Ashton. Her full title is a terrible mouthful and journalists immediately shortened it. The BBC website confidently announced her appointment as Europe's first 'Foreign Minister', using quotation marks. But the UK specifically refused to accept that title, so I think it is best to avoid 'Foreign Minister' in scripts, as it is technically incorrect, and write the EU 'Foreign Affairs Representative' or 'Foreign Policy Chief' (favoured by many newspapers). Interestingly, the High Representative is also the first Vice President of the European Commission, and will have a large diplomatic staff at the Commission, so in effect has a foot in the previously separate camps of the Council and Commission, making the job unique in the EU structure.

In summary, when writing about the EU, we should be accurate about which part of the institution is making the news, and we should make sure that the audience understands as much as possible. It is extremely difficult to explain everything in every brief story. But it is not difficult to differentiate clearly between, for example, a proposal from the Commission, or an argument between the UK and France in a Council of Ministers' meeting, or a vote at the European Parliament which will almost certainly turn a proposal into law.

The EU is much more open than many national governments, with a mass of information available on its Europa website, including minutes of meetings for those who are really interested (www.europa.eu). The European Journalism Centre, based in Maastricht, runs a useful site for journalists with references to other information sources (www.eu4journalists.com).

European courts

The various European courts can cause confusion. Two are institutions of the EU – the European Court of Justice and the European Court of Auditors.

- The **European Court of Justice** (sometimes called the European Court) is based in Luxembourg, and applies or interprets EU law.

- The **European Court of Auditors** is also based in Luxembourg, and independently scrutinises and adjudicates on the way the EU raises its income and spends the annual budget.

- The **European Court of Human Rights** is not connected with the EU, though confusingly it is based in Strasbourg, home of the European Parliament. It was set up by the Council of Europe, and applies the principles contained in the European Convention on Human Rights. Cases are first heard by the European Commission of Human Rights, which decides if they should be referred to the court.

- The **International Court of Justice** sits in The Hague and is part of the United Nations. It seeks to resolve disputes between states. It is sometimes called the 'World Court', a phrase I do not recommend. Stick to the correct title.

- Also in The Hague is the **International Criminal Court** (ICC), which is not part of the United Nations. The ICC is an independent organisation, established in 2002 under the Rome Statute ratified by 60 countries, with the aim of bringing to justice perpetrators of the most serious crimes of concern to the international community. Alongside it are tribunals set up by the UN Security Council to bring to justice individuals involved in specific conflicts, such as the International Criminal Tribunal for the former Yugoslavia (ICTY). So take care over the names of these different judicial bodies, and don't try to shorten them.

Around the world

Accuracy and consistency in reporting the world are important for clarity and credibility. But when a city or country changes its name, it can be difficult to know if we should accept the change. After all, the British have anglicised foreign names throughout history, and we are unlikely to start calling Naples Napoli, Rome Roma or Porto Oporto, or pronouncing Paris the way the locals do.

But sometimes there are powerful diplomatic reasons for changes to be accepted. It took years for journalists to start calling the capital of the most populous nation on earth Beijing, and Peking continued to be used in parallel for some time. After India gained independence, many city authorities there applied to central government to abandon the colonial usages and revert to earlier names. Some changes have not been authorised. Some have caught on better than others. So, for example, the name Bombay, like Peking, appears to be a dead duck, apart from in names like the Bombay Stock Exchange. But at the time of writing, Bengaluru for Bangalore, and Kolkata for Calcutta, have not been adopted in the UK. My advice is that if the establishment accepts a change, by which I mean the Foreign Secretary speaking in the Commons, or government press releases, then we should accept that the change has taken place.

In general terms, journalists should be familiar with the main cities in all countries. They should be wary of common misconceptions. For example, the largest city is not necessarily the capital. The capital of Australia is Canberra, not Sydney. The capital of South Africa is Pretoria, not Johannesburg. In Nigeria, it's Abuja, not Lagos. Confusingly, in The Netherlands, Amsterdam is the capital but The Hague is the seat of government. Incidentally, it is worth noting that the name 'Holland' applies only to two coastal provinces, called North Holland and South Holland. The Dutch live in The Netherlands, and prefer us to call their country by its correct name. The Dutch national football team is often called 'Holland' in English, but the official name that comes out of the hat in international competitions is 'Netherlands'. A colleague working in Dutch television told me with feeling, 'The Netherlands is correct. All over the world people use Holland, which is really incorrect!'

THE NUMBERS GAME

The use of numbers, fractions and percentages requires particular care in broadcasting. In print journalism, numbers stand out on the page and can be absorbed at the reader's own pace. In a fast-moving radio or television bulletin, anything that requires the audience to make even the simplest calculation will be a challenge to many.

Simple numbers

The first rule is not to litter your script with too many numbers, and to simplify them if at all possible. So 'nearly 500' is better than '485'. When ITV Digital went bankrupt, the losses were put at £1.2 billion. For most people this just means an unimaginably large amount of money, so 'over a billion pounds' is near enough.

The second rule is to understand precisely the nuances of maths, measurement and comparisons. If you write things that are ambiguous or inaccurate, the audience will be confused, irritated or baffled.

For example, always compare like with like. Do not say, 'Half those polled said apples were their favourite fruit; twenty per cent preferred bananas, but only one in twelve voted for plums'. You are asking your audience to make instant calculations, and surveys show that a surprising number of people in Britain are very bad indeed at maths. Leaders of the retail trade complained recently that many trainee staff can't work out a customer's change without the help of a calculator. Our audiences certainly don't listen or watch with calculators in their hands, so we must make it very easy. Personally I think that 'a fifth of people questioned . . .' is more understandable than '20 per cent . . .', and 'one in five . . .' is even better.

Incidentally, when reporting interest-rate changes, some financial journalists insist on saying 'half of one per cent', whereas in ordinary conversation most people would say 'a half per cent', or even 'half a per cent'. I understand that 'per cent' means 'out of a hundred', so half of one out of a hundred is technically correct, and 'half of out of a hundred' is not. Nevertheless I think that 'half a per cent' is in wide general use and is perfectly clear. Daniel Dodd, the Head of the BBC's Business News Unit, agrees. 'We don't have a problem with the common usage.'

Using 'double' to mean twice as much is fine. But 'triple' is not used very widely. Most people would say 'three times as many'. And some people aren't quite sure what tripling means. President George W. Bush was quoted as saying, 'We've tripled the amount of money – I believe it's up from $50 million to $195 million available.' He seemed to think that to triple a figure, you double it and then double it again, rather than multiply by three.

Up to . . .

The use of the phrase 'up to . . .' is routinely deployed by salespeople and advertisers, usually to obfuscate or even mislead, rather than to clarify. 'Up to 20 per cent off!' might mean that a couple of lines are reduced by 20 per cent, but everything else in the sale has smaller reductions. Broadcast journalists should not use this technique to hype their stories. When BBC Radio 4 reported an incident on the London underground in 2003, the script said, 'Most of the passengers were trapped for up to an hour and a half'. What on earth did that mean? I suspect it meant that the reporter did not know how long most of the passengers were trapped, but knew that no-one had been in the train for more than an hour and a half.

Generally, 'up to' is a phrase to avoid. 'Up to five thousand took part in the march' is vague and unhelpful. We should give the best estimate of the numbers and source it.

Vague numbers

Sometimes our sources give us extremely vague information about numbers. 'The police say a number of people were arrested in the raids . . .' – you should try hard to indicate the kind of number we are talking about. 'Several people' is better if the number is thought to be in single figures. 'Some weapons were found . . .' is better than the official-speak versions, 'a number of weapons . . .' or 'a quantity of weapons'. Equally, 'a percentage of the shareholders expressed dissatisfaction with the board' tells the audience nothing about the level of dissatisfaction.

We should be very careful about vague statements that clearly are designed to impress. 'A wave of arrests in dawn raids across the capital . . .' – try hard to find out how many arrests there are in a wave, and how many raids took place. 'A stockpile of weapons' is equally vague, as journalists in Northern Ireland know only too well. 'An arsenal of weapons . . .' is even worse, unless you know it is a very substantial number. If you can't indicate numbers reasonably accurately, you should source the information very clearly. 'The police issued a statement this morning saying they'd arrested a number of people in early-morning raids across the capital, and seized what they described as a stockpile of weapons'.

Number or amount?

One mistake that seems to drive some people to apoplexy is to confuse 'number' with 'amount'. 'Absolutely disgraceful', wrote one reader of the *Independent*, after reading in a leader column that 'less candidates' would be standing for election. The 'less and fewer' debate is as hard-fought as any over misuse of language. Less is a measure of quantity, and should not be applied to numbers. So it is less sugar, but fewer sugar lumps.

I certainly find it very irritating to hear people being described as a quantity of something. 'An amazing amount of Japanese are supporting England' (Radio 5 Live, 2002), which might make you wonder, 'an amazing amount of Japanese what?'

'Less' and 'amount' refer to an uncountable substance. 'Fewer' and 'number' refer to countable items.

Measurements

The UK has been using European standard metric measurements, and schools have been teaching them to our children, for a long time. The BBC TV children's news programme Newsround has been using metres rather than yards for well over thirty years. The temperatures on the TV weather charts have been in Celsius rather than Fahrenheit for over a generation (some weather presenters still convert some values to Fahrenheit to keep older viewers informed, but the practice is dying out, along with the viewers who still can't grasp that zero degrees is freezing and thirty degrees is hot).

Shops have to show quantities in metric measurements by law. I imagine that nearly everyone under the age of fifty is familiar with litres, kilos and grams. It's interesting to note that the evergreen cookery queen Delia Smith uses ounces or fluid ounces in her recipes, with the metric equivalents written afterwards, while the younger Jamie Oliver's recipes are in grams or litres first, with the old measures shown second.

Every newsroom should have an agreed house style. I would urge writers to use commonly used measures such as meters and litres more, to avoid the risk of being out of step with a very large and growing part of the audience.

Foot or feet?

Some of our traditional measures can also produce grammatical errors, which annoy many listeners and erode the authority of the news. On a game show, you might be content to hear, 'You've just won fifty pound', but you would not expect to hear on the news, 'Pensioners are to get another five pound a week'. There are a surprising number of occasions when the singular is used wrongly instead of the plural.

'In places the oil is two foot thick', said a BBC World reporter after the wreck of the Prestige oil tanker. And in September 2002, according to ITN, the flood water was 'almost four foot deep in places'. No, the oil was two feet thick, and the water was four feet deep.

Technically, the singular is used when it is part of a compound adjective (a twenty-foot drop) and the plural when part of a noun (a drop of twenty feet) or as part of an adverb (twenty feet down). So it is a twelve-inch ruler, but the ruler is twelve inches long.

If you find yourself in doubt, it's sometimes helpful to mentally convert the measure into something else, to see whether the plural or singular sounds right. For example, no-one would say, 'the oil is two metre thick'. It would be two metres thick. But it is a two-metre-thick layer of oil.

Figures in opinion polls

When quoting the results of opinion polls, especially political polls, language should be chosen with care. Professional pollsters acknowledge that even the best conducted national polls are likely to have a three per cent margin for error in either direction; we should remind the audience of that when reporting them. In recent years, some key polls used by broadcasters have been embarrassingly inaccurate. Before the May 2010 general election in the UK, the BBC's credibility had been damaged in successive elections by exit polls that proved to be seriously misleading.

So don't use language that gives greater credibility to opinion polls than they deserve. Polls can 'suggest' or 'indicate' something, but never 'prove' anything, or even 'show' what we think. The BBC is so sensitive about exaggerating the importance of opinion polls, its Editorial Guidelines devotes five pages to the subject, and includes the advice, 'Do not lead a news bulletin or programme simply with the results of a voting intention poll.'

Writing the numbers

A big difference between writing numbers for newspapers and for broadcasting is that the convention in TV and radio is to write them out in words. So 2000 is scripted as 'two thousand'. £2 million is written as 'two million pounds'. If a pay rise is 6.6%, we should write six-point-six per cent.

The reason is that, when reading a script live on air, it's quite possible to lose the flow when a number appears on the page or the teleprompter. The eye has to convert the figures into speech. It's easier for the presenter to read aloud the spoken word. A more important reason is that there are several ways of saying some figures, and you want the presenter to use the most natural version. For example, in conversation you probably would not say, 'He bought one thousand shares' but 'He bought a thousand shares'. In ordinary speech, a batsman who was out for 165 runs scored 'a hundred and sixty-five', not 'one hundred and sixty-five'. Write numbers exactly as you want them spoken.

Ages

As for people's ages, there's a big difference between the way they appear in a newspaper and the way they are written in broadcast scripts. Personally, I think that some local newspapers seem obsessed with people's ages. They are often irrelevant. In broadcasting, they are used much less. But if a person's age really helps the story, we should use a natural spoken form such as, 'Ron Knee, who's 65' rather than '65-year-old Ron Knee'. Not 'Ron Knee aged 65'. And never 'Ron Knee, 65.

QUESTION OF GRAMMAR

Some of the most challenging aspects of writing very precisely involve questions of English grammar. One theory of writing broadcast news advocates that we should largely ignore grammar. The argument is that people do not speak very grammatically, and we are trying to write how people speak. Also, Latin-based English grammar was artificially imposed on a language that had blended many different linguistic roots, so it is in some ways a technical exercise that is at odds with human communication in the real world. These arguments seem to be gaining some ground, as the leading broadcasters try to be more accessible to a wider audience, and less pompous or elitist.

I take the view that all writers of broadcast news should have a good grasp of basic grammar, because it will help them to write precisely, accurately, elegantly and without ambiguity. It will also ensure that their reports command the respect of the entire audience. Very many people hate to hear expressions on the news that they regard as either sloppy or plain wrong. It is a misconception to say we do not speak grammatically in normal conversation. Overwhelmingly we do, because without rules of the game that we all follow, communication begins to break down. We may speak colloquially, but most of the time we follow the rules of grammar.

Writing for Broadcast Journalists is not a reference book on English grammar — you will be relieved to know. There is invaluable and detailed advice on many grammatical questions in another book in the Routledge Media Skills series, *English for Journalists* by Wynford Hicks.

But it will be useful in this section on accurate writing to consider briefly just a few of the particular grammatical problems that confront radio and TV journalists trying to script the spoken word.

The split infinitive

Let's start with the infamous split infinitive. I have to tentatively put my cards on the table by using a split infinitive and declaring that the usage doesn't worry me. People split infinitives in conversation all the time. I think the people who object so intemperately when they hear divided verbs are in danger of being pedants. If we had been told that the mission of the Starship *Enterprise* was 'to go boldly' to seek out new worlds, I think we would have been less impressed with the boldness of the project. The split infinitive is in print everywhere as well. The Royal Television Society's magazine *Television* asked the question, 'Will the government's plans to actively encourage the flow of funds into the UK from abroad find their way on to the small screen?' I very much doubt whether the magazine received any complaints about sloppy grammar; '. . . to encourage actively . . .' doesn't seem to me to be preferable. (In fact, if this had been a broadcast script, the adverb 'actively' would probably have been dropped altogether.)

The split infinitive has been defended for many years. In the 1907 edition of *The King's English*, the Fowler brothers say we should split infinitives sooner than write something ambiguous or artificial, and call the opposition to the split infinitive a 'curious superstition'. And in 1947, in a letter to his editor complaining about a proofreader correcting his grammar, Raymond Chandler spluttered, 'When I split an infinitive, God damn it, I split it so it will stay split!'

Having said all that, I must confess that in my twenty-seven years in broadcast journalism, I very rarely wrote a split infinitive. Why not? Because I knew there were some irritated and irritating people out there who would harrumph and think the newsreader or reporter was an ignoramus. I think these people are dying out, and I would advise scriptwriters today to boldly write whatever seems most natural to them – but also to know when they are splitting an infinitive, and choose to do it because it sounds right.

Collective nouns

Mixing singular and plural in the same sentence is much more contentious and probably irritates more people. For many years, there has been a lively debate about whether collective nouns (government, council, union, committee, team, company) should take a singular or a plural verb. 'The cabinet are meeting this afternoon. . . . Number Ten know this is dangerous ground' (BBC TV News, 2010). Channel Four's internal style guide is firm and uncompromising. 'Collective nouns will always be singular, not plural. E.g. The Government is . . .'. But *The Complete Plain Words* by Sir Ernest Gowers says, 'There is no rule; either a singular or a plural verb may be used.'

A few years ago, BBC Radio News, wishing to be consistent, came to the opposite conclusion to Channel Four, and declared that collective nouns should normally be plural. 'The council have decided . . .'; 'the government are considering . . .'. I support this advice. Most people use plural verbs with collective nouns when they are speaking, presumably because they want to indicate a group of people, not an inanimate object. No-one would say, 'England is playing well, it might score soon'. And very few actually say, 'The Cabinet has made its decision', even though on paper it is grammatically correct. Here is an example from BBC TV News in February 2003. 'Our reporter spent the day with one family from Southampton, who explained why they had given up their weekend to join the peace rally in London.' It would have been most unnatural to write that the family explained why it had given up its weekend.

There is a strong lobby for the mathematical approach to this grammatical issue. Many newspapers reported jubilantly an error in an advertisement from the Department for Education and Skills. The advertisement included the line: 'One in five British employees have literacy and numeracy skills.' Even the normally restrained *Independent* splashed a headline, 'Grammar Advert Included a Howler', and continued, 'Officials at the Department for Education and Skills have been left red-faced after an advertisement promoting a literacy campaign was found to contain a glaring error.' As a journalist who has worked in broadcasting for many years, I'm reluctant to call this a howler. Most people would say 'One in five have . . .' rather than 'One in five has . . .' because we are imagining a lot of people, not just one. The same issue of the *Independent* carried a front-page headline in 2002, 'One in 20 women has been raped'. I think if you were telling the story to someone, this would sound rather awkward, even if it is technically correct. In fact I think it even looks a little awkward on the page. How far should we take the singular? Would you write, 'One in twenty women says she has been raped and that she was reluctant to report it to the police . . . '?

In each case, you must use your own judgement on which verb sounds most natural. But there is one rule. If you feel that a singular verb must be used in a particular story, don't change number, especially in the same sentence. It's easily done. Here are a few examples that have been broadcast.

- The National Union of Mineworkers wants a rise of fifty pounds a week for each miner; but British Coal says they'll only negotiate with the union which holds the majority at individual pits.

- The jury hasn't been able to reach their verdict.

- The TUC have decided to back the health workers. It says their strike is justified.

- Every one of those present were creditors.

Most experienced editors are very sensitive to mixing singular and plural in the same sentence. The BBC's Daniel Dodd says, 'One of the things I dislike most is the habit of switching tenses within a sentence. It sounds ugly.' ITN's Sir David Nicholas pronounces on this subject with jabbing finger and glittering eyes. 'I go absolutely mad when I hear ". . . the government have announced today that its policy will be . . ." Mixing up plurals and singulars is awful.' I'm sure you would not want to contribute to Sir David going absolutely mad.

I think one, no-one and none should always take a singular verb, because it clearly sounds wrong for 'one' to be followed by a plural. 'None of those who had read this book was able to dispute its wisdom.'

And bear in mind that data, media, criteria and phenomena are plural words – although this is a tricky Latinate zone. Many people are justifiably contemptuous when they hear a reporter saying, 'This is a spectacular natural phenomena . . .' or 'The main criteria is . . .' (it should be phenomenon and criterion). But 'data' and 'media' are very widely used now as singulars: 'The data is clear on this . . .'; 'The media has a tendency to sensationalise events . . .'. And what about referenda and referendums? Either is correct according to the *Oxford English Dictionary*. Personally, I think most people would use the latter. Maybe we need a referendum to sort it out.

His and hers

A persistent problem for a writer of spoken English is trying to avoid saying 'he or she' or 'his or hers'. The commonly used solutions do not follow mathematical grammar; for example, 'Each journalist must find their own way through this difficulty'. Sometimes using the plural noun will be the answer. So instead of saying, 'A good driver will fasten his seatbelt before he starts the engine', we can prefer the non-sexist 'Good drivers will fasten their seatbelt (or seatbelts if you feel really strongly about the maths) before they set off.'

In broadcast news, it's probably best to be relaxed about the technicalities. Nearly everyone is happy to say, 'Everyone has what they want', and 'Each of us has our secrets'. The advice repeated in this book is to consider what will be regarded as Good Spoken English, which will offend no-one, or hardly anyone, and to use the English language knowingly, not in ignorance.

Blatant errors

Unfortunately, it's not at all unusual to hear blatant grammatical errors on TV and radio. One of the most frequent and most irritating is the wrong use of such couplings as 'John and I' or 'me and John'. 'That's all for this week, so from John and I, goodnight.' (At this moment, thousands in the audience simultaneously say, or think, 'Aagh!') A book by James Cochrane about bad language is entitled *Between you and I*. He believes this common error may arise from a feeling of discomfort about using the word 'me', a sense that it is somehow impolite or uneducated. I think this comes from parents drumming into their children that it is ignorant to say 'John and me are going to the park', or especially, 'Me and John are going to the park.' It's 'John and I!' they would insist. Well of course that's right when 'I' is part of the subject of the sentence, but when it isn't the subject, it should be 'me'.

If ever you have a moment's doubt about this, just separate yourself from your partner for a second, and ask whether you would say, '. . . from I, goodnight', or 'Me is going to the park.'

As for the 'Me and John' construction – Andrew Marr, who championed less stuffy and more accessible writing when he was the BBC's Political Editor, says he absolutely hates it when he hears one of his kids saying, 'Me and Jane are going out.' But they seem determined to continue with it. My children are the same. Is it becoming the norm? Between you and me, I very much hope not.

The Plain English Campaign says that after spelling mistakes and the misuse of the apostrophe, which in broadcasting affect only captions on television and website versions of scripts, the most disliked error is the growing habit of saying 'could of' and 'should of' instead of 'could have' and 'should have'. I haven't noticed this in broadcast news scripts to date, but I have noticed 'fed up of' and 'bored of'. 'One man who's hoping the British public haven't bored of *Popstars* . . .' (ITV News). Conventionally, it should be '. . . haven't become bored with . . .', but the new usage is a little briefer, and seems to be in line with 'sick of' or 'tired of'. So it is sure to gain ground. As usual, I would counsel a traditional approach until the new usage is well established everywhere.

The confusion between 'lie' and 'lay' seems to be spreading alarmingly. I have heard several TV presenters saying such things as, 'He woke up laying on the floor'. It is a deeply irritating error, confusing the verb lie (intransitive, past tense 'lay') with the verb lay (transitive, past tense 'laid'). Pop music has played a part in confusing the two. 'Lay your head on my shoulder' is OK. 'Lay lady lay, lay across my big brass bed' is wrong, unless Bob Dylan is inviting a hen to lay an egg. You have to lay something. If you recline on the bed, you lie on it. If you did it yesterday, you lay on it.

And who will spare a thought for the word whom? In recent years it has fallen out of use quite spectacularly. Who these days would say, 'The woman whom the police want to interview'? But many listeners will know that whom should be used when it is the object of a sentence, or when it follows a preposition such as by, with, for, or from. 'This is the woman from whom he bought the gun.' 'Ask not for whom the bell tolls.' Often it's possible to turn the sentence around so that the word is unnecessary. 'This is the woman who sold him the gun.' But the word 'whom' does have its uses. Replacing it with 'who' can lead to ambiguity. 'Who did you want to help?' has two possible meanings: 'which person do you want give assistance to?', and 'which person did you want to assist you?'

And another thing. If anyone tells you that you can't start a sentence with 'And', as I have done in the last two paragraphs, they are plain wrong. There has never been such a rule, just a notion promoted by a past generation of schoolteachers who were following a rather pedantic school book of grammar. In spoken English, we do it all the time, rather than saying 'In addition . . .' or 'Also . . .' The first chapter of the authorised version of the Bible – written to be read aloud, as you will recall – has thirty-one sentences, of which thirty begin with 'And . . .'.

And as you write your scripts, don't become concerned about whether or not your sentences have a main verb. The first sentence in the previous paragraph may not be a technical sentence, but listeners can't hear whether it is followed by a full stop, a dash, a colon or a semi-colon. Writing a self-contained phrase as a short sentence makes it easier to read.

Reported speech

Journalists use reported speech a great deal, especially in broadcast news, where direct quotes spoken by a reporter don't work very well. Yet reported speech probably produces more errors than any other grammatical challenge. It is quite a complicated subject, and this is not the place for pages of technical explanation. If you are not sure about reported speech, look it up, and try to develop a sharp ear for what is regarded as right and wrong. In *A Pocket Guide to Radio Newswriting*, the BBC's Tom Fort says, 'Many writers and correspondents don't know what reported speech is. They should. You cannot write good English for radio without some knowledge of how reported speech works.' He gives some handy examples.

> Jim says he will be going to the football match.
>
> Jim said he would be going to the football match.
>
> Jim said he had always wanted to go to a football match.
>
> Jim said that when he was living in Paris, he often went to (or had gone to) football matches.

The key point is not to use the verb of direct speech in a reported speech construction, such as, 'Jim said he'll be going to the football match.' In fact, he said 'I'll be going to the football match', but in reported speech he said he'd be going to the football match.

And don't think that you have to include 'that' in reported speech: for example, 'Jim said that he would be going to the football match.' It's technically correct reported speech, but the word 'that' is normally dropped from this construction in spoken English, and is regarded by most editors in broadcast news as an awkward and intrusive word, easily deleted.

Quoting direct speech

Newspapers are full of direct quotes. In broadcasting, the listeners and viewers can't see the quotation marks, so writing direct speech into your scripts is risky. You must make it very clear who is saying these words before they are spoken. Presenters will always try to indicate by their voice that they are quoting directly. On television, it's easier: TV presenters have perfected the technique of glancing down at their script to indicate they are reading the exact words. On radio, it's much more difficult to indicate someone else's words. It's best to keep such quotes very short – usually just a phrase. I would suggest fifteen words is a maximum.

> He described the allegations as 'an appalling slur' and 'completely baseless'.
>
> As he arrived at the talks, the leader of the Firefighters' Union, Joe Black, denied they were refusing to negotiate, and accused the employers of going back on their word under pressure from the government. He told journalists, 'They are serial liars. They've lied to us, and now they're lying to you.'

SENSITIVITY

It is extremely important for broadcasters to avoid excluding, offending or insulting their viewers and listeners. Insensitive use of language can have a powerful effect on some sections of the audience. We live in an age of rapidly changing social trends. Some words that were acceptable a generation ago are not acceptable now.

The debate about the acceptability of words describing identity rages even more fiercely than those about changing grammar or pronunciation, because words can wound deeply. The argument about 'political correctness' became prominent in the late '80s, with American commentators and sociologists leading the drive against words which they believed had been used insensitively or inaccurately for too long. Traditionalists and commentators writing in the more conservative newspapers in the UK seized on some extreme examples to ridicule 'political correctness gone mad', which some used as a defence against all change: 'I'm a plain-speaking man; I call a spade a spade.' This position simply ignores the issue. Sensitive terminology is a serious element of good writing, which cannot be ignored.

Stereotyping and loaded language

Stereotyping can happen because a writer is ignorant, or thoughtless, or both. But in times of conflict, the language of broadcast news can be used deliberately as a powerful propaganda weapon. During the Balkan wars of the '90s, the state-controlled television and radio stations in all the countries involved, but especially RTS in Serbia, fuelled the conflict with so-called hate speech and propagandist language. To some listeners, it carried echoes of the Nazis' demonising of the Jews half a century earlier. During the war against Croatia, for example, the opposition forces were routinely described on the news in terms that translate into English as 'barbarians, fascists, mercenaries, butchers, criminals, cut-throats and hoodlums'. President Milosevic was invariably described as 'questing for peace', while NATO acquired a new name, 'The NATO Aggressor', by which it was always called.

In Britain, broadcasters have learned to avoid such loaded language through the experience of the long conflict in Northern Ireland, the bitter and divisive miners' strikes of the '70s and '80s, the Falklands conflict in '82, and the wars in former Yugoslavia and the Gulf. There is now a strong British tradition of impartial language in the journalism of conflict. For example, during the Falklands campaign, despite some pressure from Conservative MPs, broadcasters avoided saying 'our fleet is under attack' or 'our troops have entered

Goose Green', preferring 'the British fleet' or 'the Royal Navy task force' and 'British troops'. There was a significant section of the British audience who were opposed to the campaign. Some viewers overseas were receiving these reports, for example in Ireland and Belgium, where UK domestic channels are widely heard and watched. At such a time, the wide credibility of the information was paramount. The detached style emphasised impartiality and trustworthiness. This style has been followed by most broadcasters working in the English language in coverage of the two Gulf wars and the conflict in Afghanistan.

For most journalists or students of journalism working in English, the danger of insensitive usage is less about propagandist phraseology or hate-speech, and more about careless descriptions of everyday stories and the routines of life in a changing society. Writers must beware of insulting parts of their audience on issues of sex and gender, race and religion, and disability.

Sexism

Even in the twenty-first century, a few male journalists seem to have difficulty in accepting that some traditionally used titles and expressions annoy many women. Newspaper journalist Sarah Strickland points out that there is a bias against women embedded in the English language. The name of our species is Man. Women make up more than half the population, but using words such as mankind, man-made, spokesman, newsman, foreman, man-to-man, or the man in the street, gives the impression that women are less important, or are excluded from mainstream society. Back in 1991, Ms Strickland wrote in the *Guardian*:

> Some progress has been made; many people are now careful to use words like *chairperson* for chairman, *workers* for workmen, *humans* for mankind. Some newspapers will use *firefighters* not firemen, *official* not spokesman, *supervisor* not foreman. Using the plural can often avoid excluding women. Rather than saying, 'the good driver will always look in his mirror before he turns', you can say, 'good drivers always look in their mirrors before they turn'.
> When women began to enter traditionally male jobs, the language adapted to show that they were exceptions to the rule. Expressions like *lady doctor* have now, thankfully, disappeared, as have *poetess, authoress* and *murderess*. But we still have *actress, waitress, stewardess*. Why can't a woman be an *actor*?

I quote the above to show that sexism in language arouses strong feelings, and has done for some time. I think further progress has been made since

1991. Female actors are now the norm; firefighter is the job title. We must be aware that attitudes to language change quickly. My personal view is that broadcasters have been a little slow to recognise growing concerns about sexist terminology, which reflect an enormous social change in post-war Europe. Should we continue to use the following words, for example?

Ambulancemen. No. There are very many women working in the Ambulance Service. Say ambulance crews.

Businessmen or 'the effect on the small businessman'. No. This excludes the large number of women in business, and should be excluded from scripts. Say 'people in business', 'the business community'; even 'business-people' is preferable.

Chairman. It's not a new problem. In 1915, when the Women's Institute was founded, the people chairing meetings were called 'President' to avoid the use of 'Madam-chairman'. These days, we should try to use the title that the individual involved in the story prefers and uses. Some women who chair committees/councils/businesses use Chairperson. Some stick to Chairman. Others are called Chair. I remember many years ago a senior editor exclaiming, 'You can't call her a piece of furniture!' Well, you can. More and more people do. I think Chair is becoming widely acceptable, and will continue to gain ground in normal usage.

Fireman. No. For several years the Fire Service has called all its uniformed men and women firefighters, leading firefighters, and fire officers.

Girls. When we mean women, no. This used to be very widely used and was probably thought to be flattering. The girls in the office . . .; the girls in the frontline . . .; Britain's girls strike gold on the track. Now it's regarded as condescending. I'm told by the girls in the newsroom that they prefer to be called women.

Housewives. No. Heartily disliked by many women, as in 'the housewife's shopping basket'. To be avoided. In this context, refer to shoppers or consumers. In other contexts, full-time mother seems to be quite widely used for mums, and homemaker is preferred by some women who don't go out to work.

Manned/manning. Watch out for this one. A television report on a Gulf helpline said it was 'manned 24 hours a day' as we saw a room full of women answering phones. Open or working 24 hours a day would have avoided the sexist usage. Manning levels should be staffing levels.

Postmen. 'A quarter of postmen to cross picket lines' (*Daily Telegraph*, 2009). There are thousands of women in the Communication Workers Union, and many deliver mail. We should say 'postal workers' even in headlines, and when talking about delivery staff, there's no ready alternative to 'postmen and women'.

Servicemen. In 2003, I heard on BBC Five Live, 'We are joined by BFBS for the second half commentary, so a particularly warm welcome to all the servicemen listening in the Gulf.' There are many women serving in the armed forces, so we really should say service personnel, or even service men and women.

Taxman. Certainly not. It's a long time since George Harrison wrote a song about the 'Taxman'. These days, tax offices employ more women than men. Instead of writing 'an attempt to escape the taxman', try tax office, Inland Revenue, tax inspectors, or even the tax people.

Sexual orientation

As for sexual orientation, the terminology is changing so quickly I am reluctant to commit any advice to print. My father's generation would say, 'He's a bit queer . . .' and meant no offence by it. The word 'homosexual' is correct, but disliked by some. The word 'gay' has very wide acceptance now. But I am sure that any journalist or media student reading this book would not dream of writing, '. . . an objection to the bill from gay MP Nigel Mortenson'. Sexual orientation, which is a complicated issue in many cases, is a private matter. It should be ignored unless it is directly and openly pertinent to a story.

Race

For many years, all the major broadcasters in Britain have followed their own guidelines on references to race, colour and religion. In essence, they all say that a person's colour, ethnic origin or religious allegiance should be mentioned only if it is absolutely relevant to the story. Most will agree that this policy is fair and sensible. It avoids stereotyping and the promotion of prejudice. But under pressure of deadlines, some irrelevant ethnic references can slip through. 'The record lottery winner is James Smith, a black bus driver from Salford.' Always ask yourself whether you would use the adjective 'white' in the same circumstances. It's a more serious mistake if you are reporting crime. Many members of ethnic minority groups are infuriated if they hear something like, 'a grandmother has been mugged by two black youths', because they know the journalist would not have written '. . . by two white youths', and the report is therefore perpetuating a stereotype.

Take extra care with police descriptions of incidents. 'The car was driven by a West Indian male' may be what the duty sergeant tells you, but it would be completely unacceptable to broadcast it that way. First, 'West Indian' is almost certainly wrong – he was probably British. Secondly, the colour/nationality/ethnic background of the suspect/witness – black, African-Caribbean – is only relevant if it is part of a given description. 'The police are searching for a tall, black man in his thirties. He's described as heavily built, with a moustache and short hair.' Similarly, descriptions of white people the police are hoping to find should always include the skin colour; 'He's described as white . . .' etc.

Note that the word 'ethnic' can be misused. The editor of the BBC's African and Caribbean programme unit in Birmingham issued guidance to his producers, which said 'It is correct to refer to people from ethnic minorities. But don't be tempted to shorten it to "ethnics", which black and Asian people dislike, and is meaningless. We're all ethnic.'

Racism

Scriptwriters must take care when dealing with stories about extreme right-wing groups. When the British National Party won a few council seats and two European Parliament seats in 2009, there was some soul-searching about whether or not they could be described on air as a 'racist party'. It may be clear to all thinking people that, if BNP leader Nick Griffin believes that black footballers shouldn't play for England, as expressed in a BBC radio interview in 2009, then he must be racist. But the BNP denies racism. And the party evidently has supporters. My advice is to report the activities of such parties or groups factually and objectively, attributing any claims about racism. We certainly should not write '. . . the racist BNP . . .'. Let the audience decide on the basis of accurate reporting.

Colour

A lot of people are colour-sensitive. Geographical or ethnic origin is often more relevant and informative than colour of skin: 'Bangladeshi, Jamaican, Indian', etc. The adjective 'black', at one time considered to be derogatory, is now widely acceptable as a description for non-white people. In Britain, some Asian people are happy to be called black; others are not. The Equality and Human Rights Commission prefers to use 'black and Asian people', or 'Asian, African and Caribbean people'. 'People of colour' is being used in the

USA, but rarely in the UK, so is best avoided. 'Half-caste' is considered offensive; use 'mixed race', or refer to a person being 'of mixed parentage'. Use the term 'black people' rather than 'blacks', which carries echoes of South African apartheid and slavery in the southern states of the USA. People are people first. And always remember, colour and race are often irrelevant in news stories.

Asian

Geographically, Asia is a vast part of the world, home to many different peoples with different cultures, languages, religions and physical characteristics. Journalists should have some knowledge of the main Asian groups, and should avoid mistakes that large numbers of Asian listeners and viewers will regard as ridiculous and excluding. Anita Bhalla worked as Community Affairs Correspondent for BBC Birmingham for several years before becoming Head of Political and Community Affairs for the BBC English Regions. This is an extract of the guidance she issued to journalists to help them avoid such mistakes.

> The term 'Asian' is often used to describe someone from the old Indian sub-continent; strictly speaking 'South Asian' is correct but not widely used in Britain. Many people describe themselves as coming from India, Pakistan, Bangladesh etc., or even from regions in those countries, e.g. 'Gujerati', 'Mirpuri', 'Sylheti'. Some young people prefer to call themselves 'British Asian'.
>
> Hindu names: Traditionally Hindu names have three parts: a personal name, followed by a middle name, followed by a family name. Examples: *Kishore Bhai Patel, Bimla Devi Sharma.*
>
> Some Hindus have in the past given up their family name as a rejection of the caste system, in which case the middle name is used as a surname, e.g. *Harish Lal*, whose wife may be *Usha Devi*. A Hindu woman normally takes her husband's family name after marriage. The Hindu equivalent for Mr and Mrs, *Shri* and *Shrimati*, are not generally used in the UK.
>
> Sikh names: Traditionally Sikh names have a personal name followed by a religious title – *Singh* for males and *Kaur* for females – followed by a family name when one exists.
>
> Examples: *Manjit Kaur, Manjit Singh Sandhu* (note that many Sikh personal names can be male or female), *Ajit Singh, Resham Kaur Uppal* (*Singh* means 'lion', *Kaur* means 'princess'). It is better not to refer to someone as *Mrs Kaur* or *Mr Singh*; the full name should be used, *Mrs Gurdev Kaur, Mr Karamjit Singh.*
>
> Muslim names: All Muslims have a personal name, which is usually combined for men with a religious name, and for women with a female title.

Male examples: personal names (first or second): *Akhbar, Aziz, Hasan, Nazir;* religious names (first or second), *Mohammed, Allah, Hussain, Ali.* The favoured way of addressing a male Muslim would be by a combination of his personal and religious names, e.g. *Mr Bashir Ali, Mr Mohammed Nazir.* A Muslim should not be addressed only by his religious name, so *Mr Allah* or *Mr Mohammed* are out.

Female examples: personal names: *Amina, Fatima, Razia, Yasmin;* female titles: *Bano, Begum, Bibi, Khatoon.* So we could have Mrs *Fatima Begum,* Ms *Amina Khatoon;* but Mrs *Begum* is incorrect because it consists only of two titles, Mrs and *Begum.*

Some Muslim men and, more rarely, women may also use a final hereditary/family name, e.g. *Choudhury, Khan, Shah.*

In summary, if you have any doubts, use the full name.

An important pointer for the unwary writer is about religious buildings. Sikhs pray in a gurdwara; Muslims pray in a mosque; Hindus pray in a temple. Don't mix them up.

Religion

As with race, a person's religion should be mentioned only if it has direct relevance to the story. And all journalists should make sure they know something about the main religions that make up the diversity of faith in modern Britain. Displaying ignorance of religious practice or important events turns off sections of the audience and erodes credibility. According to recent surveys, more than a million people in Britain attend a mosque regularly. So all writers of news should know that Hindus worship in temples, not mosques, and should be aware of the main religious dates in the calendar, such as the month of Ramadan, or the festivals of Eid and Diwali.

If you feel the need for further reading on this subject, the *ITV Cultural Diversity Guide* (2003) describes all the main faiths found in the UK. You can order a copy by email: culturaldiversity@granadamedia.com

Disability

In this subject area, too, we must be aware of terminology that might give offence. It's worth remembering that one in four of the UK population either has a disability, or is related to or cares for a disabled person. Almost as many will suffer from a mental illness at some time in their lives. With an ageing population, a growing number of viewers and listeners will be hard of hearing and will have mobility problems.

As with race, we should regard people as people, and mention a disability only if it is strictly pertinent to the story. 'The disabled' gives a sweeping impression, which includes a wide variety of conditions and can imply uselessness or a general incapacity. The word is usually inaccurate as well as harsh. 'People with disabilities' is better; be specific whenever possible.

'The handicapped' is even worse. No person with a disability likes to be portrayed as a handicap to society. The similarity to the phase 'cap-in-hand' is no coincidence. In eighteenth-century horse racing, the best jockeys were sometimes required to ride one-handed, with their cap held in the other hand, hence 'handicapping'. Always try to be specific about someone's condition – if it is relevant. It is a difficult part of writing sensitively. Here is a part of the BBC's Editorial Guidelines on terminology.

- Never refer to 'the handicapped'. Words like 'invalid', 'spastic', 'retarded' or 'defective' cause widespread offence.

- Terms such as 'the blind' or 'the deaf' are often disliked. 'Crippled with', 'victim of', 'suffering from', 'afflicted by' should be avoided. 'People who have' or 'a person with' will usually be clear, factual and inoffensive.

- However, some people with disabilities will describe themselves bluntly as 'blind', 'deaf' or 'crippled'. We should respect their right to call themselves what they wish, while trying to avoid offence.

- People with an intellectual disability are now normally described as 'people with learning difficulties'. 'Mental handicap' is acceptable to some people, but others dislike it because they believe it carries a stigma.

- Learning difficulties should not be confused with mental illness.

- Try to be precise about deafness. Use 'deaf/partially deaf/deafened/ hard of hearing'. 'Deaf and dumb' is not acceptable.

- Some people who use wheelchairs often dislike the terms 'confined to a wheelchair' or 'wheelchair-bound' on the grounds that wheelchairs provide mobility, not confinement. Also many wheelchair users get out of the chair some of the time. A person who 'uses a wheelchair' or 'is in a wheelchair' is preferable.

In recent years, the medical profession has stopped using the phrase 'Siamese twins' because it is inaccurate, and is probably disliked by people from Thailand. 'Conjoined twins' is now generally understood. ITV News was careful to use this phrase when conjoined twins from Manila arrived in the USA for a risky operation to separate them. But someone had failed to tell the graphic designer, so the caption over the newsreader's shoulder proclaimed the children from the Philippines to be 'Siamese twins'.

Elements of the British tabloid press blatantly disregard the feelings of people with disabilities or illnesses in favour of sensationalism or sentimentality. So it is not uncommon to read about 'Little Gemma, crippled from birth . . .' or 'Knife-Nut Jailed'. When Frank Bruno was committed to a mental hospital, the *Sun* headlined him as 'Bonkers Bruno'. This kind of language is unacceptable on radio and television.

There is plenty of evidence that insensitive reporting of suicide or attempted suicide – particularly on television – can cause mentally unstable people to copy what they have seen. I feel sure that television news should never show people jumping to their death, or holding a gun to their head, and should never show people who have been hanged – or even someone with a noose around their neck. Good broadcast journalism requires sensitivity in the use of disturbing images and in the use of words. There is useful guidance on this from The MediaWise Trust, which provides research, advice and training on media ethics (www.mediawise.org.uk). I hope all journalists will think carefully why so many minority groups feel they are stereotyped, and sometimes insulted, by careless language in news programmes.

> The media must avoid prejudicial or pejorative reference to an individual's race, colour, religion, gender, sexual orientation or to any physical or mental illness or disability.
>
> (The Code of Practice of the British
> Press Complaints Commission)

PRONUNCIATION

Many journalists working in broadcasting, particularly in local and regional newsrooms, are required to broadcast their scripts themselves. So if you find it difficult to read aloud without making any errors, maybe you should try a different profession. It is not easy, especially under pressure. But if our journalism is to be respected for its accuracy, it is very important to be able to pronounce words correctly. As we write, we should beware of difficult words.

Newsreaders, reporters and programme presenters are expected to get the most complicated words and names right every time. It can be useful to have a pronunciation dictionary to hand, such as the *Longman Pronunciation Dictionary*. If you are writing a script for someone else to read, it's a very good idea to alert the presenter to difficult names. Some writers put a phonetic version in square brackets after the name. Find out what your presenter and producer prefer. Inconsistent pronunciation of names is regarded as unprofessional. As soon as the huge nuclear accident at Chernobyl became known, the BBC pronunciation unit set to work and declared that this little-known place should be pronounced 'Cher-*nob*-bil'. Other broadcasters and some politicians began by saying '*Chur*nobil', but soon switched to Auntie's choice.

Local radio journalists are often required to read international news. All broadcast journalists should listen to the mainstream news programmes and note the correct pronunciations. I once heard a local radio newsreader pronouncing Arkansas to rhyme with Kansas, which shows carelessness as well as ignorance. If in doubt, ask.

Some common words and phrases are regularly mispronounced, usually because the correct pronunciation is a little difficult. Here are a few to note.

- Vunnerable (vulnerable). Even the most venerable get it wrong. I think 'vunnerable' is an upper-class affectation, like 'guvverment' and 'pry-minister'. In broadcast news, it just sounds wrong.

- Nucular (nuclear). George W. Bush was not the only leader of a nuclear power who could not pronounce 'nuclear' correctly. Tony Blair struggled with it too. If you also find it difficult, think of it as two words – new clear.

- Reckonise (recognise).

- Laura Norder. The well known crime fighter.

- Secketary (secretary).

- Febuary (February).

- Burgalry (burglary).

- Joolery (jewellery).

- *You 'n Jaws*. The radio programme for conshumers.

- Ecksettera (etcetera, etcetera).

Saying it aloud

The best way to avoid stumbling or mispronouncing on air is to speak your script aloud as soon as you have written it, to make sure it sounds clear. *The BBC News Styleguide* quotes the example of a script that looks fine, but isn't so good when spoken aloud.

> There were scenes of delight in Port Talbot tonight, as news of the settlement spread.

News presenters will not thank you if you give them tongue-twisters to read aloud. For example, the word 'statistics' is notoriously difficult to negotiate without stumbling. Try to avoid it. Instead of writing, 'According to the latest statistics . . .' maybe you can write, 'The latest figures indicate . . .', or 'According to new research . . .', or drop the phrase altogether and let the figures speak for themselves. One radio newsreader had to grapple with 'the Navy's provision of efficient ships'. Another is said to have refused to read, 'she dismissed this as a myth'. A long-serving presenter in the BBC's midland region, David Stevens, had a slight propensity to spoonerisms, such as 'The South West Watershire Worcesterboard', or 'The Royal Arse Hortillery'. There isn't much a scriptwriter can do about that kind of mispronunciation, other than provide the script early, so that the presenter has time to read it through before going on air.

Do's and don'ts and won'ts and can'ts

It's a fundamental principle of writing broadcast scripts that you write them as they will be spoken. This makes them very different from newspaper or magazine articles. So most broadcast journalists will write, 'The Prime Minister won't be going to Chequers this weekend . . .' rather than 'will not be'. 'There'll be a public enquiry . . .' 'It'll be wet and windy . . .'. As you may have noticed in this book, after years of writing broadcast scripts, I find it difficult to write 'it is' rather than 'it's', or 'do not' rather than 'don't'.

Some broadcasters who deliberately adopt a more formal and precise style, such as the BBC World Service and BBC Radios Four and Three, have a slight problem with this kind of colloquial writing, and tend to avoid the shortened versions of the verbs, at least in the studio introductions. 'The Prime Minister is to drop his plans for . . .' rather than, 'The Prime Minster's dropping his plans . . .'. Follow the style of your station. My personal opinion is that the natural spoken forms are generally acceptable, and are more accessible.

There are some occasions when the full verb should be used: 'aren't' and 'weren't' can be misheard. 'The victim's relatives aren't attending the proceedings.' 'The police weren't to blame for the death.' So sometimes it's good practice to write and say 'are not' and 'were not' to emphasise the negative clearly.

STORY STRUCTURE

Having established the main point of the story for the target audience, and having decided to write it in the first line, and having promised yourself to write Good Spoken English with accurate language, simple constructions and no excess baggage, the next problem for any writer is how to order the information.

All news stories should have a structure or shape. A randomly presented collection of facts will become a jumble of information that fails to keep the interest of the audience. In broadcasting, there is quite a big difference between the structure of a short bulletin item, and the longer reporter-piece. The short item has to summarise the core of the story in the first sentence, then add a few explanatory facts. The longer reporter-piece, which follows the establishing introduction (the intro), is likely to use the story-telling technique known as narrative journalism.

Short bulletin items

News bulletins, which are essentially brief summaries of the news, are the staple journalistic product on many radio stations. These bulletins can be anything from one to five minutes long, with the longer ones including short voice-pieces or interview clips. The shorter bulletins are usually delivered as a 'straight read' from a presenter, with each story lasting no longer than fifteen seconds. Clearly, the structure of these short bulletin stories has to be extremely simple.

> Two people have been killed in a crash on the M1 in Northamptonshire involving thirty vehicles. It happened during this morning's rush hour when fog was affecting the area. The southbound carriageway is still closed between junctions fifteen and fourteen.

> A thousand baggage-handlers and check-in staff have started a two-day pay strike at Heathrow Airport. Eight flights have been cancelled so far. Kuwait Airways and Middle-East Airlines have been the worst hit.

These very compact items usually aim to encapsulate the story in the first sentence, then to give some supporting facts, favouring any information that might be directly useful to the listeners. Younger journalists may find it a little intimidating to be asked to summarise a complex story in about twelve seconds (as above). It's good advice to remember the commonly quoted formula of the five w-questions: who? why? when? where? what?

Kipling's questions

Originally this advice on how to write journalistically came from Rudyard Kipling's verse *The Elephant's Child* (1902), and included 'how?' as a sixth question.

I keep six honest serving-men,
(They taught me all I knew);
Their names are What and Why and When
And How and Where and Who.

All journalism is a process of question-and-answer. Researching and inter-viewing follows this process literally. Writing a story does it mentally. Even a short bulletin story will often answer most of these mental questions. I think that who, what and where are essential. When is often included (though listeners expect broadcast news to be extremely recent; if it all happened yesterday and we've only just picked up the story, we may choose to ignore the when!).

A short bulletin usually has to be written quickly. In many radio stations, one journalist probably has to write it all, and to rewrite the bulletin every hour or half-hour. So there can be some pressure when you are producing these compact summaries. If you are having difficulty getting started, using the ques-tion 'where?' can help.

> In southern Afghanistan, two American marines have been killed . . .
>
> At Twickenham, England have beaten Ireland . . .

This helps the newsreader to indicate a new story, and helps listeners to orien-tate themselves immediately as you whiz them around the world. In local radio, we know from research that listeners like to hear the name of their own town, and prick up their ears at the mention of a familiar place. But it would become extremely tedious to start every story with the location. Mix up the who, where and what openings.

If you decide to start with who – the person at the centre of the story – it's sometimes far from clear which person to choose, especially when one is accusing another of something. If, for example, the former Conservative Home Office Minister, Anne Widdecombe, had warned the Tory Leader David Cameron to stop behaving in a presidential manner and to listen to grass-roots opinion, you may decide that the first name in the bulletin story should be the man of the moment, rather than the critic.

> David Cameron has been warned by a senior Conservative colleague that his presidential style could be his undoing. The warning comes in a Sunday news-paper article by Anne Widdecombe, who served as a Home Office Minister in the last Tory government. She says the party leader must be prepared to listen to colleagues to achieve broad party support, rather than rely on what she calls his 'rule by dictat' backed up by an inner-circle of enforcers.

WRITING INTROS

Writing the intro often requires a discipline that is similar to writing short bulletin-stories, with the essence of the story captured in the first sentence – but not always. There are many different kinds of programme requiring different styles of writing. In case any reader is not sure what is meant here by the intro, the word does not mean quite the same as it does in the world of newspapers, where it simply means the first paragraph. (In America they call it the lead.) In broadcasting, the intro is read by a presenter, and introduces a voiced report from a correspondent, or perhaps a live interview. In some broadcast newsrooms it's called the cue. Sometimes, on a programme running-order, it's a link. Most people call it the 'intro'. These intros appear in news programmes rather than news bulletins, and tend to have a more personal touch than the short bulletin story, which is relatively anonymous.

The classic or conventional intro will tell the essential story in a self-contained first sentence. It will be quite a concise sentence, covering who and what, and possibly where or when. A length of twelve to twenty words is typical. Anything over thirty words for this opening sentence may lose impact, and is likely to make the presenter take a breath.

> Council tax bills are to rise on average next year by twice the rate of inflation'
> . . .
>
> A year-long study into the MMR vaccine concludes there's no evidence it can cause autism . . .
>
> Aid agencies now say more than a hundred thousand people were killed by Tuesday's earthquake in Haiti . . .

The classic intro will follow up the first sentence with the elements that will most affect the listener, but will not attempt to tell the whole story. The reporter is about to do that. It is very irritating to hear an intro that gives all the interesting facts, followed by reporter immediately repeating most of them. So this might be a thirty-second intro leading into a one-minute voice report on radio:

> Aid agencies now say more than a hundred thousand people were killed by Tuesday's earthquake in Haiti. Field workers for Oxfam and Save the Children report widespread devastation as far as a hundred miles from the epicentre of the quake. Many people are thought to be trapped in collapsed buildings and there's a shortage of drinking water and medicines. There's growing criticism of the slow pace of international help. Our reporter Emma Walsh has spent the day with Oxfam field officers, and has just sent this report. (Descriptive eye-witness report follows with quotes from Oxfam field officer.)

The latest development

Many reports are developments of a running story. It is generally good practice to put the latest development in the top line, but the audience must be up to speed. Don't start with the latest twist if you think the audience will not know what you are talking about.

Broadcasting and online news, unlike the morning papers, provide round-the-clock services where news stories have to be refreshed all the time. It's a matter of judgement when an update is required. Conventionally, stories have been refreshed for the main points of viewing or listening to the news – breakfast time, lunchtime, tea-time, late evening. With 24-hour news, it's becoming a constant process. I think that when a story has been reported for about two or three hours (there's been a big crash on the motorway), then it must be updated (the motorway is still closed after a pile-up this morning); and after another few hours we must start assuming most people have heard about it (police are blaming drivers who ignored fog hazard lights for the crash this morning, which killed four people).

Many journalists strive to get a 'tonight' or a 'this morning' into their first sentence. And they like to use the present tense at the start of the story, as in the examples above. It's good to be immediate. But don't make it sound unnatural.

'Hillary Clinton is on her way to Jerusalem tonight' is fine. 'Hillary Clinton is tonight preparing to fly to Jerusalem' is artificial immediacy, and isn't spoken English.

The length of an intro

The length of an intro should be in proportion to the length of the report that follows. So the eye-witness radio report on the big lead story from Haiti needed a set-up of around thirty seconds. A short, snappy voice-piece, which may be only thirty-five seconds long, requires a short and snappy introduction. But even in the crispest bulletins, a single sentence can be unsatisfactory. 'Some GM crops can damage the environment, according to the first results of a government study. John Williams reports' sounds just a little too hurried, because it doesn't give the listener a real chance to absorb the information before the voice changes and the details start to flow. Two sentences of information are usually better than one.

Longer reports require longer introductions, for several reasons. The longer report will be part of a news programme, aiming to deliver more rounded and detailed journalism, and trying to put daily events into context and explain them. So the intro will have more to say, to establish what the report is going to be about. The longer introduction also prepares the audience mentally for a longer report. The listeners or viewers know subconsciously that a two-line intro will be followed by a short despatch. A more developed intro sets them up for a more developed report.

For example, on British television, *Five News*, which targets younger viewers, uses a fast pace and quite brief reports, some less than a minute long. So the intros are likely to be no more than fifteen seconds. An intro to a standard-length report of one minute, forty seconds on ITN's news is likely to be around twenty-five seconds long, and an introduction to a six-minute film on BBC's *Newsnight* can be a minute long, with graphics establishing the main themes to be explored.

The inviting intro

The longer introduction, leading into a longer report, provides many more opportunities for a more creative approach than just encapsulating the story in the first sentence, as in the classic intro. In the past thirty years, there has been a big change in the way radio reports and television packages are introduced. In the '70s, most radio and TV intros were versions of the classic. Too much informality was frowned upon by British editors, and regarded as an American trait, driven by the need to increase ratings rather than tell the story clearly.

I remember watching a prime-time TV news programme in New York in 1980 and mentally ridiculing an introduction which, if I remember rightly, went like this: 'They say a man's life hangs by a thread. Last night, that thread broke for two firemen in Brooklyn.' I thought it was unutterably corny (or cheesy, to use the more up-to-date word), and I still do. This kind of street-corner philosophy would not be acceptable on television news in the UK. On the other hand, we have moved substantially in the direction of the USA in the way that intros in news and current affairs programmes are much more conversational and inviting than they used to be.

One reason is that writers of news are more conscious of the need to avoid repeating the headlines. As will be explored at a little more length in a section about writing headlines (Chapter 5), the news programme should be regarded as an organic whole. The headline, intro, reporter-package, live interview, and closing headline on any given story should be an integrated piece of communication, telling the listeners or viewers a complete or developing story without confusion or needless repetition.

So if the headline at the top of the programme has told us that ...

Two firefighters have been killed trying to save a Manchester school.

... the intro-writer can assume that nearly all the listeners or viewers have clearly understood that. The intro can try to capture the mood, indicate the drama of the incident, be more immediate, and be more inviting.

Six children have lost their fathers today, after a fierce fire engulfed a paint store in Manchester. It was just fifty yards from a primary school. Fire teams were trying to beat back the flames – then the roof collapsed. Two firefighters, both fathers of three children, were killed – trapped among exploding drums of chemicals.

Involve the listener or viewer – especially at the local level

The style of intro will depend on the established style of your TV channel or radio station. But an increasing number of broadcast news programmes are rejecting the boring factual first line for something that aims to be as relevant to the audience as possible, using 'you' and 'we' when appropriate. This is particularly effective in regional television and local radio, which like to be regarded as a part of the community, and as being as friendly as possible.

A few years ago, Heart FM became the most popular radio station in central England, partly because of its carefully selected music playlist, and partly because of its bright and engaging tone of voice. This included the news bulletins, which were written and delivered in an extremely conversational style, which had been developed by their News Editor, Sue Owen, later the Managing Editor at BBC Radio Stoke. She issued a Heart FM's internal style guide, which rammed home the idea that every story would be told to the listeners in a natural way, with no journalese. Here's an extract:

Be more creative in the way you write – turn it around, make it interesting, use normal language and definitely not 'newspeak' or clichés!

DON'T start a story with either a person or an organisation's name or title. There is nothing more dull than a top line which reads: 'Birmingham City Council is to end its weekly rubbish collections and replace them with fortnightly ones to cut costs.'

How about this instead ... 'If you live in Birmingham, you'll soon only see your dustbin men every fortnight instead of every week.'

Embarrassing examples we have broadcast:

> 'The West Midlands Low Pay Unit is being forced to withdraw help from fifty thousand people because of where they live. Walsall and Solihull councils have withdrawn funding for the first time in 20 years which means low paid workers in those areas will not be able to use its services.'

Argh! [writes Sue Owen], so how about:

> 'If you're in a poorly paid job in Walsall or Solihull and have trouble at work, you could soon lose one of your lifelines. The local councils have decided to stop giving cash support to the West Midlands Low Pay Unit, and that means you'll be turned away if you need help.'

Another example.

> 'Shadow Home Secretary Anne Widdecombe's been in Birmingham today giving her support to a group trying to kick prostitution out of their community.'

Yawn. Try . . .

> 'If you're sick of prostitutes hanging around outside your house, you've got one of the Tories' best known battlers on your side' and name her and localise in the second sentence.

Heart FM's style may not be right for other broadcasters. It is easier to use 'you', 'your', 'you've', 'you're' in local radio intros than on more traditional national or international channels. But *Heart News* was (and I guess still is) accurate, interesting and up-to-the-minute, and sounded relevant to the target listeners. And it was mercifully devoid of journalese. To my mind, it exposed how rigid and boring much of the scriptwriting is on radio and television. More and more news outlets are adopting this more personalised style.

Intros on television

Some news editors believe it's easier to engage the individual member of the audience directly on television than on radio. Most radio newsreaders are disembodied voices – very familiar to the listeners, of course – but strangely insubstantial! The eye-to-eye contact of TV makes it easier for a presenter to be less formal, especially in the second half of a news programme. You can't play around too much with the intros to serious, tragic or worrying stories at the top of the programme. Even there, the opening words should not have the tone of an official announcement. But later in a full news programme, or in the so-called 'second quarter hour' on a 24-hour news channel, good writers can employ the engaging style. Questions are quite popular.

> Do you worry that your kids might be taking drugs? A Mori poll of teenagers says two out of three seventeen-year-olds have experimented with illegal drugs – with cannabis the most popular substance, followed by ecstasy. Only two per cent of those polled said they had used hard drugs like heroin.

The first sentence is clearly expendable. But it could serve to attract the attention of many viewers, as well as creating a bond with the presenter.

> Do you ever drive with a mobile phone in your hand?

> Now, where do you think was the favourite holiday destination for the British last year?

> Does natural childbirth lead to happier children?

The question-intro should be used sparingly. But it does have its place in longer broadcast-news programmes, particularly on television, where visual contact with the presenter makes a chattier approach more suitable.

Graphics in TV intros

Many TV news programmes use a graphic to emphasise the subject of each main story in visual terms. This may be electronically inserted over the newsreader's shoulder, or be on a screen next to the presenter. There are some clear rules about the way an intro script should be written if a graphic is being shown with the presenter.

The graphic image will have been chosen to encapsulate the story; maybe a petrol pump handle for rising fuel prices, or Israeli and Palestinian flags for a relaxation of travel restrictions in the West Bank. If you are the scriptwriter, it is essential that you see this image in advance; ideally, you will have helped to choose it. Remember that every viewer will glance at it, the moment your intro starts. The power of the image on television is overwhelming. These intro-graphics are supposed to help the viewer to adjust immediately to a new story, not to confuse them. So the first line of your script should refer to the picture.

The petrol pump image would not work well with an intro saying, 'OPEC oil-producers, meeting in Dubai, have decided to cut production immediately to halt the slide in oil prices . . .'. It must say: 'Petrol prices are likely to go up by as much as three pence a litre in the next few weeks . . .' (a much better intro anyway). The Israeli and Palestinian flags (not a very good idea because it is a boring and hackneyed image, and many people may not know the Palestinian flag immediately) must accompany a top line mentioning Israel and the Palestinian Authority or the Palestinians. The pictures and words must work together straight away.

Sometimes the graphic accompanying the newsreader will include a well known face – the Pope; the President of the United States; Prince Charles. The script must mention the person as soon as possible. Otherwise there is a subconscious period of waiting until the picture is referred to by the presenter. For example, a picture of the US President does not work too well if the intro says, 'Twenty-eight billion dollars for the reconstruction of Iraq are likely to be voted through Congress later today . . .'. If that's the best intro, use a picture of the Capitol. If the President's political victory is the main point of the story, rewrite the intro so that he is mentioned in the first line.

If two faces are on the graphic, perhaps to indicate a planned meeting between the Prime Minister and the President of Russia, then write the script so that the person on the left is named before the person on the right. From left to right is the way we are used to scanning images.

If there are words printed on the graphic behind the newsreader, the script must use exactly the same words early in the introduction, so that the viewer can read them and listen to the script simultaneously. The viewer's eye and ear must work together to follow the story. (There is a little more on this subject in the section on TV news graphics in Chapter 5.)

The 'split-intro' on television

Many television news programmes have two presenters. It's regarded as a friendlier presentation style compared with the single, authoritative 'anchor'. The double-presentation style is particularly popular for regional news programmes and breakfast television, where the man–woman combination is well established.

In the past, the two presenters would read complete intros alternately. In recent years, the 'split-intro' or 'split-link' has become the norm, with both presenters sitting close together in the same camera shot and sharing the link. For example:

> Presenter one: 'It looks like the fire that destroyed most of St Joseph's School in Weston at the weekend was started deliberately. The police say they're treating the case as arson.
>
> Presenter two: According to Bristol Fire Service, school fires have become their most frequent callouts. They say on average there's a fire in a school twice every week. They're planning a new information drive aimed at school-children. Emma Stevens reports.

This kind of split-link works only if it is quite concise. This one is twenty-three seconds long, with the script divided fairly evenly between the two presenters. It means each presenter will be in shot, listening to the other in a duly enthralled manner, for little more than ten seconds. Much longer than this, and the non-speaking presenter can become an awkward-looking distraction.

Special occasions

For really major stories, the intro should capture the sense of occasion. It should be deliberately slowed down if the news is grave. And it should capture the mood, as well as relating the facts. Most writers believe that on this kind of occasion, less is more. There is no need to inject drama into dramatic events. 'A series of bomb attacks on London's transport network has killed at least thirty-seven people and injured seven hundred others' (BBC Radio 4 News, 7th July 2005). Facts, rhythm and dignity are required. Also required is a summary of the overall story.

This was the thirty-three-second introduction by newscaster Peter Sissons to BBC1's *Ten o'clock News* on 11th September 2001. After the initial sum-marising sentence, it uses the present tense to describe the situation tonight, as it introduces the first report.

> Good evening. America came under attack today from international terrorists
> – on a scale that made it more an act of war. The centre of New York is still
> smouldering, with America's two tallest buildings in ruins. Terrorists also
> struck, with remarkable ease, at the heart of America's defence, the Pentagon.
> Also in Washington, other government buildings, symbols of American power,
> were emptied as the terror spread. Air traffic is paralysed. Coast to coast, all
> key installations are on high alert. And amid the nightmare, the only estimate
> of fatalities is that they could run into many thousands.

It must have been a difficult intro to write, bearing in mind that most of the viewers would have known what had happened already. But the principles for writing the intro for the exceptional event are not much different from those required for the routine story. The core of the story is encapsulated in the first punchy sentence, in this case, 'America came under attack today from international terrorists – on a scale that made it more an act of war.' (The reference to an act of war proved to be prophetic, as in subsequent months the USA's 'War against Terrorism' became the long-term response to the events on that day.)

This was Jane Hill's studio introduction as she presented the BBC evening news on the day of the space shuttle *Columbia* accident in February 2003.

> Good evening. Flags are flying at half mast across the United States tonight. Seven astronauts lost their lives when the space shuttle *Columbia* broke up, forty miles above Texas, on its return from a sixteen-day mission. Debris has been found across hundreds of miles. President Bush has led the mourning, calling it a day of great sadness for the families and the nation. NASA has suspended all shuttle flights and launched an investigation.

In this case, the first sentence could be deleted. But the decision to start with flags at half-mast captured the mood of the USA, and acknowledged that most viewers would already have heard about the *Columbia* disaster, which had happened several hours earlier. Also, the intro immediately followed the programme headlines, which had shown the key image of the shuttle breaking up and given the key facts.

The intro uses short sentences. There are no descriptive adjectives. It is plain and simple. And it is only twenty-five seconds long because this was the start of a fairly short weekend news bulletin, and the reports had to be quite compact.

Exclusive?

Should our intro mention that the story is an exclusive? You might think that the perfect news programme would be composed entirely of exclusives, and the audience would be mightily impressed as one followed another. It would be a serious mistake to think this way. The tabloid press may have 'exclusive' splashed across nearly every page, but in broadcasting it usually sounds like serious oversell and self-consciousness.

In the past, the policy of both ITN and BBC news was to avoid the word 'exclusive', except for unusually enterprising and important stories. Brian Barron's interview with the deposed Ugandan dictator Idi Amin, a year after he had fled and disappeared, deserved the adjective 'exclusive', because so many journalists had been looking for him, and it had been a very difficult operation to penetrate Saudi security to reach him in secrecy.

More recently, I think the word 'exclusive' can be heard in intros more frequently, particularly in regional news magazines. I think it sounds uncomfortable for routine stories to be called exclusive, and by trumpeting that we've found a story ourselves, we might be reminding the audience that newspapers are much better at uncovering original stories than broadcasters, who apply most of their energies to the complex logistics of electronic coverage rather than door-knocking or investigations.

As an alternative to saying 'exclusive', the vogue construction of 'The BBC has learned that . . .' or . . . 'ITV News has discovered that . . .' is particularly irritating. It makes the broadcaster seem to be the subject of the story, and raises expectations of a momentous revelation – expectations that invariably are dashed. How about this one from BBC Radio Four in March 2003? 'The BBC has learned that the population of ruddy ducks is to be culled because they are aggressively mating with the indigenous species of white-faced ducks.' I would cull this phraseology quite aggressively. Put the news first.

Intros written on location

Reporters working on location, and preparing to send their radio despatches or television packages back to base by satellite, phone or internet, will usually write a studio intro. It is important that the commentary in the report follows the intro logically, without repeating information. Modern technology means that an increasing number of reporters have laptop computers with links to their newsroom, so that intros can be sent directly to the producer. Others may text their intro, or may still find it easier to dictate it over the phone in the traditional way. Sometimes the report, sent by ftp, line or satellite, and recorded at base, will begin with the reporter speaking the suggested intro.

The important thing to remember is that this intro will almost certainly be rewritten, with the programme producer and the presenter probably involved in the rewriting. The producer in the newsroom is in command of all the latest facts from various sources; the reporter on location may not have the full picture. The producer also knows how much will be said in the programme headlines, and where each individual report sits in the whole programme. Other reports may be covering different angles on the same subject. Presenters like to use their own phraseology, and will usually rewrite the intro information in their personal style.

So intros sent from reporters on location, regional offices or overseas bureaux should not be regarded as the finished article. These suggested intros are usually called cue material, indicating that they contain the information that should be in the cue, but not necessarily in a finished form. The BBC's highly regarded correspondent, Brian Barron, who died of cancer in 2009 after a career of nearly forty years as a location correspondent, usually in the more challenging parts of the world, always sent back to base intro information that he called cue guidance.

Here's an example of cue guidance sent by Barron following a rare trip into North Korea.

> Daily food rations in the hard-line communist state of North Korea have been drastically cut. The World Food Programme says the new limit is below

survival level. North Korea has been hit by drought followed by floods. The first ever British Embassy has just opened in Pyongyang, though western nations continue to pressure North Korea to abandon missile and nuclear weapon development. BB sent this exclusive report from the world's most secretive and isolated state, which is hostile to western journalists.

As you can see, this is not written in Barron's usual fluent style. He knows it will be rewritten. It is essentially what it claims to be, guidance on the facts that should be covered in the intro, which his report will follow. It gives the writer in the newsroom suggestions on acceptable phrases, such as 'hard-line communist state' and 'the world's most secretive and isolated state', and suggests that maybe the producer would like to give this report the 'exclusive' tag!

If you are a journalist in a newsroom, writing intros based on the cue guidance or cue material sent by the correspondent in the field, make sure the essential facts proposed are included. Otherwise the report itself (which you won't be able to change when it arrives just before transmission) may not make sense to the audience.

Casualty figures in the intro

Any casualty figures in cue guidance should be checked carefully. You will often want to include them in the first line of an intro, but they can change up to the last moment before transmission. So if the cue guidance says, 'Twelve people have been killed and nearly a hundred injured in a suicide bombing . . .', it indicates that the latest casualty figures will be in the cue, and these were the latest the reporter knew at the time of sending the report. They may not be definitive.

For this reason, correspondents on location rarely include casualty figures in their reports unless they are broadcasting live. They expect the latest figures to be in the intro.

The intro in summary

For many years, Sian Williams has presented BBC Breakfast and has probably written a thousand intros. On the corporation's College of Journalism website (www.bbc.co.uk/journalism), she summarises the technique of writing an intro that will be faithful to the facts, will lead smoothly into the report, and will make the viewers want to watch.

Find out as much as you can about the story. Highlight the bits you think are important, and then establish what is known as the *top line* – the key part of the story that you want to sell to the audience. Know your audience. A script that you write for BBC3 [youth channel] will be different from the script for a Radio 4 audience [older/educated]. You're selling a story to that audience, so put your best line at the top to hook them. Bear in mind that your headline and first intro must work together. For example, for the story about the plane landing in the Hudson River just off New York, the headline was: 'Hailed as a hero – the pilot who crash-landed his plane into New York's Hudson River'. The intro really needed to say something else, so we started with a quote from one of the survivors, ' "The engine blew and everyone started saying their prayers" – that was one passenger's account of the terrifying moment when a US Airways plane lost the use of both of its engines over New York.' Read your intro script back aloud in case you stumble over some words. Don't tell the whole story. Double check the facts. Check them with the correspondent. You can never be too sure.

NARRATIVE JOURNALISM

Patterns and stories

The western journalistic tradition of turning information into stories taps into some of the fundamental ways in which we think and view the world around us. Neurological scientists tell us that our brains receive a huge amount of information every second, and we automatically filter these signals provided by our senses, concentrating on just a few that are important at any one moment. This filtering follows patterns learned from birth. We recognise familiar patterns, from the basic rhythm of night and day to more complex patterns of movement, which enable us to do something very complicated such as driving a car. In his television series *The Human Mind*, Professor Robert Winston demonstrated that, while we all find it difficult to remember a large number of bare facts, our memory works very much better when it is asked to recall narrative patterns. 'When we invent simple stories to memorise facts, we set up lines of communication into the key receptors of the brain.' Story-telling helps us to identify with something, and to remember it.

The techniques of narrative journalism borrow quite a lot from stories in literature or folk tales. Very often, our news stories will have a central character. The character may be a person. Sometimes it is a group of people – the Red Cross mission in Iraq, England football fans in Turkey, the Ulster Unionist Party, or the residents of a Welsh village. Sometimes it is a place – a hospital, a school, or a factory. It might be a thing – the Mir Space Station or the Elgin Marbles. Sometimes the central character is just the main event – the bus bomb in Jerusalem, or the earthquake in China. If you ask yourself, 'who or what is this story about?' and you are not quite sure of the answer, perhaps you can adjust the angle or line of approach to make sure it has a central focus.

For example, a story about analysts in the City of London anticipating tax rises in the next budget (not much of a central character there, unless it's the Stock Exchange) might be better told as a story about the Chancellor and his need to fund public spending through unpopular measures; or it might be a story about low-paid taxpayers and pensioners who are increasingly fearful of more taxes to come. The angle of approach can make it easier for the audience to identify with the narrative.

As in any fictional story, our factual narratives should introduce the audience to the character (central subject) immediately, persuade them to be interested, and hold their attention until the end.

Pyramids or lines?

For many years, there has been a tendency in print-journalism training to describe news stories as 'pyramids'. I think this means that the point of the story is sharp and succinct, and it is supported by more detailed information in layers. This conventional view suggests that, to shorten a story, the sub-editor can simply cut from the bottom without altering the core meaning or losing any essential facts. I am not convinced that this idea helps us to write broadcast scripts.

When I first started working in broadcast news, the pyramid theory had been adopted from newspapers. It was expected practice to present your radio or television report to the producer with an overall duration, and one or two so-called 'early-outs', or optional early endings to the report, to help the programme finish precisely on time. These early-outs, timed to the second, would indicate the end of a sentence, or the end of a clip of interview, when it would be possible to cut back sharply to the studio presenter, to save a few seconds. I am pleased to say that this awful practice has almost disappeared. Broadcast news stories should be written as an organic whole according to the time allocated. Often the last sentence is the one that provides most insight, impact or food for thought.

I prefer to think of broadcast news stories as linear. They should start by attracting your attention, then quickly develop your interest, and progress to either a conclusion or a question about what will be the next chapter. If you think of this line of interest as a simple graph, the line shoots up at the start, as you attract the interest of the audience, it plateaus as you add explanation and context, then rises again as you carry the story forward with new and interesting information.

Chronology

> Georges Franju: 'Movies should have a beginning, a middle and an end.'
> Jean-Luc Godard: 'Yes, but not necessarily in that order.'
> (Film Symposium in Monaco, 1960)

This well known observation by the French film director Godard is a clue to why his films had an unusual quality. They were intriguing, sometimes baffling, sometimes coming together only in the final reel. I don't think this artistic approach works in broadcast news, where we must be sure that a mass audience understands everything as clearly as possible, from the beginning to the end.

Very often, the best structure of a broadcast news report follows the chronology of the event. This may seem obvious, but it is certainly not the case in newspaper journalism.

An account of President Sarkozy's 2008 state visit to Britain in a morning paper (reporting what happened the day before) would be very dull if it said 'first he did this, and then he did that'. The report would aim to pull together strands and moments in a mosaic style, to create a portrait of how the day would be remembered, with some comment about the true significance. For example, the *Independent* began with the main points of his address to Parliament: '. . . he heaped praised on Britain and called for the two countries to write a new page in our common history', then related the charm offensive of the President's wife Carla Bruni, who 'curtsied confidently as she met the Queen. And she received a taste of old-fashioned British chivalry when the Prince of Wales kissed her hands as she stepped off the plane at Heathrow.' In broadcasting, dislocating time like this is risky, because it can confuse the listener or viewer. This is particularly true of television, where images have a natural time-line. If we see the French President addressing Parliament, then greeting the Queen earlier, then pictures of his arrival at the airport, it seems time has gone into reverse, and simply won't work. The key points from the address and the overall impression of the visit should be in the headline and introduction, but the reporter's package is usually best as a chronology.

It's interesting to note that modern technology reminds broadcast journalists that stories develop over time. Tape recorders can tell you precisely when a piece of sound was recorded. Cameras stamp the images they record with time-code. More significantly, computer-editing for radio and television is based on the idea of a 'time-line' that appears on the screen. We can see that time is the logical pattern of our narrative and helps us to relate the story clearly.

Picture sequences on TV

The BBC's brilliant correspondent Brian Barron, interviewed for this book, explained how TV reports must have a logical structure.

> When I moved from radio to TV in 1971, one grizzled newsroom editor voiced the mantra, 'You need a beginning, a middle and an end to any television package you are going to do.' I think that more or less still holds up, though there are an infinite number of possibilities of how to cover those three points.

Barron did not recommend putting these three basic sequences in reverse order, because television is composed of sequences of shots, which are edited together skilfully so that the viewer scarcely notices the edits. Many television reports are composed of sequences of sequences.

They tend to make sense if they follow logical patterns. For example: limousine drives up – children wave flags – the Queen emerges – the mayor steps forward for a handshake – crowds applaud – Queen enters building – inside she inspects exhibition. Obviously the picture editor is not going to use a shot of the Queen inside the building followed by her entering it.

Equally, it is disruptive for the viewer if one moment it is daylight, then we see a night-time shot, then it's daylight again; or if the pictures jump between interior and exterior shots. Even jumping between the present and the past sometimes happens, when a shot of archive film is used too briefly in the middle of a report. Writers of television news have to use the chronology of events and familiar sequences much more than newspaper journalists.

Sport gives us a good example of this difference between print and broadcasting. Football reports in newspapers routinely describe the winning goal, then describe the goals that were scored earlier in the game. This style follows the idea that news stories will begin with the latest or most dramatic development, then will recap the background. I have once seen a football report on a TV news programme following this idea – showing the last goal first. It did not work very well. If the big talking point of the match was whether the ball crossed the goal-line in injury time, then maybe you can show that controversial moment first, then relate the events that led to the moment of controversy. But in the vast majority of cases, keeping to the chronology is best. Showing the goals in the right order makes sense to the viewers as a summary of what happened.

When the England rugby team won the World Cup Final, it was settled in the last minute of injury time by a drop-goal from Jonny Wilkinson. Nearly all the newspaper reports began with that heart-stopping moment, but the TV news highlights on all channels stuck to the chronology, building up to the winning kick. In the same way, relating the events of a news story in the order they took place will confuse no-one. The intro can highlight the main talking point of the day. The reporter's account of the event is usually structured best as a chronology.

Setting the scene first

The main exception to the chronological structure is in the reporting of a precise news event that happened earlier, when the script will first need to set the scene now. This is often necessary on television, where only aftermath pictures are generally available. This is Gavin Hewitt's 2002 report for the BBC *Ten o'clock News* on a serious rail crash at Potters Bar, which had happened that morning. Note that he uses first the pictures that were taken first, to establish the scene shortly after the accident, and therefore has no difficulty in starting the narrative with the frightening moment when the loose carriage was careering along the station platform, before going back to the moments leading up to the accident.

> This was the scene at Potters Bar station today at around one o'clock. The last of four carriages of a train from King's Cross to King's Lynn lying across the platform wedged under the station roof. The train had been travelling at over ninety miles per hour when its last carriage began shuddering. People on the platform were terrified as the carriage, having broken loose, tore through a waiting room and slid towards them. [Short interviews with passengers who had been on the platform.]
>
> The first sign of trouble came as the train approached a bridge just outside the station. The driver reported feeling a bump. The last carriage sideswiped the bridge; pieces broke loose, falling on the cars underneath. [Interview with witness.]
>
> A section of the wheels flew off and the carriage mounted the platform, turning on its side. The first three carriages continued down the track. Those inside knew the train was in difficulty. [Interview with passenger describing how they all hung on as it rocked.]
>
> A major incident was declared . . .

Hewitt's report went on to describe the rescue operation, including interviews with some passengers who had been pulled from the wreckage, and with local people who had run from their houses to help. It ended by looking ahead to the accident enquiry, saying that investigators were focusing on a set of points just outside the station, and reflecting that this was the latest in a series of damaging accidents on Britain's railways.

Ending the report by looking to the future is fairly common practice. On television, many correspondents will put their 'piece to camera' at or near the end of the report, so that they can sum up in a direct and personal way, and suggest what is likely to happen next. Appearing on camera in this way can also overcome the problem of what to show when talking about how the story might develop. It's quite difficult to film the future. The concluding piece to camera has become something of a cliché in recent years. Beware of writing something trite just to try to throw the story forward in time, such as, 'tomorrow will bring more challenges' or even worse 'only time will tell'.

Other familiar patterns

Time is the most obvious familiar pattern that will help us to relate the story clearly. It is interesting to note how many television feature-reports from foreign countries begin at dawn and end in the evening. Or sometimes they relate a journey, which takes us through an area in a set period of time.

Another pattern is the circle, with the report starting and finishing with the same person, place or scene. For example, 'Joan Smith has been waiting for a hip operation for two years. Today she was told her operation had been postponed, for the fourth time . . .' is a well established type of opening, which introduces the audience to a human example illustrating a general problem, in this case the over-stretched health service. We can relate to Joan. We hear from Joan about her pain and discomfort. Then the report moves on to explain the problem. The structure of this reporter package will be much more satisfying for the audience if, after a sequence at the hospital, and perhaps an interview clip with the Health Secretary, it returns to Joan at the end (still waiting and getting angry), rather than apparently forgetting about her.

5
Different techniques for radio and television

SIMILARITIES AND DIFFERENCES

Many of the principles of writing for radio and television news programmes are the same. In both media, we try to write Good Spoken English, avoiding journalese, clichés and jargon. We use short and simple sentences, without too many adjectives and adverbs. We try to be accurate at all times, in vocabulary, terminology, basic grammar and pronunciation. We use sensitive language, which will not offend sections of the audience.

But there are also significant differences between radio and television. In my view, radio is a little more straightforward – partly because the flow of information is free of the need to find good pictures; partly because it can be prepared relatively easily and quickly; and partly because for many years it has been an individual activity. A radio journalist working entirely alone can research the story, record all the interviews (checking the batteries and sound levels beforehand), record the commentary, edit the recorded material, and even read the introduction live on air and press the button that plays the report.

Television requires more teamwork. Even today, with lightweight digital cameras and laptop computer-editing bringing more opportunities for multi-skilling and individual newsgathering, most TV news reports require a large number of people to bring them to the screen.

Students of broadcast journalism preparing to go into the profession should be aware that there can be some hostility between news professionals working in radio and television. They seem to occupy three camps.

First, there are the radio loyalists, who believe their medium is the only pure journalism – it is a medium of ideas, argument and analysis, undistorted by the sensationalism of TV or the need to find pictures for everything. It is the ultimate medium for the fine writer, where the spoken word reigns supreme. They will tell you that the pictures are better on radio – meaning it is the medium of the imagination. Even now, in the twenty-first century, there is a lingering resentment that radio – the senior service of broadcast news for decades – was supplanted in the trendy 1960s by the infotainment upstart, television.

Secondly, there are the specialist TV journalists, who love the daily challenge the medium imposes. They will tell you that TV is adrenalin-land. Trying to produce a television news programme can be like riding the Grand National blindfold. It is highly competitive, and the logistics are frightening. But the effort is worth it. The impact of television is enormous, and the satisfaction of producing a fine TV report is unparalleled in journalism. Teamwork is crucial. TV journalists tend to be talkative extroverts, because the production process works only if there is a constant flow of clear communication, whereas a radio newsroom can sometimes resemble a library.

Thirdly, there are the growing numbers of broadcast journalists who are comfortable in either medium, and also enjoy writing versions of their stories for the website. It is clear that, in the years to come, there will be more multimedia news organisations, and more multi-skilling will be required. Having worked in both radio and television throughout my career, I hope that people entering the profession of broadcast journalism will enjoy working in all forms of audiovisual media. But it is important to have a very good understanding of the different qualities of the two disciplines of broadcasting, and the best use of language for news online.

WRITING RADIO NEWS

In some ways, radio is untouched by progress. Essentially, it is the same product as when it began in Britain in the 1920s. And that is its enduring strength. Despite the arrival of the biggest mass medium – television – and later the internet, ninety per cent of the UK population use radio for an average of twenty-four hours every week. Radio still enjoys a high rating as the most trusted news medium. It is a mass medium that does not seem to address the 'mass', but speaks to the individual.

As for the best way to write news for radio, the essentials have already been covered in earlier chapters. Write as you would speak to an individual listener, in a fairly formal but conversational style. Simplicity and clarity are the main principles, particularly when you are sitting in the newsroom, writing the short summaries. Not counting the unscripted live reports or two-way interviews with reporters, written radio news stories come in four broad types.

- The **copy story** or **straight read**, which is read live on air with no illustrative clips of interview or actuality sound.

- The **reporter-piece** (still called a despatch on BBC World Service), where the newsreader introduces a location report voiced by the correspondent.

- The **short package**, containing one or two short clips of interview, which may be little more than a minute in duration.

- The **package** or **full package**, which can range from ninety seconds to several minutes, and might deploy a range of radio techniques – actuality sound, extracts of speeches, interviews, vox pops (short interviews with members of the public expressing their opinions), an unscripted descriptive passage by the reporter on location, or even music.

The copy story follows similar principles to the writing of intros, described in Chapter 4. It should encapsulate the essential story in the first sentence, then add explanation, and try to ensure a balance of views in as short a time as possible. The writer in the newsroom is in no position to use descriptive words, so the copy story style is pared down and concentrates on facts and clarity, often in short, punchy sentences.

Each newsroom will use its own format, but all will have templates in the computer so that everyone can see the essential information clearly. Most formats have a story title (or 'slug'), the name or initials of the writer, the date and time of the bulletin, and the duration of the story, which in most computer systems is calculated automatically at three words per second. Copy stories are typically around twenty seconds. Even in longer-form bulletins, they are seldom more than thirty seconds. So a typical copy story might look like this:

Wind Farms (slug). Anne Smith (writer). 27.2.10 (date). 12.00 (time of bulletin).

An environmental group claimed this morning that the development of clean energy in Britain is being obstructed by a conspiracy backed by the nuclear industry. At an enquiry into a proposed offshore wind farm in the Bristol Channel, Greenpeace say the opposition campaign is funded by nuclear power companies determined to scupper the growth of green energy. The Campaign to Protect Rural England say the conspiracy allegation is nonsense. They say their supporters oppose windmills simply because they ruin the landscape and don't generate much electricity.

0'29"

The script for a package would be the intro, followed by the exact duration of the package, and importantly the last five or six words, called 'out-words', so that the studio presenter or engineer will know exactly when it is about to end, and will not be caught by surprise.

Using actuality and description

With the exception of copy stories, the other types of radio report all seek to use the reporter's voice, and in the case of packages, actuality – interviews or natural sound that add reality, interest, variety and pace to the reporting. Using the voice of the reporter on the spot, or interviews with people involved in the story, adds credibility as well as immediacy to the journalism.

The distinctive quality of radio reporting from location is that the journalist's words can express the sense of being there, so that the listeners can capture the atmosphere. For example, a full package on the wind farm enquiry might include the whooshing noise of a wind turbine with some description from the reporter, the sound of waves on the shore as the reporter describes the proposed wind farm which will be visible from a holiday beach, interview clips with spokespeople from Greenpeace and the CPRE, vox-pops with people living near existing windmills, and perhaps the babble of the enquiry room as the package concludes with a look ahead to the arguments likely to be heard in the coming days.

I believe that radio packages should not end with a clip of interview. This literally gives one contributor the last word, and the last word can be disproportionately influential. Not all radio journalists agree with me about this; Radio Four's *Today* programme went through a period of several years when the programme style was to end packages with a telling clip of interview. Most producers think that the reporter should 'wrap' the story and end the package with his or her own voice. A pay-off immediately after an interview clip is not enough (for example . . . end of interview clip . . . 'Joan Bloggs, Independent Radio News, Nottingham'). The report sounds incomplete; in effect, it still gives the interviewee the last word, and it can sound as though the interview clip came from Joan Bloggs.

Writers of radio news tend to look for opportunities to use the present tense, because it sounds immediate and is quite succinct. So 'Elton John is suing his former manager . . .' is preferred to 'Elton John has announced that he'll sue . . .'; 'Interest rates are up a quarter per cent . . .' rather than 'The Bank of England has raised interest rates . . .'.

The present tense can also be used on location for descriptions of events, but it should be used very carefully, and only when there is sufficient drama for this rather dramatic style to seem appropriate. For example:

> Mortars slam into the villa. Helicopter gun-ships strafe the site, and two aces are crossed off America's pack-of-cards most-wanted list.' (Independent Radio News, July 2003).

Here are a few words of advice about writing location reports for radio news from experienced professionals interviewed for this book.

Richard Sambrook, former Director of BBC News:

> In radio you have to paint a picture with the words. People will have an image in their head as they listen to it. With television, of course, they have the image in front of them.

Clare Morrow, former Controller of Programmes YTV and for several years a radio correspondent:

> On radio you have got to create the scene. If you are trying to paint a picture of what an explosion or a fire was like, people need to be able to 'see' that the flames reached the top of the building. In radio you are trying to create the picture. In television you are trying to think of words that give complementary information to the pictures.

Karen Coleman, former BBC radio correspondent and Foreign Affairs Editor at Newstalk 106 in Ireland:

> Radio requires an intelligent understanding of the story and particular care with words. In many ways, it's easier in TV to let the pictures tell the story for you. In radio you have to be more imaginative in the language you use. You want to be able to convey the real picture. A radio journalist should describe the scene. With experience you learn how to do that.

Lyse Doucet, BBC World Presenter and an experienced foreign correspondent on radio and TV:

> Think of all your senses when you write for radio . . . colours, sounds, even smells . . . the stench of death . . . the sharpness of tear gas. Think of painting a picture, and look for detail. A colleague in West Africa reporting on refugees fleeing Nigeria wrote how one man was dragging an anchor with him. It was the detail everyone remembered! But it also gave an insight into the panicked and confused thoughts of people forced to leave everything behind.

Big stories need more description

As a general rule, a big story needs a little more description than a routine one, because listeners have suddenly become more attentive and want to be able to capture the sense of occasion. BBC Radio Four introduced its series of reporter-packages on 11th September 2001, a few hours after the attacks on America, like this:

> An astonishing series of acts of terrorism has been perpetrated in the United States. Countless numbers of people have been killed and injured when at least three apparently hijacked passenger aircraft were flown into buildings in New York and Washington. The twin towers of the tallest building in New York – the World Trade Center – have been destroyed, reduced to rubble. Huge billowing clouds of dust and smoke have engulfed the southern part of Manhattan Island . . .

The television reports did not need to describe the huge billowing clouds; we could all see them. The radio coverage then used the time-honoured chronology to relate the events of the day. After hearing from terrified eye-witnesses who had seen the first plane strike, the Radio Four coverage switched to BBC reporter Steve Evans, who had been in the World Trade Center when it happened.

> I can tell you that I'm looking up at the World Trade Center. There is a cloud of grey smoke in a very clear sky coming from the top of it and now in the last thirty seconds another explosion half-way down the building, and you can see the rent in the side of the building from that explosion. I was in the base of the building when this happened. First of all there was a huge bang, and it felt as though a construction company or something like that dropped a weight from a very very great height. The building physically shook. I initially thought no more about it, thinking there's a bit of a problem on a building site. But then seconds later there were two or three more very big explosions, and this building, this huge building, towering into the sky, again physically shook, and at that point people came screaming past me saying – 'Just get out! Just get out! Just get out!'

I realise that descriptive passages on radio tend to be the exception rather than the rule. Most radio journalists will go through their careers reporting many more court cases and political disputes than stories involving huge billowing clouds, the stench of death or the sharpness of tear gas. But my personal view is that radio has become less adventurous in recent years, and rather less atmospheric. I hope a new generation of radio reporters will rediscover the descriptive passage, and even when covering everyday stories, will try to use short sections of atmospheric sound, and look or listen for those little details that bring events to life.

WRITING TELEVISION NEWS

Television makes enormous impact. According to Eurobarometer surveys, which track lifestyle trends across Europe, more than seventy per cent of the population regard TV as their primary source of information. So far, the internet has made little impression on the popularity of television, though I suspect that will change in coming years.

The impact comes from television's visual power. 'Of course', I hear you cry. 'TV is pictures. Everyone knows that.' Well, it's interesting how many aspiring television journalists do not seem to know that. I have seen countless television reports, in different countries, which are essentially radio reports, with pictures slapped on top. General pictures, used to cover an essay from a reporter, are known in broadcasting jargon as 'wallpaper', because the picture-editor is asked by the journalist to 'cover that with some pictures'. This is dreadful technique. It dates back to the days of news being covered on film, by people who had been trained in the film industry, teamed with journalists who had learned their profession in newspapers or radio. Demarcation was accepted. 'You look after the words, squire. I'll worry about the pictures', a news cameraman would say to a reporter.

And back at base, the film would have to go into processing for at least forty minutes before editing could begin. So, while this was happening, the reporter would hammer out the script and record it, so that editing could begin immediately the wet film emerged from the processing bath. In the twenty-first century, it is unforgivable for TV reporters to write their scripts without knowing the available pictures in great detail, and how they will be edited to show the story in the best way.

Write commentary first or edit the pictures first?

Computer-based editing has made it much easier to edit the pictures first and write the script afterwards, or, when making a package, to record pieces of commentary while picture editing is in progress, using a lip-microphone to record directly on to each sequence of shots as it is edited. With non-linear digital editing, if the pictures and words don't quite match, shots can be swapped around, shortened or lengthened in a few seconds. But it's much better for the script to be adjusted. A shot has a natural length. A script line can be any length you want. If it is a very late story, it may be marginally faster to record the commentary first and slap on pictures. Even then, the script should be written with a very precise idea of what pictures will be seen at every moment.

Martin Bell, one of the best television correspondents I have worked with, who left the BBC to campaign against 'sleaze' as an independent Member of Parliament, became so accomplished at editing the pictures and then recording commentary in segments that he would not write a script at all. He would watch and listen to the editing intently, perhaps pace up and down for a few moments, then grab the microphone and record a short section of his report directly on to the edited pictures. I first saw him doing this back in 1980, at the Republican Convention in Detroit. The words matched the pictures perfectly, and the editing happened very fast indeed.

I am certain that the best television news packages have the pictures edited first, so that the shots can be chosen to flow together in a natural sequence and at just the right length for each shot. The journalist will dictate the structure of the piece, and will take a keen interest in the individual shots, perhaps asking the picture-editor for a particular image, which he or she knows can be reflected in the commentary. These days, more and more newsrooms are training their journalists to edit the pictures themselves. This guarantees that the reporter will be thinking in pictures and sequences, and is much more likely to result in a symbiotic relationship between images and words.

Unlike Martin Bell, most reporters write a script after taking notes during the picture-editing, whether or not they are editing the pictures themselves. These notes mark the precise times when key images appear, or interview clips are to be introduced. This is a long-established technique called 'shot-listing'.

Shot-lists

Time codes on the linear editing machines or on the non-linear computer screen have made shot-listing easier in recent years. Some journalists write the shot-list on their computer as the edited pictures take shape, and refer to it carefully as they write their script. Others prefer to use the older technology of the notebook, to scribble ideas alongside the shot-list. The notes for a ninety-second package might look something like this.

0–3″	Sound of chanting 'four more years' as Obama enters hall for campaign rally.
4–13″	Barack Obama and beaming Michelle mount stage and wave from podium. Crowd wave banners. Note placards saying 'Change'.
13–17″	Afghanistan vets in front row.
17–32″	Obama clip 1 (Finish the job).
32–36″	Shot of Hillary Clinton looking determined.
36–39″	Large Statue of Liberty balloon is held up.
39–58″	Obama clip 2 (Economic recovery theme).

58–1'12"	Protesters behind police cordon outside calling for more jobs, chanting 'America doesn't work'. 1'07" to 1'09"
1'12"–1'24"	Piece to camera (stand-up).
1'24"–1'30"	The Obamas shake hands with supporters.

With detailed notes like these, it's not too difficult to write a script that allows short pauses for the natural sound, and uses visual references throughout, by mentioning Michelle Obama and Hillary Clinton at the right times, mentioning that the president's big challenge is disenchantment with his 2008 promise of 'change', that he is campaigning on the twin messages of security and jobs – starting to bring the boys home from Afghanistan while insisting he will never flinch from the battle for freedom and security, and creating jobs at home in a sustainable recovery – but not coming into contact with the unemployed demonstrators, who were kept well away from the rally.

Short stories and longer packages

Shot-listing works for television stories of any length, where moving pictures are involved. These can be very short stories or long special reports. There are still a few occasions in TV news when no illustration is possible, so some stories must be written for a presenter 'in vision', addressing the camera directly throughout. Different news organisations use different jargon for the various types of story. In broad terms, the following are the different kinds of TV story a journalist may be required to write.

- **Vision story** – the studio presenter is in vision with no illustration.

- **Vision/inset** – the presenter is in vision, but with a caption electronically inset.

- **Vision/plasma** – the presenter is in vision, with a caption or relevant moving pictures on a plasma screen in the studio.

- **Vision/still** – the presenter begins the short story in vision and then talks behind a full-screen 'still' or caption.

- **Vision/OOV** – the presenter continues reading 'out of vision' as moving pictures are shown.

- **Wipe-story** – a sequence of short, illustrated stories, with the presenter reading live out of vision, and the director 'wiping' from one story to the next. These short sequences are sometimes called a 'Nib' (news in brief) or a 'Fru' (Foreign news roundup).

- **Package** – the bread and butter of TV news programmes for many years, the package is usually written and voiced by the location reporter, but is sometimes written by a specialist correspondent back at base, or a journalist pulling together various picture sources.

More and more frequently, correspondents are integrating all these techniques into a sophisticated studio-based package, where the newsreader will link to the correspondent standing at a video wall with moving graphics, who then links into various video sequences, including more graphics, before handing back to the presenter.

When writing the simpler short stories for OOVs or wipe sequences, it's a good idea to edit the pictures with a long and steady shot at the end. Before you cut the pictures, you'll know the producer is expecting a maximum of – say – twenty seconds. So ensure that there is a shot-change at about fifteen seconds, and that the last shot is held at least until about twenty-five seconds. This means there is no danger of the story running out of pictures (a black screen is a serious error in a news programme), and ensures the audience will not be shown a new shot just before the director cuts to another story, which is irritating and leaves a feeling that the story ended prematurely.

Writing to pictures

It is difficult to over-estimate the need for the script to follow the pictures in TV news. The head of journalism training for the French public television networks, Didier Desormeaux, tells his trainees about a research project in Paris, which showed that during a TV news programme, seventy-five per cent of a typical viewer's brain concentrates on the pictures, while only twenty-five per cent is attentive to the words being spoken. Research also shows that viewers believe TV news is 'the news in pictures'. They expect to see the story rather than hear it.

The more arresting or dramatic the pictures are, the less attention the viewer will pay to the commentary. So television journalists are well advised to consider the pictures all the time. The words should not compete with them, but should work with them.

Here are some pieces of advice from successful TV news professionals.

Sir David Nicholas, former Editor in Chief, ITN:

> Write tightly to the picture!

Karen Coleman, formerly a foreign correspondent in radio and TV:

> Television is about pictures. You don't need a pile of words, especially if
> you have strong images. There's a big difference between radio and TV.
> You should look carefully at the pictures, then choose the words to
> complement those pictures while telling the story.

Bob Jobbins, former head of news at BBC World Service radio and World TV:

> In the best television news programmes, the writing together with the
> pictures produces the impact. TV writing at its best is really pared down.

Clare Morrow, for many years in charge of journalism at ITV Yorkshire
Television:

> In TV you are trying to think of words which give complementary
> information to the pictures, additional information, information that the
> picture can't tell you. Less experienced journalists tend to describe what
> they see. What's the point? The two forms of communication, pictures
> and words, should work together but do different jobs.

Tim Orchard, former senior programme editor at BBC TV News:

> Writing commentary to pictures is a difficult line to tread. Don't write
> against the pictures; in other words, don't write about something while
> the viewer is seeing something completely different. On the other hand,
> don't write a commentary to the pictures which points out the bleedin'
> obvious! The secret is finding words which complement the pictures and
> don't fight against them.

Words and pictures are complementary

So what does all this mean in practice? The first clear principle is to asso-
ciate the words with the pictures, but not describe them. If our report starts
with a shot of a tanker on rocks, we do not write, 'The ship was wrecked on
the rocks ...' but 'The Panamanian tanker was loaded with fifty thousand
tons of light crude ...'. Shots of the drug squad smashing down the door of
a house do not require the commentary to say, 'The police used sledgeham-
mers to break down the doors ...'. Say how many officers were involved, and
that this was one of five raids happening simultaneously across the city ...
TV commentary explains what we see without describing it.

In his book *News From No Man's Land*, the BBC correspondent John Simpson
expresses it like this:

> Good quality television reporting, and there is quite a lot of it nowadays,
> cannot be done by writing an excellent script alone. The pictures have
> to be accentuated, their full meaning brought out and enhanced, if the

report is to be effective. Sometimes you hear a reporter launching into the purplest of prose, paying no attention to the pictures, and you know that he or she is off on some private planet which has little to do with communicating with the audience.

Simpson goes on to confess that he found it very hard to learn how to write for television news.

As a radio journalist who did a good deal of work for newspapers, it seemed strange not to be describing in words exactly what had happened. By comparison, writing a television news script felt like playing chess in several dimensions. But then television news is more complicated than any other type of journalism. That's its attraction.

What am I looking at?

One tip that might help simplify this multi-dimensional chess game is to make sure your commentary helps the viewers to know what they are looking at. This is particularly relevant to locations. On television, many places look much like any other. So don't be afraid to say, 'On this industrial estate on the outskirts of Swindon . . .' or 'Here in the mountains to the east of Kabul . . .' or 'Inside the committee room . . .'.

If a report changes location, make sure the commentary explains the change near the beginning of the new sequence.

The ACAS talks resume tomorrow with union leaders expressing confidence that a deal will be done . . . [switch visual location from outside ACAS to car workers] . . . On assembly track number three at Cowley, the men who make the Mini aren't so sure . . . .

For the Republican faithful, this was enough to provoke a ten-minute ovation . . . [scene change to exterior shot of conference centre with faint sound of cheering from inside] . . . Outside the conference centre, no sign of demonstrators. Because . . . [demonstrators behind barrier] . . . they were penned back here, two blocks away, by two hundred police, well out of sight of delegates, and out of earshot . . . .

Television commentary often uses words such as 'this' and 'here' in a way that would not work on radio or in print. In some ways, television commentary can resemble a series of captions to a storyboard or strip-cartoon of pictures.

BBC Breakfast showed pictures of people walking through an airport. They would have been meaningless without the verbal 'caption', by which I mean the concise line of commentary, which had no main verb, and would not have worked on radio.

Back in Britain this morning, the lucky ones who managed to get on the last flight out of Kenya.

A *Six o'clock News* television report on train delays caused by the record temperatures in the summer of 2003 started with a caption-phrase on a good opening shot of railway lines seeming to wobble in the heat haze. 'The sweltering shimmer across Britain's railways this afternoon.'

It's particularly important for the script to identify people. If the picture shows a close-up of one of the main characters in the story, you should identify the person immediately, unless it is someone incredibly well known.

Even fairly unspecific street scenes can work well if the scriptwriting follows the pictures and explains them. Here, John Simpson describes Belgrade preparing for a night of NATO bombing in 1999. He was working under restrictions, so the range of available pictures was quite limited.

> The all-clear siren sounds, for the time being. By now, it's after five, the time when Belgrade starts to change. The café culture is over for the day. Now people make tracks for home. And the illusion that life is normal begins to fade. The trams stop running at eight o'clock. This is the last one. As the evening wears on, Belgrade becomes a different, more frightening place. The uncertainties and fears grow stronger. No one knows what the night will bring . . .

The siren, shots of empty cafés, people scurrying through the streets, a tram, frightened faces, are all used precisely. Notice the chronology. And notice how short the sentences are – a Simpson trademark style when he is trying to convey tension.

Brian Hanrahan has always been particularly adept at writing to the available pictures. He also reported for the BBC on the Balkan wars. During a tense period of political manoeuvring in Belgrade, with media access to the talks denied, the only shots available were of the restaurant at the front of the national parliament building.

> Most politics in Yugoslavia goes on behind closed doors. It takes a crisis to force them ajar and give the public a glimpse of what the politicians are doing. And with more parties in parliament than tables in the dining room, it's an opportunity for endless intrigue.

Pictures from the library or archive

Sometimes library pictures have to be used because there are no new shots to illustrate the subject. Even then, they should not be used as wallpaper.

The commentary should try to use the strength of the images. When the BBC's Ben Brown reported on the arguments over equal opportunities legislation and the Army's recruitment policy, he had to use library shots of soldiers in action. A clause at the end of the first sentence relates them to the story.

> Every single member of the British armed forces must be fit enough to fight on the front line, according to Sir Charles Guthrie, as fit as these soldiers in the Gulf for example. Sir Charles believes that allowing the disabled to join up could threaten Britain's very ability to wage war . . .

It's good practice to refer to library pictures in the commentary, rather than rely only on a fleeting caption on the screen. For example, library pictures of Russian troops pouring in to South Ossetia at the start of the short war with Georgia in August 2008 might well have a caption saying 'South Ossetia, August 2008', but it is helpful to the viewer if the commentary also says, 'When ten thousand Russian troops entered South Ossetia to engage the Georgian army on the ninth of August 2008 . . .'. Otherwise the viewers will be trying to read the caption, while looking at the interesting pictures, and listening to the reporter telling them something else. Good commentary always helps viewers know what they are looking at by steering them through the visual narrative.

The present tense

The present tense is used a great deal in broadcast journalism, usually to describe situations rather than specific actions or events: 'The refugees are desperate. Mrs Aziz says she can't remember how long she's been here.' And it can be used for what people have said recently: 'Mr Clegg says that's a deliberate misreading of the coalition policy . . .' rather than 'Mr Clegg said it was . . .'.

On television, it is sometimes possible to use the present tense to relate events that have already happened. I guess this is because there is a strong sense of immediacy for the viewers as the pictures unfold. Present-tense narrative has the effect of injecting more drama, so it should be used sparingly, and when the story really does qualify as dramatic. Here the BBC's David Shukman reports on a Tornado mission over Serbia.

> This is where the air war starts. A two thousand pound bomb, the largest the RAF has, is loaded into an RAF Tornado in Germany. These weapons are meant to break the Serbian military and force Mr Milosevic to the peace table. The planes begin their mission – two men in each – six bombers in all – many other aircraft in support. The sight is formidable, but so are the complications . . .

Once again, we can note the chronological narrative unfolding, and the use of very short sentences and phrases.

The play-on-words and the pun

The struggle to relate the words to the image on screen has led many TV reporters to use a play-on-words to find the connection. It's particularly popular at the regional television level, where stories are not always tragic or dramatic, or when rather dull visuals require ingenuity in the commentary to make them interesting. This is risky territory. It is difficult to write useful guidance on this because it is so subjective.

Personally, I like subtle pointers to the pictures in the choice of words. At its simplest, we could write, 'It was a dazzling entrance . . .' as we see the film star flinching from the flash bulbs, or 'City analysts expect the Chancellor to box clever . . .' as we see him holding up the red box on budget day. I enjoyed the last line of a regional television report about a multi-storey at Stratford-upon-Avon winning the Car Park of the Year Award: 'The pay and display's the thing!'

The BBC's Martin Bell reported on a British poet winning a top literary prize in the USA, and wrote his television commentary in rhyming couplets. His delivery was so measured that hardly anyone noticed.

But the joke or pun can easily be a groaning distraction. You might just get away with, 'It was a hairy moment . . .' as David Beckham emerged from the hairdressers in plaits to face the press, because it's a fun story. But I urge all readers of this book to resist puns, particularly in animal stories. They've all been done already, and amuse only the very young, the very old, or the very indiscriminating. Banish from your mind any thought of 'barking up the wrong tree' or 'thereby hangs a tale' in doggy stories.

How about this from a regional TV company, which I will not name out of charity. It's the end of a short package about the top cockerel at the agricultural show.

> And while the prizes might be poultry, this cock of the north is hoping he can pullet off.

At this point, the cockerel was seen attacking the reporter. Thousands of viewers were urging him on. The serious point is that puns in television commentaries have to be very good ones if they are going to work for most viewers. They tend not to work in serious reports. A play-on-words is seldom the best way to relate pictures to the script.

There's nothing to [subediting] really ... it's just a matter of checking
the facts and spelling, crossing out the first sentence, and removing any
attempts at jokes.

(Michael Frayn, *Towards the End of the Morning*)

Natural sound on television

A student of broadcast journalism might be forgiven for thinking that the
domain of television is pictures, and the realm of radio is sound. Curiously,
sound plays as important a role in television news as it does in radio news.
Some would argue it is even more important on TV. This is because the staple
diet of radio news is the concise voice-piece or despatch from the reporter –
the voice only, with no real sound. The short radio package may include interview clips, but not much atmospheric sound.

Television news, on the other hand, has a staple diet of packages composed
of sequences of moving pictures, and these picture sequences are not silent.
They carry real sound with the images throughout.

'Natural sound' is sometimes called 'actuality', 'real sound' or 'international
sound'. Whatever you call it, good natural sound is essential for good television packages. It brings reality to television. We do not live in a silent world.
The TV screen is two-dimensional. The sound gives depth to the picture. It's
the third dimension of a rounded reality.

For television news professionals, sound has always posed particular challenges.
In the past, it was difficult and expensive to record sound on location. That's
why the early cinema newsreels, Pathé and Movietone, for example, put music
on all their reports. The stories had been filmed largely with silent Bolex
cameras. The film was 'mute'. Edited with commentary alone, it sounded flat.
So expert music-finders were employed to provide appropriate non-copyright
music, joyful and happy for the Queen at Ascot, doom-laden and threatening
for war in the Balkans.

In the digital age, all cameras record good quality sound on at least two sound-
tracks. Yet some journalists refuse to acknowledge how important the sound
is. Some view their pictures at high speed, which means they cannot hear
any good sound. And many produce 'block-scripts' or 'wall-to-wall scripts',
which give no opportunity for the viewer to hear the real sound or capture
the atmosphere.

Ian Masters, for many years the Controller of Broadcasting at the Cardiff-
based Thomson Foundation, trained broadcast journalists around the world.
He regards the lack of real sound as one of the most common faults in TV
news package-making.

Journalists should not write 'wall to wall' and never write over gripping sound. I remember watching a news piece on the last steam locomotive journey in an overseas country. The cameraman produced a fantastic set of pictures with wonderful hissing and sounds of steam belching. The journalist dipped the sound on the lot and wrote over everything. The emotive sounds of the steam engine would have said more than the yapping journalist.

The best journalists, camera-operators and picture-editors listen for good sound all the time. Writing the script for a TV package should always take account of the need to pause briefly for the sound to be clearly audible. This is called, in broadcasting jargon, 'letting it breathe'. Don't try to write block script across pictures of football fans singing, a police car roaring past with sirens blaring, a caged tiger leaping at the bars with a roar, the baby gurgling at the camera, the applause, the laughter, the aircraft talking off from the carrier, the roof coming off in the hurricane – in fact, anything captured on camera that needs no words – at least for a few seconds.

Lyse Doucet:

> Sometimes pictures don't need words. Let them breathe. Let people take in the full impact. Don't feel you must keep talking. It will only distract.

Clare Morrow:

> Commentary should come after the pictures are edited. This also allows you to hear the natural sound, and adjust the words to make it come through. You may not have noticed it on location. Natural sound makes the viewers feel they are there!

Sir David Nicholas:

> A great stylistic requirement in my old company, ITN, was that you used natural sound mixed up with the script as much as possible. If someone wrote a script which squeezed out some very effective sound, my old editor would jump on you from a great height.

Natural sound is often most effective when the report changes locations. For example, if the scene moves from a quiet upland sheep farm in Shropshire to the weekly market in Shrewsbury, the commentary script should pause for two or three seconds at the start of the first shot of the market, so that the viewer can hear the general hubbub, or the sheep baaing as they are herded in to the pens. Picture editors look and listen for 'edit-points' when they can move the action along or change location. A classic edit point is a door closing. Whether it's a car door or a classroom door, the bang or click allows the picture editor to cut effortlessly to a different location. But the picture-editor's craftwork is time wasted if the journalist writes an essay all over the natural sound.

Using graphics

Viewers of television news can see three basic types of image on their screen. They can see the news studio; the outside world (either on live location shots or, more often, recorded on tape or memory-card); and graphics. These graphics are electronically inserted images, designed to help the communication process. They can be name-captions (generally known as 'supers', short for superimpositions), maps, still pictures, animations, key quotes, key numbers, bullet points, charts, graphs, currency exchanges, sport results, or weather captions.

Up to the late '70s, graphics in British TV news were hard to handle. They had to be hand-produced by artists sitting at large drawing boards in the newsroom, and shown on screen by pointing studio cameras at them. Even simple name-supers were printed on to black cards and placed before a camera in a purpose-built caption-scanner. Computer-based electronic graphics, which developed in the '80s, were fabulous in comparison. They were sharp, three-dimensional and capable of animation. Since then, electronic graphics devices have become dazzling in their capability, and they have become cheaper.

Yet many news programmes around the world still do not use graphics very much. Editors say they are too expensive, or too time-consuming, or both. I believe that some television journalists are afraid of using graphics. They don't know how to make them work well. They think graphics spell trouble and waste time, and they find it much easier to cut a TV package without worrying about inserting graphics.

Broadcasters in the UK are generally more ambitious in the use of graphics than their counterparts in the rest of Europe. The BBC, ITN, Sky News and the regional companies use graphics a great deal. They are used for a number of reasons:

- to **identify** speakers and library pictures, or places via a map

- to **clarify** information, particularly when numbers are involved

- to **explain** complicated stories

- to **emphasise** the main points of a report or a statement

- to **illustrate** when no pictures are possible, for example in a court case, or if the only way of receiving a report or conducting an interview is on the phone

- to **indicate** a change of subject visually, usually as an inset or screen-graphic next to the presenter.

Graphics also help to give the programme style, through their typeface, colours and general design, which will be chosen to match the opening titles and the studio set. And they provide visual variety, which keeps the viewers' attention.

Full-screen and integrated graphics

The simplest form of graphic is a full-screen caption, such as a chart of football results, currency changes, or the main points of a government bill. In recent years, graphics have become more and more integrated with television's moving images. The latest computer systems allow movement within the graphic, such as swirling backgrounds, zooms to highlight locations, or animated lettering. And now the reporter and the graphic can be integrated visually. Many graphics are shown on one side of the screen with the presenter in the studio, or reporter on location, also in shot. Sometimes a specialist correspondent will stand in the studio beside a plasma screen and explain the background to a story with the aid of a series of carefully produced graphics, which include some moving pictures. And sometimes the reporter on location will be filmed on one side of the screen so that graphics can be inserted alongside. Television weather forecasts have used this technique for several years, to take the presenter out of the studio and into the real world, with its real weather.

Whether graphics are used full-screen or integrated with other images, the principles of writing the script remain the same. Remember that the moment you present a graphic on to the screen, the viewers will look at it! So the script must immediately help them to interpret it or to read the words.

Writing to graphics

The reason we throw a graphic on to the screen is to make it easier for the viewer to understand our story. If we show words or numbers on the screen, we are inviting the viewers to read them. And if they are going to read them, in just a few seconds, we cannot expect them to listen to something completely different at the same time. This logic leads to some clear rules for writing to graphics.

- Don't put too many words on the screen at the same time. Information on graphics should be taken in very quickly, almost at a glance. A screen full of text is almost impossible to read. Most viewers will not bother to try.

- Make sure the visual effects are not too distracting. Swirling backgrounds, which make it difficult to read the words or numbers, are counter-productive.

- The words in the script must precisely match the words on the caption (in much the same way that a graphic shown with a newsreader's intro must match the words closely, as outlined earlier). It's not good enough to show a caption reading ... '19% of secondary school children have played truant' and write a script that says, 'According to the survey, [caption] nearly one in five children over the age of eleven have skipped school in the past two years'. The information is broadly the same, but it is far too difficult for a viewer to try to read the caption and listen to different words at the same time. And a list of sport results should be scripted in precisely the order they appear on the screen.

- The caption must be on the screen long enough for the audience to read and understand it. Even a short caption-statement like the example above (19% of secondary school children have played truant), which would take three to four seconds to read aloud, should be on screen for at least seven seconds. So the accompanying script should have an extra phrase at the end, so that the caption does not disappear too quickly. For example:

(Commentary behind pictures)	'Last year's truancy initiative seems to be having little impact . . .
(Caption: 19% of secondary school children played truant)	According to the survey, nineteen per cent of secondary school children have played truant at some time in the past year. The Minister says something must be done.'
(Pictures continue).	(Interview clip with Minister).

Spellings on graphics

As a footnote on writing to graphics, it is worth emphasising that this is the one part of broadcast journalism where spelling really matters (apart from the need to spell accurately if you are required to deliver a version of your story to the station website). One careless mistake on a television graphic looks ghastly. It will be noticed by thousands, maybe millions, and severely damage the reputation of the journalism. So check and double-check that your graphics are correct.

It is very useful to have a good dictionary and an atlas to hand. This may seem obvious, but I have been in newsrooms that did not have them. Nor do some newsrooms have their own spelling guide for graphics. Any credible news organisation needs to be consistent. For example, Al Qaeda can be spelt in English at least twelve different ways. On your caption, should it be al-qaida, or Al Qa'ida or Al Qaida? Is it Colonel Gaddafi or Ghaddafi? You don't want to waste time trawling the internet to find out. I think all television news graphics areas should have a copy of a style guide from a quality newspaper, such as *The Times Guide to English Style and Usage*, which is full of recommendations on spellings and punctuation.

Probably the most common error on television graphics involves the infamous apostrophe. Its misuse drives normally placid folk into a frenzy of letter-writing to the papers. There is even an Apostrophe Protection Society, and a rival Society for the Prevention of Apostrophe Misuse (SPAM). It seems that more and more people are leaving school confused by this small punctuation tick. We have probably all seen shop signs, some of them expensively printed, that use apostrophes on simple plurals: Best Sausage's, Kitchen's and Bathroom's, even the baffling Xma's Tree's.

I'm confident that no professional journalist could produce such howlers on simple plurals. But bear in mind that 'people in their 90s' is a simple plural. 'The 1990s' is also plural. But an apostrophe appears in 'the '90s' to show we've dropped something.

I'm less confident about the potential confusion between forms of the possessive. Remember that the apostrophe comes after the letter 's' for plural possessives; so 'the board member's decision' refers to one board member, and 'the board members' decision' refers to more than one. If the plural form of the word does not end with the letter 's', the apostrophe treats the word like a singular, for example 'children's books'.

But the possessive 'its' has no apostrophe at all. 'The board took its decision.' The apostrophe in 'it's' denotes that a letter is missing: it means 'it is'. So 'the board took it's decision' is wrong. It's not it's, it's its.

An example of a full TV package

So what do all these principles of writing television news mean in practice? Here's an example of a full-length TV news package, which illustrates many of the above points. It was a report from Uganda shown on the BBC main evening news a few years ago. Though the location may be a little more colourful than many in the UK, the package did not have any dramatic events in it. In fact the story was little more than a situation-report. The background is quite interesting.

BBC News was becoming concerned that television coverage of Africa tended to show only wars, famines, abuses of civil rights and disease. The whole continent was in danger of being stereotyped. So when the International Monetary Fund was preparing to decide on extensions of huge loans to two former British colonies, one of them Uganda, it was decided that Business Correspondent Peter Morgan should make a quick and relatively cheap trip to both countries, to explain the situation on the ground. His special reports were shown on successive nights and were about three minutes long.

But how do you film the Ugandan economy? It would have been relatively easy to write a short essay about the progress the country had made during a period of relative stability, and cover it with pictures of Ugandans at work. But that would not have been good television news.

Intro.

(Newsreader in vision).	The world's poorest nations have been told to do more to end corruption and to encourage free trade. In return, the International Monetary Fund is offering them more help to relieve their debts.
Graphic animation zooming in on Uganda (Newsreader OOV)	So far the only country in Africa to qualify for extra help is Uganda, where a period of stable government has led to an economic revival.
Graphic (economic growth and inflation figures)	In the past five years, the economy has grown by forty-five per cent, while inflation has fallen from two hundred and forty per cent to seven per cent now.
Graphic animation (picture of Peter Morgan)	In the first of two special reports, our International Business Correspondent Peter Morgan looks at Uganda's journey from basket case to role model for Africa.

Package

Early morning tea picking	(Sound of tea picking) A new dawn. In war-torn, famine-cursed, Aids-ravaged Africa. In Uganda – for decades plundered by the cruellest dictators of a savage continent – today they're picking PG Tips.
Tea processing shed. First shot is a sack thrown towards camera.	(Sound of sack landing in front of lens). This plantation, deserted during twenty years of anarchy, has now been brought back into production by a British company which can prosper as long as peace lasts.

continued . . .

Interview Harry Percy, tea planter	'The soils and the climate are good enough to produce yields and quality of tea that are the equal of anywhere in the world. But it is no good unless you've also got security. For years that wasn't available here. Now it is and we're really making progress.'
Busy street scenes in Kampala. First shot is stylish women in dark glasses. Interior greenhouse growing roses. First shot is close up of rose being snipped. Interview Vincent Senyonjo, rose grower.	In Uganda's capital Kampala, designer shades abound. Twelve years of peace and a kind of democracy have allowed commerce to flourish. (Sound of snip) New industries are taking root, so close to the equator roses bloom seven times each year. These flowers are being sold in Europe in ever growing numbers. 'Oh yeah – for the next five years we are very confident that the prosperity will continue and we estimate that by the year two thousand we shall have five hundred acres of flowers.'
Kampala's outdoor market, with close-ups of money changing hands.	(Noise of market) Uganda has been growing three times as fast as Britain for a decade. It's brought down inflation by adopting the rigid policies of the International Monetary Fund, privatising industry and cutting government spending. But not everyone is happy.
Metal security gates being unloaded from a lorry	(The clang of the gates on the ground) Uganda's new rich are buying security gates to keep out the poor. The benefits of economic revival have not been evenly spread.
Vox pop lorry driver with gates	'The poor man is getting poorer, and the rich man is getting richer and richer.'
Parliament building. Shots of Vice-President being introduced to Morgan.	Uganda has a parliament, but opposition parties are banned. Its Vice-President, and incidentally Africa's most powerful woman, rejects persistent criticism that this no-party state, or 'movement system' as she prefers, encourages competition.
Interview Dr. Wandira Kazibwe, Vice-President.	'You know I don't believe that a system is corrupt. Individuals are corrupt, whether they are in the Movement System or in the Multi-Party System.'
Children in school singing and clapping.	(Sound of kids singing) Yet for these children to inherit a genuinely developed country there's so much to do. Though some debts have been written off, Uganda still spends more repaying loans than it does on education. Two thirds still live in absolute poverty.
Workers clearing jungle on tea plantation.	(Sound of machetes hacking the jungle) Back on the tea plantations they're hacking undergrowth, extending cultivation. But here you're just a rifle shot away from the warring Democratic Republic of Congo; Rwanda lies just to the south.
Morgan piece to camera with workers clearing jungle behind him.	'Ugandans are working hard to impose order on chaos in the very heart of Africa. But too much war on their borders and too little democracy at home mean their achievements, however impressive, remain extremely fragile. Peter Morgan, BBC News, in Kasaru Western Uganda.'

It's a fairly routine feature-package, but was an effective one, because it was carefully constructed and written.

The structure followed familiar patterns by starting at dawn and progressing through a busy day, taking us on a journey from the plantation, to the tea-processing sheds, into the capital, to a rose-growing business, to the market area, to the government building, to a school, and back to the plantation for the final sequence.

Each new location was signalled with about three seconds of good natural sound, with the commentary pausing each time to allow the atmosphere to be heard. This is what is meant by 'letting it breathe'.

The script, while a little more discursive than the very short sentences that are often used in hard news stories, is still very succinct. And it works well because it refers very closely to the pictures throughout. It's a neat idea to show schoolchildren when talking about the future, and the script connects them directly to the economic outlook by referring to their inheritance, and uses education spending to explain the size of the debt-burden. There is even a subtle play on words. The reporter chooses to say that new industries are 'taking root' rather than 'appearing' or 'opening up', because we are seeing rows of flowers. The final images of jungle clearance symbolise the economic point in the final summary, 'Ugandans are working hard to impose order on chaos in the very heart of Africa.'

Headlines on TV

Most news programmes begin by headlining the main stories. Some give viewers a reminder of the main stories half-way through, or just before the commercial break, so-called 'half-way-heads', which are often followed by a taster of what is still to come in the programme. Some programmes use 'closing heads' at the end of the programme.

The first few seconds of a news programme are very important, and can be quite complicated to produce. The programme editors take a keen interest in the headlines, often writing them personally with suggestions from the presenter. But other journalists in the newsroom frequently will be asked to 'write the heads', or at the very least to suggest a headline for the main stories they are working on.

Writing headlines isn't easy. Newspapers employ experienced senior sub-editors who specialise in this particularly succinct form of writing news. In broadcasting, headlines cause endless arguments, particularly in television.

Radio headlines tend to be concise summaries of the main development. Television editors are looking for the key images of the day, as well as the right words. So good TV headline writing relates the words directly and immediately to an interesting picture.

Why headlines?

It's worth considering briefly why we have headlines at the beginning of news programmes. Some argue that we must have some kind of menu to tell the audience what's in the programme. But why? Newspapers don't have a list of five headlines in the same large typeface down the centre of the front page. And there is some evidence that headlines encourage people *not* to watch or listen!

The long-established American television networks, ABC, CBS and NBC, have been in fierce competition for viewers over many years, and have often scheduled their early evening news programmes directly against each other. They had always carried three or four headlines at the start of each programme, until a few years ago ABC broke with tradition. After a very short animating logo, the programme went directly into the first story. The decision startled their rivals. Why no headlines?

The reason was that ABC executives had noticed from audience research a proportion of their viewers turning on the prime-time news, then switching channels immediately after the headlines. This was bad news for the ratings. It was clear that some people were checking the news headlines to reassure themselves that nothing of huge importance had happened, then switching back to the sport, movie or game show. ABC had decided not to give the viewers that switch-over point. If viewers wanted the day's news, they would have to stay tuned. Within weeks, CBS and NBC had followed suit. Since then, headlines have made a comeback on all networks, but they are used more flexibly. On nights when there is clearly a big first story, that is sometimes covered in full first, to be followed by a menu or headlines of the rest of the news. And, these days, the headlines are written much more carefully, to try to keep people tuned.

An inviting style in headlines

Television headlines are not a news summary. They don't have to try to tell the whole story in a few seconds. They are an invitation to watch the news programme, and should be written in an inviting style. The difficult decision for broadcasters is whether we abandon those firm principles of writing good conversational English when it comes to the headlines. We don't tend to talk to each other in news headlines. Imagine coming into the house and informing your partner, 'School run snarl-up; hundreds delayed by traffic lights on the blink . . .; Bargains galore as Marks and Sparks mark everything down . . .; And why Mrs Brown snubbed the games mistress.'

Yet this kind of headline style is a widely accepted convention in broadcast news, providing opportunities for some very succinct writing, and some witty phraseology. Alliteration and rhyme can work quite well. For example, BBC *Breakfast* used a picture of an elderly woman eating breakfast muffled up in her coat and hat, with the headline:

> Millions in debt. Why so many people must choose between eating and heating.

This 'Why' formula is a useful device for indicating a subject and telling the audience they'll find out more later – if they stay tuned. A main verb often isn't necessary, especially for a short first sentence or phrase.

> More misery for rail travellers – now many face two months without trains . . .

> Turn away from the Taliban – the new American plan to win hearts and minds in Afghanistan . . .

> And blowing a fuse – why it all went black in Blackpool

The inviting style of headline also reduces the danger of the headline words being repeated in the first line of the story intro. The headline and the intro to a story should always be written in a complementary way, without direct repetition.

Clichés in headlines

It's a fine dividing line between a good, sharp headline and an awful piece of journalese. Headlines are fertile ground for the cliché. The requirement to write very succinctly, and with some impact, draws some writers to the monosyllables we see every day in newspaper headlines: rap for reprimand, bid for attempt, clash for disagreement, slam for attack. 'Chancellor set to curb spending' (*Five News*) is not spoken English. 'Germany's unemployment crisis deepens as elections loom' (*BBC World*) seems over-dramatically doom-laden. Can elections loom? 'Three die in M6 fog smash' (*ITV Central News*) has abandoned any notion that the presenter is telling the news to individual viewers; he is apparently reading aloud a newspaper headline. I also dislike this use of the present tense when people have been killed or injured. Describing a specific act that has taken place by using the present tense – 'Baby dies as fire rips through block of flats', 'Six are hurt as scaffolding collapses' – is not at all the way we speak, and dramatises tragic events in an insensitive away.

My personal view is that journalists should try hard to write headlines that sound natural, refusing to use journalese, and refusing to drop the definite article. In radio this is a little easier than in television. Research shows there is much less channel-hopping on radio than TV. Listeners to a radio news programme are more likely to listen to it all. So the need to be especially brief and intriguing isn't quite so pressing as in the ruthlessly competitive world of television. And in radio, the obstacle of matching words to pictures is removed, leaving all the headline options available to the journalist. Television headlines are more like captions to pictures, and will inevitably use less natural language, sometimes using phrases without verbs: 'Oxbridge out of fashion – fees up, applications down'. But this is far removed from using tabloid vocabulary and clichés.

Howlers in headlines

The BBC training department has collected a few embarrassing headlines over the years, and urges its journalists to double-check that there can be no double meanings, such as 'Byers accused of lying on Railtrack', 'Safety experts say school bus passengers should be belted', 'Grandmother of eight makes hole in one', 'Prostitutes appeal to Pope'. But surely 'How do you solve a problem like Korea?' is pretty brilliant?

How long and how many headlines?

TV headlines vary in length depending on the style of the individual programme, but they are usually around four to seven seconds long. Some programmes that favour a very fast pace cut the headline pictures to three seconds each. This puts the headlines on the edge of comprehensibility for many viewers. Certainly, anything shorter than this will take the picture away before the audience has had a fair chance to see it. The best pictures for TV headlines are simple and bold. If you are going to talk about a person, make sure it is a good single shot, in close-up if possible. Steady shots from a camera on a tripod work well in headlines, so that the image moves inside a fixed frame. Mixing or wiping between four different five-second shots will become a visual whirl if the camera is moving in a different direction on each shot.

The number of headlines depends on the length of the programme and its individual style. But most TV editors would agree that two headlines doesn't feel right, neither promoting the main story of the day on its own, nor giving the viewers an adequate menu. Six or seven headlines (the norm in some central European countries) seem to me to be too many, and turn the opening sequence into a full news summary before the real news programme starts. For half-hour news programmes in the UK, four headlines has become fairly standard.

If the headlines are to use a clip of natural sound, it must be very short and very clear. On days with a dominant main story, the first two or three headlines might well cover different angles of the big story.

Split headlines

Quite a lot of TV news programmes, especially breakfast programmes and regional news programmes, which use features as well as hard news, will split their headlines. The day's dominant story or the main top stories will be the hard news, with crisp, visual headlines, then there will be a studio link from the presenters along the lines of '. . . and also in tonight's programme . . .', then there will be one or two human-interest headlines designed to keep people tuned throughout the programme.

A mini-production

Good news programme editors and presenters try to make their headlines irresistible and stylish. They are, in effect, a mini-production in themselves, particularly on television. Using some natural sound is becoming the norm.

Here's a typical example of headlines on a day with no really outstanding story. It comes from the BBC News at Six in February 2010.

Presenter in vision:	The right to die. A best-selling author calls for a special panel to decide who should be helped to take their own life.
Pictures of Pratchett	Terry Pratchett, who has Alzheimer's, wants assisted suicide made legal.

Clip of Pratchett interview	'If someone of their own volition wishes to die, it's in society's interest to allow them to do it as peacefully as possible.'
Presenter in vision:	Also on tonight's programme . . .
Still picture of victim	The young mental health worker killed on a home visit – her employer admits she should never have been sent alone.
Pictures of students	More applicants less cash. English universities say hundreds of thousands could lose out on places after government cuts.
Sliding cars on icy roads	And new figures suggest we've slithered and skidded through one of the coldest winters ever.

The BBC's College of Journalism website has an interesting video showing the editor, senior journalists, and the presenter Huw Edwards discussing options for the headlines for the *Ten o'clock News*, then Edwards writing the script. Here he describes the essence of TV headline-writing, and emphasises how important it is to get it right.

> Headlines must make people sit up. The main purpose is to convey the main essence of a story – and make the viewer want to know more. The first thing to do is select the four or five stories which will offer the viewer a good mix. Each viewer should see something that will hook them. Decide the facts that must go into the top line, and clearly the available pictures help make the decision. The words must work with the pictures precisely. A simple, concise style is always best – you don't always need complete sentences. But watch out for legal problems and balance because it has to be so short. It's good to use clips of people speaking in the headlines – usually well-known people, and the clip must be concise and clear. Headlines must never be boring but must never sensationalise.

Closing headlines

Closing headlines are different, and should be written differently. They are not an inducement to watch or listen. The main reason to recap the main headlines at the end of the programme is to capture the viewers and listeners who tune in after the start of the programme, because they know the closing headlines will give them the top stories they've missed. Figures show that about one in four viewers of a typical early evening television news programme tune in after it has started. The closing headlines also remind the rest of the audience of the main story, giving the programme a sense of ordered priories, a clear structure, and a strong finish.

The closing headlines also provide an opportunity to update the main story. It is unsatisfactory to repeat the words of the opening headlines. Try to refresh the phraseology. A neat headline like, 'Where were the gritters? Were councils caught out by the cold snap?' would be an irritation if repeated at the end of the programme, and should be replaced: 'Councils have blamed the Met Office for failing to issue an ice-warning in time for them to get out the gritters.'

And if the programme style is to give the main three stories at the end of the programme, I recommend that they are written in their natural order, with the lead story first. On some radio stations there has been a fashion to write the closing headlines in reverse order, ending with a flourish on . . . and tonight's main story . . . . I don't think this works very well because it forces the presenter to begin the closing headlines with a down-bulletin story, which is editorially curious and confusing for the listeners.

24-HOUR TV NEWS

In recent years, there's been a rapid growth in the number of continuous news or 24-hour news television channels across Europe. British viewers with digital reception can now pick up the BBC News channel, CNBC, Bloomberg TV, as well as the pioneers of the genre, CNN and Sky News. Internationally, BBC World News has grown a substantial audience, Euronews has the biggest audience in Europe for an international news channel, and Deutsche Welle TV and France 24 are just two of many overseas broadcasters providing an English language service.

There are also more radio channels. As digital radio receivers become more affordable, there will be many more. While music stations still have the biggest audiences, talk radio has a solid share of the market, both nationally and locally. In Britain, the news and sport station BBC Five Live has been voted station of the year more than once. Since the '80s, BBC local radio has become an overwhelmingly speech-based service, with long sequences of live news, information and current affairs at key times of the day.

Producing news stories for these news-based stations and channels is particularly demanding, especially for television. Scriptwriting is often done under great time pressure, and each script should be particularly conversational to match the informal and dynamic style of rolling news. In fact, quite a lot of the news on 24-hour channels isn't written at all, because new technology now permits so much location reporting and interviewing to be live.

Rob Kirk, Editorial Development Manager at Sky News:

> Twenty-four hour news is insatiable. It has a remorseless appetite for live broadcasting, on the hour every hour, sometimes more. This tests a correspondent's ability to find the right words – under tremendous pressure – to the utmost. It's a particular skill.

Julie Etchingham, Presenter, Sky News:

> The programme segment I work on consists of almost all live material with very few packages. Therefore scripts are quickly becoming a thing of the past, as you ad lib to the next interview. Anything that is written beforehand needs to be snappy and to the point, to fit in with the pace of the programme.

Sir David Nicholas:

> The new dimension in broadcasting these days perhaps doesn't involve writing at all. Because so much now is ad lib live coverage, including court reports and parliamentary debates. So there is a requirement for a new skill which was not so important in my day; that's to be able to be able to speak tightly, coherently, logically and fluently. There's so much continuous news and live location broadcasting. It's a new skill, and I think on the whole the younger reporters are very good at it.

Live on location

On location, the report might be a live but 'straight' account of the story. It might well be a 'two-way', with the studio presenter interviewing the journalist. It might be a live link into a recorded package, followed by a live interview with one or two people on location before a hand-back to the studio. And these live sequences are allocated a duration by the producer, and are expected to finish exactly on time.

It's a little easier on radio. The reporter can hold a script, or at least a sheet of notes, to help get the facts and structure right. I would advise brief notes in the hand, rather than a detailed script, because the immediacy of live broadcasting is audible. Reading out a script loses the spontaneity. To be precise, I would advocate notes on postcard-sized cards rather than A4 sheets of paper, which are inclined to rustle and flap about in the breeze. File-cards are easier to handle, especially when you have a microphone in your hand.

In television, you really do not want to be seen referring to notes. The reporter with the microphone in one hand and the clipboard in the other is a very old fashioned image. A clipboard makes you look like an estate agent; a notebook makes you look like a police officer giving evidence. And the modern style is not to stand stiffly to deliver your information, but to 'walk and talk', to demonstrate things, and to use hand gestures to emphasise the words. It's quite hard to do it with a script in your hand. To be honest, it's quite hard to do without a script in your hand.

Robert Hall has specialised in this kind of live and dynamic location reporting for many years, with ITN and the BBC. He says he rarely writes things down.

> There's no point. I work out what I need to say, and in what order. It's important to have a walk-through with the camera operator so that we both understand how the sequence will look. If there's time, we might do this two or three times. But the script is in the head.

Personally, I think there are many television and radio journalists who are brilliant at this kind of natural story-telling. And I know it's not as effortless as it looks. First, it's essential to know what the studio presenter will say before handing over to the location reporter, or in a two-way, what the presenter will ask. Secondly, for television reports, it is essential to know in detail what will be in shot, and to rehearse any camera movements. Thirdly, it can be useful to write down a few telling phrases, names or statistics you know you are going to use, and look at them to help the memory. But then put the piece of paper out of sight! Live reporting means that you tell the audience what you know, not recite what you have just memorised.

Live in the studio

Back at base in the 24-hour news operation, it's important for the journalist to make sure the studio presenter has the right information at all times – in the usual scripts, intros, headlines and 'coming-up' sequences – but also when there may not be enough time for conventional scriptwriting.

Maxine Mawhinney has been a lead presenter for the BBC News and BBC World News channels for many years, capable of conducting informed interviews on nearly any subject at a moment's notice, and always staying calm under pressure. She says writing scripts for continuous news requires the same disciplines as writing for bulletins or news programmes, but the main difference is the speed at which scripts have to be produced.

> Scripts can't be agonised over all day as the channel never stops and the information has to be constantly updated. The headlines, quarter-heads and half-heads have to be reviewed all the time as the stories move. As for breaking news, this isn't scripted. It's usually ad-libbed by the presenter using agency copy he or she has pulled up on to the computer, or information sent by the gallery producer [in the studio control-room] or the assistant editor in the newsroom. So there is nothing on Autocue and no one writes it, until it finds its way into the running order for the next news update.

So the job of the journalist is to brief presenters, particularly about live interviews coming up, as well as to write scripts. As well as sending messages to the presenter's computer, notes can sometimes be posted on the teleprompter or written on old-fashioned sheets of paper. A quickly typed sheet, or even a hand-written note (clear writing, large print), saying, for example, how to pronounce the interviewee's name, how many years she's been foreign minister, and when she's going to Washington for the showdown meeting, will be invaluable for a hard-pressed presenter switching between very different stories. Here are some pieces of advice from the BBC *World News* presenter Lyse Doucet.

> Every presenter is different. If news is breaking fast, some presenters can busk it from agency reports and ad lib. Others need more help so they will need more information on the Autocue. If you are working regular shifts in a TV newsroom, try to understand each presenter's needs. Their job is to look calm in the midst of chaos. Your job is to give them as much clarity as possible, at a time when the situation is often *unclear*.
>
> If it's breaking news, and there are only ten lines of the first news agency reports, don't put all ten lines in the intro. I've seen the alarmed look on the correspondent's face when the presenter reads all the known information and then turns to the correspondent and says, 'What else can you tell us?' (Real answer – Nothing.)
>
> Don't be sloppy. I once had an intro saying twelve people had died from 'hospital actions'. It should have been 'hostile actions'. Being fast is no excuse for being inaccurate. Check, check, check. One source of information is usually not enough. Three news agencies quoting the same source doesn't always count. Attribute all information.

In essence, 24-hour news should embrace the same principles and good practice of any credible news programme. The main differences in writing it are that you must be fast, sometimes be prepared to put the key and verified information in note-form for the presenter, and be ready to speak live on location, with a 'virtual script' in your head. It's interesting to note that continuous news channels, broadcast substantially without scripts, tend to be relatively free of journalese and clichés.

6
Writing online news

It represents the emergence of a new information ecosystem that will
have a more profound impact on human civilisation than did the
printing press.

(Al Gore, former US Vice-President,
The Virtual Revolution, BBC2, 2010)

Tim Berners-Lee created a new way of allowing communication to work
in extraordinarily connected ways.

(Stephen Fry, quoted in the *Observer*, 2010)

Since Tim Berners-Lee's Hypertext system was first used in 1991, the World
Wide Web has expanded at breathtaking speed, and is profoundly changing
journalism. News outlets are converging so that distinctions between print,
audio, TV and telephony, all delivered to a personal interactive screen, are
becoming blurred.

TV and radio stations must now have an online presence to accompany and
complement their broadcast services. (So do newspapers. Indeed, the growth
of online consumption with portable devices like the iPad may one day elim-
inate the need for expensively produced printed papers being driven around
the country in vans and pushed through your letterboxes by kids on bikes.)
In TV and radio, the station's online service has already become much more
than an afterthought. It has a symbiotic relationship with the broadcasting,
particularly with radio. Local radio stations, for example, now have instant
response and feedback from listeners via message-posting, email and text –
more than they ever got on the phone. They also have a new source of
information. For example, if severe weather strikes your region, suddenly the
radio station's website becomes a support network, with listeners sharing their
experiences, calling for help, and offering it. The newsroom now has a wealth
of immediate information about what is happening, and can pick up human
stories. It also provides a practical community service, which increases its
audience and enhances listener loyalty.

The bigger network stations can offer much more in-depth analysis, with their correspondents providing background features on the website and, in many cases, blogging their observations and advice. Television news now has a massive source of immediate pictures and quite good quality video whenever a big story occurs. (BBC News has a special interactive section, with more than a dozen journalists checking and distributing to programme editors the thousands of pieces of information and pictures received from viewers, listeners and online readers every day.)

VERSIONING YOUR STORIES FOR THE WEBSITE

So it is essential for broadcasters to compete online with fast, trustworthy and attractive web versions of their news services, which offer opportunities for the audience to contribute. These online sites are effective and affordable only if the broadcast staff supply versions of their stories for the web as a matter of routine. When TV and radio journalists were first asked to do this by their managers, there was much grousing and grumping about extra work for no real purpose, other than to seem to be switched on to new media. The grousers have gone silent now, as they see how many younger people in partic- ular use these online news services, and how they extend the reach of the journalism worldwide.

So the ability to write a web version of your story has become very important for most broadcast journalists. Some newsroom computer systems will allow you to put your text directly on to the site with a few clicks. Many journal- ists simply send their stories to a specialised editorial and technical team, who format the material. Audio, still pictures and streamed video are usually launched on to the site by specialists.

A DIFFERENT WRITING STYLE

So is writing online news the same as writing for radio or television, or is it like writing for newspapers? Online news editors say that it is closer to print journalism than broadcasting, for the simple reason that people read most of the information, rather than hear it. Broadcast journalists who need to version their material for the web have to un-learn the techniques of writing the spoken word, and write print-English. But it is a special form of print. Consumers use it in a different way from a newspaper or a book. The screen is quite a small frame; it uses pictures a great deal, it is brightly coloured, and it is constantly inviting you to look at something else. Online news has to be written very sharply, very concisely, and very personally.

All the best practitioners agree that what makes online journalism stand out is the combination of lots of visual interest and very short sentences, with the text on the screen broken up.

For example, on a typical day with no outstanding news story, a major broadcaster's website will have perhaps twenty-five stories headlined on the front page, ten of them with still pictures or video clips, and each with a summary of the story in less than twelve words. Click through to a story and each sentence will be laid out as a paragraph, and will be short and to the point.

When big stories happen, there's an opportunity for lots of angles and background information, as well as the first-hand journalism. Here is part of the BBC News Online front page two days after the 2010 Haiti earthquake. The main story, headlined 'Race to help Haiti quake victims', was a pull-together or overview written in London using the BBC's own reports and agency material.

> Hundreds of thousands of Haitians are awaiting the start of a global rescue effort in the wake of the country's devastating earthquake.
>
> BBC correspondents say the situation is increasingly desperate, with no coordinated rescue plan so far and aid only trickling in.
>
> The search for survivors continues but rescuers have little lifting equipment and are often using their bare hands.
>
> Tens of thousands are feared dead and up to three million affected.
>
> US Secretary of State Hillary Clinton has said the disaster is 'unimaginable' and pledged long-term American assistance.

This central story went on to quote aid groups and UN peacekeepers on the ground, the UN's Coordinator for Humanitarian Affairs, the Head of Médecins du Monde, the British International Development Secretary Douglas Alexander, US President Barack Obama, and spokespeople from the US military, The World Bank, and the World Food Programme.

Prominently boxed was 'At the Scene – BBC Correspondent Matthew Price', with a click-through for his graphic first-hand account, headlined 'Living sleep among dead at Haiti hospitals' above 'click to play' for his TV report. The online story had clearly been rewritten for the web.

> There is a body lying outside L'Hopital de la Paix in Port-au-Prince – but it is the sight that awaits you inside the hospital grounds that is most alarming.
>
> It is as if a massacre has been perpetrated here.
>
> Dirty white sheets cover some of the dead, others lie out in the open – some, their limbs entwined with another's.

Many are the bodies of adults, but here to the right, a baby on her back, her belly bloated and pronounced.

She is wearing a silvery blue top – just lying by the curb, abandoned.

A man stirs to the left. He unfurls a blanket that covers the ground and lies back down. The living are sleeping among the dead.

As Price walks on into the hospital, there is more description than is required in the television commentary, with vivid details (he describes how the screams and whimpers echo down the corridors) and a series of personal stories.

A week later, the BBC Online site had fourteen background pieces and ten video reports from Haiti to choose from. Again, the eye-witness report was prominent, this time from correspondent Karen Allen:

[Headline] Uncertain Future for Haiti's Amputees

[Picture of human example Emmanuel Etienne in hospital]

[First sentence in bold – almost like a second headline] Emmanuel Etienne may be badly injured in a field hospital set up on an old tennis court but he feels like a lucky man.

Doctors had planned to amputate his crushed leg after he was trapped in the rubble of a three-storey house but they have pumped him full of antibiotics and given him extra blood.

Now they have changed their minds. They can salvage the damaged limb after all.

For the 22-year-old, an avid football fan, his odds at returning to a relatively normal life have just improved dramatically.

'I was terrified I was going to lose my leg,' he says. [This quote is also featured separately in a box]

'It's hard enough in Haiti having both of them let alone just one – I don't think I would have lived very long.'

It is estimated that some 2,000 people have had limbs amputated as a result of the earthquake. [etc.]

A NEW KIND OF JOURNALISM

As the miraculous internet developed in the '90s, the BBC took a strategic decision to invest in this new information network. If the BBC was to be the most trusted and most popular source of broadcast news at home and around the world for many years to come, it would need to have the best online news service in Europe. Mike Smartt, an experienced radio and TV journalist, became Editor-in-Chief and was influential in shaping the way the content for this new medium was written. Here he outlines some of the principles of writing effectively for online news services.

> I think it's a combination of writing for broadcast and for print. It's written for the eye so it has to be read like a newspaper, but it's a little more pithy. It's more personal, like radio; more like talking to an individual. It's deciding what's the most arresting and interesting aspect of a story, putting it at the top, then writing it an interesting way.
>
> Analogies with newspapers are quite striking. If you walk into the BBC Online newsroom, you will see a similar set-up to a newspaper. We have subs; we have chief-subs; we have reporters (we call them broadcast journalists), and we have assistant editors – the people who construct the front pages of each of the different sites, such as the international and UK versions, and the specialist sites on health, education and so on. Almost all the people we employ have at some point been newspaper or magazine journalists. We target them. Then we have to teach them the tasks that a broadcast-journalist faces, so that they can handle audio and video.

Smartt draws parallels with continuous radio or television news channels. But whereas there is less writing in 24-hour broadcasting because so much of it is live, web journalism demands *more* writing.

> The big difference between online and a newspaper, which may be published once a day with several editions, is that online news is a 24-hour process. You are perpetually updating. There is no such thing as a deadline. The deadline is when you press the button and it goes off to the server. You may do that again with an update three or four minutes later. To keep track of what you have written is quite difficult. We often find stories with repetitions at the bottom because they have been updated at the top, but the writer hasn't looked lower down to see if there is duplication. Very often the difficulty is in deciding when you have to completely deconstruct or reconstruct the story and start again rather than writing a quick update.
>
> It's a *new kind of journalism*. The writer has to understand the website as a whole. The story he or she is working on may just be one of a number of stories on the same subject. The main story and the sidebars have to complement each other, and you have to know how to link to other angles, the archive or outside sources.

FASTER AND DEEPER

Mike Smartt and his colleagues and competitors were among the early news online pioneers. Now the web has become much more competitive, is technically faster and has enormous capacity. At the time of writing, the Editor of BBC News Online is Steve Herrmann. He says one of the most challenging aspects of working in online news is to be both quick and comprehensive.

> Speed really matters because your reader is only a click away from a myriad of other news sources, and with the growth of social media, the rate at which news – or indeed rumour – can spread has got even faster. Of course that still doesn't mean that you don't first have to be right!
>
> At the same time, the almost unlimited capacity to provide explanation, additional content, angles, depth and well-chosen external links is a major strength of online journalism. It's also a challenge. On a major story, you are in effect becoming an editor as well as a writer as you assemble around your own story the best collection of links, associated content, pictures, graphics, video and audio. The ability to tie together multiple angles of the story from various sources so that people can make sense of them quickly and easily – even as the story is unfolding – is a key part of the job.

FRESH AND EASY

Aminda Leigh has been writing news and features in English for European websites for several years. She emphasises the importance of refreshing the material.

> It's vital to update a developing story, even if it means just altering the headline and the top line. When writing breaking headlines for news tickers, it's especially important to synthesise the facts into one simple phrase encapsulating the new element. Once you have uploaded the headline ticker, you must immediately refresh the actual story.

And everything must be easy to read.

> Research shows that many internet users shy away from reading long articles. Make sure the key points of your story are near the top of your text. If your story has a lot of material, break it up into linked items on separate pages, with links for more in-depth information.

MORE THAN WORDS

All online editors say that, with nearly everyone now able to access the web via broadband, the journalism must contain pictures, video or audio to enhance the text as much as possible. We know that a picture is worth a thousand words (or, as Napoleon said, 'a good sketch is better than a long speech'), but a website picture that is not clearly captioned can cause confusion. Every picture must have a punchy but informative caption that doesn't describe the image, but may answer some of the time-honoured questions: who? why? when? where? what?

Here Aminda Leigh gives us her top ten tips for successful internet journalism.

1. Keep it short and sweet. People don't have the attention span to read screeds of material and they often don't like scrolling down pages and pages of text. If you have a long article, split it up with linked headings at the top, to allow readers to jump directly to the relevant part of the story.

2. Insert plenty of breaks in your text. Readers can be daunted by great chunks of writing. I tend to put one main idea in each paragraph.

3. Put the story in the top line (though not necessarily in the headline – that should be a teaser to get the audience to click on your story). The main facts must be easy to find.

4. Keep your sentences clear and simple. Complex phrases with lots of sub-clauses are difficult to understand. And avoid needless repetition.

5. Use language that can be understood by everyone, bearing in mind that your material is likely to be read by an international audience.

6. Use bullet-points for stories with detailed facts or figures. For example, on a story about changes to the tax system, instead of writing a lengthy description of the changes, a bulleted list would be a clearer way to get the information across.

7. Highlight pertinent information. This obviously depends on your website style, but the internet is a visual medium, so to make important things in the text stand out, I tend to use bold as a way of emphasising. Don't just highlight one word, highlight the pertinent phrase.

8. Link to other pages. The beauty of the internet is that you don't have to put all your information into the main article. Additional information or background can be written separately with clear links.

9. Links to pages outside your site should open in another page, so that your site is still open and ready to be surfed again.

10. Check spelling and punctuation very carefully before you put your material online. Remember that automatic spellcheckers won't necessarily pick up mistakes caused by sloppy typing (for example, writing 'form' instead of 'from'). Read through every word, and always look at your work once again after you have put it online to see if there are any problems with HTML, links that don't work, etc. Any mistakes should be corrected immediately. You soon lose credibility if your online work is inaccurate or sloppy.

It's clear that all broadcast journalists must develop the ability to create a web version of their story quickly and confidently. Some may spend periods of time, or at least a full shift, at the specialist online desk. Being able to write a great deal during a normal shift, without losing concentration, is one of the special skills required of an online journalist. Working under this kind of pressure, internet journalists should all have ready access to written style guides, as newspaper journalists do, for quick reference on spelling, punctuation and formatting, for consistency and for accuracy.

NEWS TO MOBILE

Providing broadcast stories for the website may not be enough in the future. News to mobile phones and other devices is a huge growth area. In some parts of the world, such as Nigeria, it is now the dominant way in which people receive their news. It requires an even stricter discipline of brevity and clarity. The BBC's Steve Herrmann says:

> The big growth in the use of mobile devices to access news and much more besides means we have new opportunities to present and package our journalism. Much of the same logic applies – writing for the eye and the small screen means keeping it brief, clear and direct and using short sentences and paragraphs. But as these devices evolve, so will people's habits and preferences. A good online journalist will spot how technology is changing the way people want to get their news and work out how to evolve the way we do things.

BLOGGING AND TWEETING

More and more people seem to be getting at least some of their news and information from blogs and tweets. While much of this international traffic is personal or non-journalistic, the institutions have embraced the new information networks with enthusiasm. No self-respecting government minister or European Commissioner would retain credibility without a regular blog! Advertising agencies plant messages on Twitter.

For broadcast newsrooms, these new communication channels need serious consideration. Many well known correspondents and presenters have blogs. Some broadcasters put out stories on Twitter (which is currently limited to 140 characters at a time, so can be little more than a headline and a plea to go to the website). The emerging writing style of blogs is as informal and chatty as possible. It tends to be more personal. But all blogging journalists must make sure they don't drop their guard as they chat away at the end of a long, hard day's broadcasting. A blog is publication. As the BBC's guidelines say on this point, while encouraging their journalists to write informally on their blogs: 'We've stressed that there is still a framework of editorial standards they must work within. . . . Our news blogs are checked by a second journalist before publication.'

7
And finally . . .

ORWELL'S SUMMARY

Every journalist should develop his or her own style, avoiding clichés and stale formulae. In broadcasting, never forget that the words will be heard, not read. There is no better summary of the way the spoken word should be written than the advice given by George Orwell in his 1946 essay *Politics and the English Language*.

- Never use a metaphor, simile or other figure of speech which you are used to seeing in print
- Never use a long word where a short word will do
- If it is possible to cut out a word, always cut it out
- Never use the passive where you can use the active
- Never use a foreign phrase, a scientific word or a jargon word if you can think of an everyday English equivalent
- Break any of these rules sooner than say anything outright barbarous

WHAT OF THE FUTURE?

The English language is probably changing now more rapidly than it was in Orwell's time. The internet is altering the way we absorb information and accelerating the globalisation of the language. Another new influence is texting. Most schoolchildren have mobile phones and seem to text each other all the time, in a specialist version of the language that has been invented in just a few years. Recently, a government minister urged parents to learn text language so that they can join in and communicate with their children more easily.

New words are admitted to the *Oxford English Dictionary* every year. In the most recent major review, no fewer than three thousand words were added, including many that spring from changing social trends, such as heightism, wussy, ladette, and bling-bling. A large number of new usages have emerged from the internet, including twitterati, to groom, cyberslacker (one who surfs the net at work), and data smog (the impenetrable mass of information available online).

Many young people are determinedly avoiding correct usage and cultivating a new, cool style. Anne Barnes, a senior GCSE examiner, reports that English papers are becoming riddled with 'fashionable errors', such as 'gonna' and 'I was well bored', and says one candidate even wrote his answers in text form. She made it clear that if u txt yr xms, u fail.

So in the years to come, there is likely to be a growing tension in broadcast journalism between the need to write and speak conversationally in a way that appeals to younger viewers and listeners, and the need for absolute accuracy, which many in the audience expect to hear in news programmes. There is no doubt that more and more writers are employing a less formal approach. But I am sure that slang and sloppiness should be avoided, no matter what kind of style an individual radio station or TV programme adopts. In the future, will we hear a political correspondent reporting, 'The Prime Minister was like so not having it, and went like per-lease! And the Leader of the Opposition turns round and is like Doh! you know?'? I hope not.

I think it is more likely that broadcast journalists will have to develop new skills alongside the ability to write. These skills will be driven by new technology. They include the ability to help audiences to navigate through more and more information as web users get used to the idea of being able to go immediately to the information they want. In a presentation to the BBC 'New Tools Festival' in Belfast in 2009, the Executive Editor of the BBC College of Journalism, Kevin Marsh, expressed it like this.

> As search engines become more sophisticated people want to go straight to the facts that are pertinent to them. Google and Yahoo now see themselves as media companies, but they don't create anything. They connect people to what they are likely to want to know. So the big skill needed in modern journalism will be flexibility. Writing skills must be combined with the ability to direct or guide people through a blizzard of information.

Whatever the challenges of interactive and converging media, it is clear that writing well for TV and radio remains a core skill for broadcast journalists. Broadcast news has become the model of the spoken word, because it communicates clearly, concisely and precisely. We want all our listeners to follow the narrative effortlessly, and to be interested by it. We want all our viewers to follow the pictures easily, and to understand what they mean. And we want to be authoritative and respected. Good Spoken English carries with it credibility.

More than twenty-five years ago, the experienced BBC newsreader Andrew Timothy was asked to contribute to a BBC report on the standards of spoken English. He described his academic qualifications as negligible. But his conclusions have been widely endorsed by most commentators, and are still relevant today:

> We know that English is a living language. We know too that if the language is to remain living and lively, it must change and adapt to circumstances in an ever-changing world. However, there are still such things as correct grammar, the right and wrong way to pronounce names and innumerable English words, some in daily use, others less well-known.

*   *   *

If the trumpet give an uncertain sound, who shall prepare himself for the battle?

(*Corinthians* I: XIV v.8)

Appendix
Dangerous words
An alphabetical checklist

An alphabetical reference list of words and phrases that can spell danger for the unwary scriptwriter

> Here are a few of the unpleasantest words that ever blotteth paper.
> (Shakespeare, *The Merchant of Venice*)

We all have our pet hates in the use of English, and we will not always agree. To one writer a phrase may be an over-worked cliché; to another it may be a familiar and colourful colloquialism. And 'banned' words can easily become out of date, as language develops and new usages become generally acceptable. So this list is not prescriptive. It is advice drawn from my own observations and experience, and from other guides on writing, which have distilled the experience of many fine journalists over the years.

Here then for your consideration is an alphabetical selection of the more commonly used, or misused, pieces of cliché journalism. As you read this list, make up your own mind. Is this usage accurate or not? Is this phrase fresh and elegant, or stale and clumsy? I hope many journalists will keep this book handy, to use for quick reference, or to refresh their ideas periodically.

Admit Be careful. It strongly suggests an admission of guilt. It also suggests that the action 'admitted' by this person, company or government department is true. The word is weighted with value judgement. 'The Health Secretary admitted that in some areas MRSA targets would not be met.' When reporting what someone said, there are several possibilities: acknowledged, disclosed, confirmed. 'Said' might be best. Choose the one most apt for the circumstances. During 'the Troubles' in Northern Ireland, the BBC sought an alternative to the phrase, 'have claimed responsibility', which offended some people because it sounded boastful. The phrase 'have admitted responsibility' was preferred for a time, but to some ears sounded uncomfortable. Gunmen or bombers do not normally admit wrong-doing. Neutral phraseology is generally better. 'In a statement, the so-called Continuity IRA said they had planted the bomb.'

Admit to   Is nearly always wrong. You admit an error or misdeed, you do not admit *to* it.

After   Used too loosely, too often. 'Two people were killed after their car ran into a stationary lorry.' No, they were killed *when* the car ran into the lorry.

Ahead of   This irritating phrase has become enormously popular with broadcasters in recent years, despite the fact that it is seldom used in normal conversation: 'ahead of tomorrow's semi-final'; 'ahead of tonight's Commons vote'. What is wrong with 'before'? Or even occasionally 'in advance of'? It can also lead to a little confusion because the phrase refers not only to time, but to preference. 'Wembley has been chosen as the site of the new national stadium ahead of Manchester' (BBC TV News).

AIDS   This is a difficult subject in more ways than one. AIDS (acquired immunity deficiency syndrome) is not a disease, but a medical condition. HIV is a virus, not a disease. To use the expression, 'the HIV virus' is technically tautology, but is widely used. A person who becomes HIV-positive may develop full-blown AIDS. Only then can we say he or she 'has AIDS'. Death is usually caused by 'an AIDS-related disease'.

Albeit   An archaism meaning though or although, still used, rather surprisingly, in some sport reports. Does anyone ever say this word in normal spoken English? I don't think so.

Alleged   'Sir Norman faces a charge of alleged fraud' is wrong. There is no such charge. He is either charged with fraud, or facing allegations (try to give the source) of fraud.

Amid   Does anyone say this word in conversation? 'Amid fears that'? No. But it's heard regularly on the airwaves, particularly when tight security is in evidence, and in some sport scripts. 'England's test series ended prematurely amid a washout at the Oval.' (BBC Radio Sport, 2002.) The best correspondents manage to avoid it. And we should all avoid 'amidst'.

Amount   Increasingly being used as a synonym for number rather than quantity. It is an amount of sugar, but a number of sugar-lumps. I first noticed this in April 1997, when BBC Radio 4 reported that 'There's been an increase in the amount of days-off caused by stress.' My stress level tends to rise as I hear this usage more and more often. Surely it is an ugly error to say: 'The amount of people using Gatwick Airport has fallen seven per cent and the amount of people using Stansted has fallen two per cent.' (Economics correspondent speaking on BBC Radio 4, October 2009.)

Announce   It is not quite the same as 'said'. It implies disclosure of established fact, like the announcement of the Bafta winners. It means 'to make publicly known', so should not be used in any context where there might be dispute or doubt.

Another   This is sometimes used a little loosely in broadcasting, when the updates continue minute by minute. If I write, 'Another person has died in the legionnaires disease outbreak in Cumbria . . .', can I use the same script half an hour later? It's better to say, 'A third person has died . . .'.

Anticipate   This is a word in transition. Technically, it means to forestall or foresee, or to deal with in good time. So the goalkeeper saved the penalty because he anticipated where the ball would be directed. But it is now very widely used as a synonym for 'expect' or 'look forward to'. My advice is to use it only in its traditional sense, to avoid irritating the initiated.

Anxious   Has two popular meanings, which can be confused in listeners' minds; best used to mean troubled or worried, rather than keen or eager.

Apprehend   Officialese. Catch, arrest or detain.

Assassinate   Should be reserve for the killing of political or religious leaders, not any murder with some kind of political context, such as sectarian killings in Northern Ireland, or the murder of a journalist.

Assistance   As in 'rendered assistance'. Helped. (*See* Officialese.)

At this moment in time   Now.

Axe   Classic journalese word. 'Toyota aims to axe up to 750 jobs at its main UK factory, workers have been told' (*Guardian*, 2010). 'Fifty jobs are to be axed at a Wolverhampton cardboard factory' (BRMB Radio, 2010). 'Axe' is a punchy monosyllable with a strong violent association, but is not usually used in speech. Try lose, cut, cancel, reduce or drop, depending on the context.

Baby   Used as an adjective, it is often redundant. '. . .gave birth to a baby girl'.

Backlash   An overworked journalism word. It suggests violence, or at least a very strong or angry reaction.

Bad news   It's a good idea to avoid using 'bad news/good news' value-judge-ments. The listeners and viewers can decide for themselves. Rain may be bad news for holidaymakers, but good news for farmers. Interest rates going up is certainly a bit of bad news for mortgage-holders and other borrowers, but it's good news for the growing number of pensioners.

Banks   'High street banks' has become something of a cliché. They are not always in high streets. After deregulation, many former building societies and even large retailers are now banks. Many people now use online banking. 'The main banks' is preferable. And now that many building societies have become banks, 'mortgage lenders' may be preferable when talking about home loans.

Banned   In broadcasting, we must take care with this word. Do not say, '. . . the leader of the banned Loony Party . . .'. It sounds like the leader of the band. Say instead, 'Joshua Smith, the leader of the Loony Party, which is banned by the government . . .'. Or use 'prohibited'.

Basis   The BBC's internal World Service Radio Guide says succinctly, 'On a regular/daily basis' is an ugly phrase. Why not 'regularly', or 'every day'?

Beleaguered   Journalese.

Bid   A journalese classic. In normal conversation, you would not say, 'The weather foiled my bid to get to work', or 'Management and unions are meeting in a bid to solve the dispute'. You would certainly never say, 'Eleventh-hour bid', or (heaven forbid) 'Last-ditch bid'. In an auction, or at a poker game, or referring to a financial package such as the Olympics bids, yes. Otherwise, try 'try'. Or 'attempt'.

Billion   In Britain, this used to mean a million million. Now we and the rest of the world have adopted the American definition, which is a mere thousand million. Incidentally, since the financial collapse of 2008, the USA has been counting its debt in trillions, which in the UK used to mean a million million million. Don't even try to think about it. The English-speaking word has accepted the American maths (sorry, math), which is a paltry thousand billion.

Black box   'The black box flight recorder' is a widely used phrase, and is well understood. But people working in the aviation industry know that for very many years the box has been painted fluorescent orange. So 'flight recorder' is more accurate, and 'black box' on its own should be avoided.

Blaze   Another journalese word seldom used in normal spoken English. Would you say, 'I hear there was a blaze at the school last night'? Some journalists like 'blaze' because it is dramatic, and avoids too many uses of the words 'fire' and 'firefighters'. But many fatal fires are not blazes. 'Fire' is nearly always better. If the ffs are ffalling over each other, try 'outbreak' or 'incident', and don't be too concerned about repeating the word 'fire'.

Blow   Setback; disappointment; reverse.

Blueprint   Cliché. It's a proposal, a plan, or even an action-plan, which is what a lot of people say.

Blunder   Like 'bungle', it would be a mistake to use this word very often. It's defined as a serious mistake made clumsily and ineptly. So 'blunder' should not be used for any error of judgement. When Brazil scored against England with a freak long-distance free kick in a World Cup quarter final, the BBC *Six o'clock News* spoke with apparent relish of the goalkeeper's 'blunder'. A little unfair, I think.

Bombshell   Journalese.

Bonanza   Tabloidese.

Boost   Journalese. Major boost, major journalese.

Bored   It really should be 'bored with . . .' rather than the rather boring modern usage, 'bored of . . .'.

Boss   A slightly old-fashioned slang word, still used by newspaper journalists because it is short and punchy. 'Manager', 'Chairman', 'Chief Executive' are much better because they are accurate and precise.

Brainchild   Idea would be a better idea.

Breakthrough   Use very sparingly, and attribute the claim. It may be a perfectly fair description of the key moment of progress in difficult negotiations. But most medical and scientific advances are small steps on long and complex paths.

Call on   'Call on' can mean either 'visit' or 'urge'. In broadcasting, there's a danger of the listener having a moment of confusion. 'He called on other members to support the plan' would be better with a simpler word – 'asked' or 'urged'.

Calm   'Calm but tense' is a cliché that is also a contradiction in terms.

Casualties   Do all our listeners and viewers know that this means all those killed or injured in some way? It's better to say 'dead or wounded' or 'dead and injured', and better still to give the numbers in each case. And remember that the figures should be attributed to a specific source if possible, such as the police, the army or rescuers.

Centred around   It's a sloppy phrase because it's illogical. 'Centred on' is much better. 'Based around' is equally irritating to many listeners. And 'focused on' is clearly sharper than 'focused around'.

Chaos   Much over-used, as in 'It's chaos on the roads as the bank holiday gets under way' (BBC Radio 2). Really?

Cheap   Goods are cheap. Prices are low.

Chiefs   As in education chiefs. Journalese. When the chief and the deputy are involved, it sounds like the Wild West Show.

Chronic   It annoys many people, especially those in the medical profession, when they hear 'chronic' used to mean extremely serious, acute or severe. A chronic condition is lingering or long-lasting, the opposite of acute.

Claimed   It should not be used when the more neutral 'said' will be better. 'Claimed' carries with it an element of scepticism. It certainly should not be used simply to avoid a repetition: 'The Leader of the Opposition said hospital waiting lists had got longer in the past six months, but the Health Secretary claimed they had actually fallen.' *The Times Guide to English Style and Usage* says, 'The word carries a suspicion of incredulity'.

Clampdown   Personally I would clamp down on the use of this word, though I concede that some people do use it in speech – but not often.

Clash   Leave it to the Titans.

Cocktail   'Cocktail of drugs' has become a mind-bending cliché.

Commence   Official-speak for start or begin.

Compared with   'Compared with . . .' is preferred by most writers to 'compared to . . .'. Strictly speaking, A is compared *with* B when you are stressing the difference; A is compared *to* B when you are emphasizing a similarity. 'Shall I compare thee to a summer's day?'

Constructed of   Made of.

Crackdown   Journalese, particularly as a noun.

Crescendo   To say that the noise rose to a crescendo is wrong. Crescendo is a gradual increase in volume or intensity. So the noise, or music, rises to a climax.

Crisis   Like 'chaos', this word has been degraded by over-use. It is also a value-judgement, better left to people being quoted. Use with care. When Manchester United had three midfield players injured, was it a crisis – as described by Radio 5 Live? For one of the most valuable clubs in the world, surely not? If they had been facing bankruptcy, now that would have been a crisis!

Crucial   Another over-used word, which is often deployed by newspaper journalists to dramatise events. Try 'important'.

Crunch   In many stories, it's journalese likely to get your editor's teeth gnashing. But 'credit crunch' was terminology used by the US Federal Reserve more than forty years ago, and when the phrase came into circulation during the lending crisis of 2008/09, it was a convenient short name for the problem, soon understood by all.

Cutbacks   Cut the cutbacks, because 'cuts' is better.

Daring   When used to describe a crime or a military action, it can be taken to indicate our admiration or approval. Best used in this context only when quoting a source.

Dead on arrival (at hospital)   This phrase usually comes from an Ambulance Service duty officer reading the official log to a journalist. In most cases, the main fact will be that the victim was killed in the accident or crime. That is how we should report it. (*See* Officialese.)

Deal   A commonly used journalism word because it's admirably short. But does it suggest shoddy dealing? Try 'agreement' or 'arrangement'.

Death toll   Journalese because it's not spoken English. Is it not better to say, 'at least a hundred thousand people have died in the Haiti earthquake', or 'it's now known that a hundred thousand people were killed', rather than 'the Haiti death toll has reached a hundred thousand'?

Decimate   Best avoided. Technically it means to destroy one tenth of. But it is now widely thought to mean to destroy a large proportion of. Confusing. (It was interesting that at the start of the first Gulf War, the Pentagon announced that the Iraqi Airforce had been 'decimated'. Journalists assumed this meant that most of the planes had been destroyed. It became clear later that many of the pilots had flown to safety in other countries. Perhaps one in ten aircraft had been destroyed.)

Defuse   Means to remove the fuse from, or to reduce tension. It must not be confused with 'diffuse', which means to scatter or spread around, or as an adjective, spread over a large area, verbose or imprecise.

Described as   Described by whom, please?

Different   'Different *from*, not *to* or *than*', says *The Economist Style Guide* firmly. Most writers believe 'different from' is right. 'Different than . . .' certainly isn't. 'It's one of the factors making this recession a bit different than the ones before', opined a senior BBC Economics Correspondent in December 2009. No, different from, please.

Dilemma   Not just a tough decision to be made, a dilemma is a choice between two unpalatable alternatives.

Disinterested   Means impartial, neutral, or having no personal interests involved. Uninterested means not interested.

Dissociate   The correct form of disassociate.

Dozens   Journalists working on international channels should remember that outside Britain, most people haven't a clue what a dozen is. Likewise a score. These are vague words, which all journalists would do well to avoid. 'Several' is another. Can we say how many exactly?

Draconian   Some reporters seem to like this word whenever they mean 'severe' or 'harsh'. Strictly speaking, it should be used to describe very harsh or cruel laws. (Draco was a Greek judge who handed down death sentences for parking chariots on the pavement.) When found in news scripts, deal with it severely.

Dramatic   'Dramatic' and 'drama' should be used on the air very sparingly, and only when a sense of theatre is involved in the event. If there be drama in an event, it should be apparent to everyone.

Drugs   This word does not mean very much. Are we talking about cocaine or aspirin? Try to be specific – heroin, cannabis, LSD, ecstasy, amphetamines – even in headlines.

Dubbed   Journalese. In broadcasting it usually means 'as described rather cleverly by the tabloid newspapers'. Or in some cases described irresponsibly by tabloid newspapers: 'GM Crops, dubbed as Frankenstein Foods . . .' (GMTV, March 2004).

Due to   Try not to confuse this phrase with 'because of'. Play at Lords was stopped (verb) because of rain, but the stoppage (noun) was due to rain. 'Due to' means 'caused by'.

Duped   Journalese.

Effectively   Widely misused to the mild irritation of pedants and scholars. It is not the same as 'in effect'. Effectively means successfully. 'In effect' means to all intents and purposes. 'The South Ossetia war is effectively over' (BBC 5 Live, 2008). No, I think they meant the war was, in effect, over. Tom Fort's *A Pocket Guide to Radio Newswriting* says, 'Effectively is another battle almost lost, I fear, but still worth fighting.'

Electrocute   Technically this means to kill by electric shock. So if the victims survive, they have not been electrocuted; they suffered or received an electric shock.

Emotional appeal   Cliché. 'Emotional plea', worse cliché.

Enormity   Means monstrous wickedness. (*See* section on accuracy, pages 52–58). For great size, use immensity. Or large scale. Or great size!

Ensure   Means to make certain; you insure your property against risk; you assure your life.

Epicentre   The spot on the Earth's surface directly above the focus of an earthquake. So the word should not be used merely as a pompous alternative to 'centre': 'Travel is restricted in the Chinese province thought to be the epicentre of the Sars outbreak' (BBC Radio 2 News). Perhaps the writer was getting confused with the word 'epidemic'.

Epidemic   Are you sure it's an epidemic? Quote who says so. And beware of the possible confusion in the listener's mind with 'endemic', which means 'regularly found in a particular group of people'.

Evacuate   To evacuate means to empty. So, to be strictly accurate, places are evacuated. People are evacuated only when they have been given an enema. Nearby houses were evacuated, or people were moved from nearby houses – not people were evacuated from nearby houses. But John Allen's *BBC News Styleguide* regards this distinction as nitpicking and unsustainable, and concludes, 'Let the people be evacuated.'

Ex-   It's OK to read about an ex-policeman in the newspaper, but it isn't spoken English. Try 'former', or just say 'who used to be a policeman'.

Exceeding (the speed limit)   Speeding.

Exceedingly   Very.

Excess of   More than.

Execute   People are executed only after due legal process. The word should not be used to describe illegal actions, even when groups use the word themselves to imply legitimacy. 'The kidnappers have threatened to execute the hostages ...'. ('If anyone moves I'll execute every last one of you!' screams Hunny-Bunny as she holds up the diner in the film *Pulp Fiction*. At least that is the gist of what she said! Well, no, she was threatening to murder them.)

Eyewitness   Try using 'witness'.

Facilitate   A rather horrible officialese word; 'help' or 'enable' is better.

Fact that   This is almost always a circumlocution, as in 'owing to the fact that ...' Try 'because'.

Farther   Not the same as 'further'. Farther is applied to distance, both literal and figurative. Further means in addition to. 'Nothing could be farther from the truth'. 'A further point is ...'.

Fatwa   A legal opinion delivered by an Islamic court, not necessarily a death sentence.

Fewer   Not to be confused with 'less'. Fewer numbers; less quantity. But quantity seems to include the concept of a single measurement, so it is 'less than two years' and 'less than two miles'.

Fighting for his life   A dreadful cliché. Seriously ill people/babies are usually unconscious. We should stick to the fact that they are 'critically ill'.

First It is an adjective and an adverb. As an adjective, check carefully. Is it really the first? And 'first ever' is tautology. As an adverb, I think 'first' is better than 'firstly', first because it is crisp and easier to say, and secondly because 'firstly' irritates some people. This little word has been the subject of surprisingly fierce argument by scholars over very many years. De Quincy called 'firstly' a 'ridiculous and most pedantic neologism'.

Flaunt Means to display something. Flout means to ignore something disdainfully. You will be flaunting your ignorance if you mix them up.

Fleet Street It's no longer a handy phrase to describe Britain's national press, because all the leading newspapers and news agencies have migrated east to Docklands. Only to be used when talking about the past.

Following Too often used instead of 'after', or 'as a result of', or even 'as'. Also too often used at the start of a sentence.

Forced to This is a judgement rather than a fact. 'Police were forced to open fire' (ITV News) would be better as the straight fact, 'Police opened fire'. (*See* 'Had to'.)

Forensic This has become a tricky adjective in recent years. Do you know what it means? According to the dictionaries, it does not mean 'scientific', it means 'concerned with law courts'. Originally the word comes from the Latin 'forum', meaning the court. So 'forensic scientists' not 'forensic experts' help the police to prepare their case. I have recently started asking classes of media students if they know the meaning of 'forensic'. About 250 have been asked so far. None has got it right. And correspondents I respect have been heard to use such phrases as 'forensic teams are still searching the house and garden here in Soham' (BBC TV News). I guess all the viewers understood, and very few tut-tutted. Nonetheless, many police officers and the people directly involved in the profession of forensic science know the real meaning, and will be unimpressed by the reporter's imprecision. And there's a nice sense of satisfaction in using the word precisely. So I would advocate such uses as 'scientific teams' or 'forensic scientists'.

Fresh Becoming stale from over-use by journalists, as in 'fresh talks are to be held'.

Fulsome Take care. It means excessive, cloying or gushing. Over-generous rather than generous. So to report that the Prime Minister gave fulsome praise to the Chancellor is rather unflattering to both of them.

Gambit It is not a synonym for tactic. It is a technical term in chess meaning the early sacrifice of a piece for advantage later.

Getaway As in 'he made his getaway' is journalese. Better to say he 'got away' or 'he escaped'. When the police tell us 'he made his getaway on foot', perhaps journalists should write something more natural, such as 'he ran off'. And 'he made good his escape' is classic police-speak which should not get into news scripts.

Going forward   Meaning 'in the future'. It's a ghastly example of corporate-speak which seems to have become widely popular – normally with the insincere and pretentious. All I can say is, please avoid it in the future.

Gone missing   Most editors dislike this phrase, arguing that people do not 'go missing'. They are missing, or have been missing since, or they've disappeared. Others are more relaxed about the phrase because it is used in ordinary speech, and 'disappeared' or 'vanished' can suggest that the person has dematerialised, which would be a pretty strong twist to the story. I'm a bit of a traditionalist on this one, and believe that Fred West's victims, Lord Lucan and Osama Bin Laden all 'disappeared' in their different ways.

Green Paper   Traditionally in the British Parliament, and increasingly at the European Commission, this means a consultative document, which may turn into a draft bill, or White Paper. But 'Green Paper' means little to many people; it would be wise to add a line explaining what it is.

Growing tension   Is it a cliché? For how long can tension grow? Quite often, the tension must be continuing.

Gunned down   Journalese from the *Dodge City News*.

Gunshot wounds   This phrase is used surprisingly often by broadcast journalists, and is irritatingly imprecise. 'Bullet wounds' is correct. If a shotgun is used, it should be 'shotgun wounds'. You can hear a gunshot, but I don't think it can draw blood. There must be confusion in the minds of the viewers and listeners between gunshot and shotgun. It's not too difficult to avoid the 'gunshot wounds' cliché in a script. Try hard to find out whether a handgun, a rifle, an automatic weapon or a shotgun was involved in the incident.

Gutted   Try 'burnt out', unless your script is about fish.

Had to   As in 'Gatwick had to be closed' (BBC Radio 2) or 'The village had to be evacuated' (IRN) may be contentious. 'Forced to' as in 'Police were forced to use plastic bullets' is even worse. Stick to the facts.

Hammered out   Used too often for agreements or negotiated settlements; leave it to the Union of Metalworkers.

Head   As a noun it's fine, but as a verb, as in 'Jane Smith is to head the enquiry . . .', is less natural, and 'to head up' is plain horrible.

Headache   Not appropriate for every problem. Use sparingly.

Helping the police with their enquiries   Police official-speak and now journalese. The suspect is possibly being rather unhelpful. 'Being questioned' or 'being interviewed' is much better.

Historic   Means notable in history. Used too frequently. Will this story really find a place in the history books? And when it certainly will, such as Nelson Mandela's release from prison, the word seems to be on every bulletin. Use with extreme care. Incidentally, 'historical' means belonging to history.

Hit out   Like 'lash out' and 'slam', these macho monosyllabic phrases are not normal spoken English. Try 'criticise' or 'condemn'.

Hopefully   'Hopefully she'll reach the summit before the weather closes in' (BBC Radio 4). She may well be climbing hopefully, but our reporter means 'It's hoped she'll reach . . .'. But this word is now understood so widely to mean 'it is hoped' that it is probably pedantic to complain about the new usage. However, BBC World Service's internal style guide still says uncompromisingly, '. . . is misused to such an extent that it may be a lost cause. Do not use'.

Hospitalise   American word for admit/send/take to hospital, which pops up in agency copy, but is not used in speech by most people in Britain. (*See* section on Americanisms, pages 34–39.)

However   In the sense of nevertheless, this word is hardly ever used in spoken English. To be avoided in broadcast scripts.

Hurt   Another of those short newspaper headline words that have percolated into the text of stories. It is better to say 'injured' in an accident or 'wounded' in battle.

Imply and infer   'Imply' means to suggest without stating directly. 'Infer' means to deduce. So a speaker implies what the listener infers. 'What are you inferring?' (wrong). I am implying that journalists should not mix up these two words.

Important   *The Economist Style Guide* advises – if something is important, say why and to whom; use sparingly.

In collision with   Police-speak for 'collided'; quite often it's possible to say, 'the bus hit a car', or 'a train hit a van', without implying blame or attracting a lawsuit. (*See* section on officialese, pages 23–26.)

In connection with   'Being questioned in connection with' is official-speak for being questioned about something.

Industrial action   Usually means inaction, which can come in many forms. If it is an indefinite strike, say so. Or if it is a work-to-rule, or an overtime ban, say so. If a trades union is threatening industrial action, try to specify the precise nature of the threat if you can.

Inferno   Fire. Consign 'inferno' to the blaze, along with 'blaze'.

Inflammable   Surely only the English language could come up with the inconsistency that 'incombustible' describes something that won't burn, and 'inflammable' describes something that will, as does 'flammable', which is being used more and more instead of 'inflammable' to avoid any dangerous misunderstandings. I guess that 'inflammable' will be consigned to the flames before too long. But for now, it means combustible.

Infrastructure   Is this not official-speak jargon?

Inform   Tell.

Initiate   Start or begin.

Innocent victim   People killed or injured when not committing a crime are invariably innocent, so the adjective can often be dropped. Does it imply that other victims are somehow guilty?

Involved   A word very popular with journalists, which can be used too often and too vaguely. Originally meaning complex or tangled, it should really be used only when that kind of entanglement is involved. There are many other words that are more apt for each circumstance: 'flexible working is *included* in the agreement'; 'two hundred staff are *engaged* in the strike'; 'the chairman is *implicated* in the fraud'.

Ironically   This is a particularly irritating example of journalese. The word is rarely used in normal speech, but is regularly wheeled out by writers who do not know what it means. Irony is a subtle concept. Look it up in the dictionary. It is not the same as paradox or coincidence. Bryson calls it 'the use of words to convey a contradiction between the literal and intended meanings'. It certainly has nothing to do with the man of the match missing a late penalty. If you spot a curious paradox, coincidence, or even a genuine irony in a story, the listener is quite capable of noticing it too. All in all, it's a word to avoid.

Jail   Prison is better, but the verb 'jailed' is much more widely used than the rather archaic 'imprisoned'. 'Sent to prison' is probably best. In broadcasting, don't spell it 'gaol'. Newsreaders may easily misread it as 'goal'.

Jets   It is surprising that we still hear 'an attack by fighter-jets' or 'jet fighters were scrambled'. Do we really believe that some fighters in the twenty-first century have propellers?

Joyriding   This word, invented by a tabloid journalist in the '80s, conveniently summarised the growing problem of youths driving stolen cars at speed. But it soon became clear that the word greatly upset the families who had been affected by death or injury caused by these incidents. No joy for them. The police believe the word glamorises the offence of 'aggravated vehicle-taking'. In 1992, the BBC issued guidelines to its staff to avoid the word 'joyriding' unless it is attributed. It's better just to describe what happened, or at the very least say 'so-called joyriding'.

Justify   Do not use this when you mean 'defend'. Not 'the Chancellor justified the tax increase' but 'the Chancellor tried to justify' or 'defended' the increase.

Key   As in key issues, key decisions and key meetings, it's becoming rather a tedious adjective. Likewise 'keynote' for a speech or address.

Kick-start   An economists' cliché, best left to motorbikes.

Languishing   In jail, of course. Do not allow this cliché any freedom in your scripts.

Lash out   When referring to verbal criticism, this is a tabloidese exaggeration.

Last ditch   Cliché.

Launch   This is another of those monosyllables that has become a routine word for the journalist. Not only boats are launched nowadays, but also campaigns, books, initiatives, plans, schemes and websites. Must we use this word every time? And surely it should not be used as an intransitive verb, as in 'BBC Three launched in 2003'.

Lay and lie   These two verbs are confused more and more, but there really is no excuse for a journalist to get them wrong. Lay is transitive, with past tense laid. Lie is intransitive, with past tense lay. Pop music has been very influential in mixing them up. Bob Dylan implored the lady to lay across his big brass bed. Lay what? The coverlet? Eggs?

Learned   It has become fashionable for news items to begin with 'The BBC has learned . . .' or 'Sky News has learned . . .' to indicate an exclusive, without using the word 'exclusive'. I dislike this trend. The broadcaster is not the main point of the story, which should come first. It also sounds like a confession that broadcasters hardly ever have original stories. Can you imagine reading in a newspaper, 'The *Telegraph* has learned that . . .'? This introduction should be reserved for very occasional and very significant exclusive information.

Less   Is not the same as fewer. (*See* Amount.) Less refers to quantity and fewer to numbers. Less football, but fewer matches. 'Less than a hundred people turned up' is an ugly error, which many people watching or listening will dislike.

Literally   If we are scrupulously accurate in our reporting, the word will be tautological. But when it is used in metaphor, it becomes fatuous. 'He literally flew down the back straight' (BBC Local Radio, 1987). Remarkable story!

Luxuriant   'She spent the money on a luxuriant lifestyle.' No, it was luxurious. Luxuriant refers to something that grows profusely.

Magnitude   Size.

Major   A much over-used adjective, often superfluous, especially when describing a speech.

Management   Without the definite article, this is union-speak. Say '*the* management' or '*the* company'. (*See* section on the definite article, pages 33–34.)

Manhunt   Was the title of a rather exciting American TV series many years ago. But it is not spoken English. Police search, or murder hunt, is better.

Manufacture   Make.

Mass   Is celebrated or said, not held.

Massive   An over-used word. It means very large and solid. Hardly the adjective for security, or a heart attack.

Meanwhile   Classic journalese. This word is hardly ever used in normal speech, and is very rarely used by top-class correspondents. Unfortunately, it is all over broadcast news, popping up relentlessly as a link-word between two loosely connected stories. 'Meanwhile' is loved by sport reporters for reasons unknown. If you have two related stories or sporting events, please try cutting the 'meanwhile', and let the reader's voice indicate the connection.

Meet with   This American and international usage is disliked by some British listeners. I think that 'meet' or 'will have a meeting with' is still preferable, because it will irritate no one. (*See* section on Americanisms, pages 34–39). *The BBC News Styleguide* is uncompromising: 'In North America, people *meet with* other people. Everywhere else, they *meet* them.' As for 'met up with', the broadcaster John Humphrys calls this a hideous American import, and has offered a bottle of bubbly to anyone who can explain how the phrase differs from 'met'. The bottle is still sitting in his office.

Mercy   As in mercy flight. 'Relief flight' is better. Mercy dash? Please no! As for 'mercy-killing', it's an emotive journalese phrase which is best avoided.

Miraculously   Elliot's *A Question of Style* asked in 1979, 'Who are we to determine God's work?' As with many adjectives designed to dramatise a story, when spoken by a broadcast journalist, it sounds like over-sell.

Mob   Should not be used as an alternative word for crowds, demonstrators or rioters, unless you are quoting someone.

Morgue   An Americanism. In Britain, bodies are taken to a mortuary. They might then be subject to a post-mortem examination, not an autopsy.

Moribund   Sometimes used in business reporting, as in 'the German economy is moribund'. Take care. It is sometimes taken to mean 'lacking in vitality', but technically means 'about to die'. Many viewers and listeners will not know what it means, so it's a word to avoid.

Move   As a noun meaning development or decision, it is journalese.

Nationwide   Is the name of a financial services group that sponsors football; and years ago was the name of a very good BBC TV programme. 'National' is preferable for events, trends or surveys that take place across the whole country (though in Britain there can be confusion between the nations of the UK, so more precise phraseology might be necessary, 'across the UK' or 'a survey in Scotland').

Near miss   When two aircraft pass each other at uncomfortably close range, most people call it a 'near miss'. Some editors and those in the aviation industry are surprisingly agitated by this description, arguing that it is a 'near collision' or an 'air miss'. The Civil Aviation Authority obfuscates this uncomfortable subject by calling it an 'airprox incident'! I think that 'near miss' is very widely used and understood, and I have no objection to it. But check with your editors before you use the phrase, in case it sends any of them into a flat spin.

New   Sometimes used unnecessarily. 'In a new report from the Consumers' Association.' I think the audience assumes that items on the news are new.

Non-payment of   Legal jargon for 'not paying'.

None   Should take a singular verb, being a shortened form of 'not one' or 'no one'. 'None of our aircraft is missing'. But most people would say 'none of our aircraft are missing', and I think the precise usage is getting close to being archaic. When you think none of the older listeners and viewers care any more, then feel free to use the plural, as I have just done. But I reckon there are still plenty of people around to spot the perceived error, and I advise writers to stick to the singular.

Normality   This Americanism has almost become the norm now. But not quite. In the UK, things do not get restored to normality, they are restored to normal. And they certainly should not be 'normalised'.

Numerous   Many.

On the increase/decline   or even 'on the up'. Increasing or declining is better.

Ongoing   An unpleasant and unnecessary word.

Only   Try to make sure that it goes in the right place and qualifies the right word if there is any danger of confusion. 'Only he swore at Beckham.' 'He only swore at Beckham.' 'He swore only at Beckham.' The sentences have different meanings. But do what sounds most natural. I can't imagine Michael Caine in *The Italian Job* exclaiming, 'You were supposed to blow only the bloody doors off!'

Opinion polls   Should be treated with great caution. In recent years in Britain, there have been a succession of embarrassingly inaccurate opinion polls. The BBC Editorial Guidelines say, 'Do not use language which gives greater credibility to the polls than they deserve.' So opinion polls 'suggest' or 'indicate' rather than 'show', and they never 'prove' anything.

Order to   'In order to . . .' is very formal language bordering on officialese. The word 'to' on its own is much more natural

Oust   Journalese, or at best boardroom-battle jargon.

Over   For reasons unknown, this has become a journalese word, as in 'Police are questioning a sixteen-year-old youth over the death of . . .'. Surely they are questioning him about the crime, not over the crime. 'There are concerns over . . .' should be concerns about, and 'fears over' is better expressed as 'fears of'.

Pair   Meaning two people being sought by police, is journalese. 'The pair were spotted in Blackpool.' Duo is worse. Trio is sometimes used in newspapers for three missing people or suspects. These short words are used to avoid repetition as well as for brevity, but they are not used much in speech. 'The two suspects' or 'The two missing people' is better and only slightly more wordy.

Participate   Take part in.

Per cent   Some financial journalists insist on saying 'a half of one per cent'. I guess this is because 'per cent' technically means out of a hundred. So to say 'half a per cent' or 'a half per cent' is the equivalent of saying 'a half of out of a hundred'. Nonetheless, I reckon that the vast majority of people will tell each other, 'interest rates have gone up half a per cent'. It's perfectly clear, and to use the technically correct phraseology is in danger of sounding pedantic.

Plea   Journalese.

Pledge   Usually journalese, as in 'campaigners have pledged to carry on the fight'.

Plunge   Fall, unless into water.

Poised   About to; ready to.

Police in   'Police in . . . (wherever)' opens news stories far too often. Try it a different way. If you must start the story this way, say *'The* police . . .'. (*See* section on the definite article, pages 33–34.)

Pre-   This prefix can be unnecessary. Pre-planned, pre-conditions, pre-record are tautology.

Press conference   This is clearly acceptable. But many broadcasters prefer 'news conference'. Broadcast journalists are not the press.

Prior to   Officialese. A pompous way of saying 'before'.

Pro-life campaigner   Originating in the USA, this self-adopted name is politically contentious. Most script-writers stick to 'anti-abortion campaigner'.

Probe   A medical word, describing what doctors do and use. Does not apply easily to police officers or committees of MPs.

Protagonist   The principal character in a drama. Technically there can be only one, but now it's generally accepted that there can be a few main characters – the protagonists. So to say 'the main protagonists' is a waste of a word. And it does not mean adversaries, as some seem to think. That would be 'antagonists'.

Pushing the envelope   Originally referring to a fighter aircraft's known operational limits, this rather irritating phrase is sometimes used to describe anything which seems to be extending the boundaries, from a computer program to a rugby performance. It has pushed its way into the envelope marked 'journalese'.

Quantum leap   A cliché, which is also technically inaccurate. Quantum physics is difficult for most of us to understand, but I'm told 'quantum' means enough to change the state or sufficient to be altered. The *Concise Oxford Dictionary* describes a quantum leap as 'a sudden transition in an atom', though it also acknowledges the phrase can mean 'a sudden large increase or advance'.

Quit   Journalese. Resign. Leave. Give up.

Quiz   As a noun meaning a TV or radio programme, yes. As a verb meaning to interrogate, no.

Refute   Means to prove something wrong, not merely to argue against it, deny it or reject it.

Regretfully   Not to be confused with 'regrettably'. The first means with feelings of regret. 'Regretfully they said their goodbyes.' 'Regrettably their mother could not be there to see them off.'

Rendered   (. . . first aid); gave it.

Repeat   'Repeat again' is a tautology. 'Again' is usually superfluous with 're-' words such as reaffirm and reiterate. To be technically correct, 'iterate' means repeat, so to 'reiterate again' is to re-re-repeat.

Request   Ask.

Responsibility   'The dissident republican group the Real IRA have claimed responsibility' can sound like a boast, and offends many listeners who think planting bombs is irresponsible. 'The dissident republican group the Real IRA say they planted the bomb' is better. Incidentally, things cannot bear responsibility for anything. Bad weather can't be responsible for higher potato prices. It's the cause.

Rocks   In Britain, rocks are too big and heavy to throw. Only the Americans have the muscle to throw rocks. We Brits throw stones, and the occasional brick.

Row   This journalese monosyllable should not be an automatic synonym for any debate, dispute, argument or difference of opinion. Save it for the verified shouting-match.

Rubbish   In more formal English, this is a noun, not a verb. And in Britain we do not talk about trash, and we very rarely mention garbage, though garbage is rising! I confess I quite like to hear a political correspondent, in the less formal style of a two-way interview, using rubbish as a verb: 'The Leader of the Opposition rubbished the plans . . .', but that is not acceptable on the lips of a newsreader.

Rush to hospital   Emergency patients are always taken there as quickly as sensible. And ambulances are not always in fleets. Try to give the numbers involved.

Safe haven   Some people are irritated by this phrase because a haven is by definition a safe place of shelter – originally for ships. An unsafe haven would be a contradiction in terms.

Scene   This is an officialese word often used by fire and police officers. 'Four appliances attended the scene.' 'He was pronounced dead at the scene.' Journalists should try to avoid using the word in this context.

Scheme   A popular news-script word. But it is not used very often in conversation. And does it suggest scheming or dishonest dealing? Try plan, idea, project or proposal.

Secret talks   'Secret talks are continuing to settle the postal workers' dispute . . .' (BBC Radio 2). This sounds rather ridiculous. If they are secret, how does Radio 2 know they are taking place? If they are at a secret location, we should make that clear.

See   Try to avoid endowing inanimate things with the power of sight: 'BA saw its profits nosedive . . .'; '1903 saw the first manned flight . . .'.

Set   According to one TV script, Prince Charles was 'set to step into a row', which in my view is condensed journalese. 'Set' is particularly popular in sport scripts, when an injured player is 'set to make a comeback'. Try to confine its use to jellies and tea-tables.

Sewerage   Sewage is waste; sewerage is the system that carries away the sewage.

Ships   Used to be feminine. In my view they have now been de-sexed in general usage and news bulletins, but preserve their femininity in commentaries describing ceremonial occasions.

Shot in the arm   Not only a cliché; since the spread of hard drugs, the imagery is questionable.

Shun   To be shunned, because rarely used in spoken English.

Sighed with relief   Aaah. Cliché.

Situation   As in 'crisis situation'. It is an unnecessary word and can lead to a listener irritation situation.

Smoking gun   Has in recent years become a cliché meaning a crucial piece of evidence which indicates guilt in a crime. Take care. Yes, it's a dramatic metaphor. But can papers in the Vatican archive, indicating that during the Second World War the Pope did not protest vigorously enough about the Jewish genocide, be described as a 'smoking gun'? (BBC Radio News). Surely you would not describe it this way when relating the story to a friend.

Some   In the '90s, this suddenly came into vogue, as in, 'Some two hundred people . . .' Do we mean 200, or more than 200, or at least 200, or about 200? 'Some 200' is imprecise, and rather pompous. It seems to work in solemn reports, or in descriptions of state occasions, but for routine stories it seems pretentious. It certainly isn't the way most people speak.

Spark off   Cliché.

Spell out   Cliché.

Spree   Tabloidese.

Standstill   'Overnight snow brought motorways almost to a complete standstill' (BBC Radio 2, 1991). In Dublin, RTE journalists were once instructed in a memo from the editor to bring this kind of convoluted usage to a halt!

Stepping up   As in 'Thompson is stepping up his attack on bad English usage', is out of step with Good Spoken English.

Stricken   As in famine-stricken or poverty-stricken is archaic usage, except in the scripts of some cliché-writers.

Strike action   Journalese. In conversation we would be unlikely to say, 'London tube drivers are threatening strike action'. The drivers are threatening to strike or go on strike.

Subsequently   Later. And 'subsequent to . . .' means after.

Substantial   Unless quoting a source directly, it would be more natural to say 'large' or even 'big'.

Suffer   As in 'He suffered a broken leg' is officialese. In real speech, you would be much more likely to say 'He broke his leg'. And 'She suffers from cancer' is better expressed as 'She has cancer'.

Sufficient   Enough.

Sustain fatal injuries   Die.

Sweeping changes   Is this now a cliché?

Swoop   Hawks do. Police don't. Even at dawn.

Taliban   Note that it's plural. It means 'students'.

Target   Is this used too often by journalists? It's a metaphorical word. You can aim at a target, hit it, miss it or undershoot it. But can you stay within it? Is it the same as an objective or planned expenditure? Maybe writers can give 'target' a temporary respite.

Temporary respite   A respite can only be temporary, so you can cut the adjective and save half a second.

That   This is used much more in written English than in the spoken language. 'He insisted that the congestion charge would be a boon' is technically correct reported speech, but most people would say, 'He insisted the congestion charge would be a boon'. Elliot describes this word as 'the most intrusive, over-used and usually irrelevant word in sentence construction'. So *that's* what it is!

The then   As in 'the then Scotland Manager' is an ugly expression. The quest for brevity should never lead to unnatural usage like this. Say 'So-and-so, who was the Scotland Manager at the time . . .'.

Today   With rolling news channels, and many big events reported live, the audience is likely to assume that they are watching or hearing about today's events. Many years ago, when satellite technology was making its first impact, the ITN notice board displayed a slogan from the editor: 'Todayness has impact'. Surely not today? And where does the writer put the word 'today'? 'The Select Committee looking into the origins of the Iraq war will meet today relatives of some of the troops who died' (*BBC Breakfast*, October 2009) It sounds unnatural. This morning, this afternoon, tonight, may have more relevance. If they are to be used, I suggest such words or phrases words are put in their natural place: 'Later this morning/this afternoon the Select Committee . . . will meet relatives of some of the troops who died . . .' or 'members of the Select Committee are meeting . . .' (you don't have to write 'today').

Toddler   Tabloidese. One small step away from tot, or even tiny tot.

Top-level   Overused.

Total   Often a meaningless adjective. 'Total shutdown.' 'Total extinction.' (Total and utter? – Rik Mayall in *The Young Ones*.)

Tracker dogs   Journalese. As is 'sniffer-dogs'. 'Police with dogs' is usually perfectly clear.

Tragedy   Another over-used reporter-word. Properly derived from Greek drama, it should indicate an important person's downfall initiated by his or her own actions. In modern usage, the word at least requires a sense of scale if it is not to be devalued by over-use.

Transpired   Does not mean 'took place' as in 'The Mayor had a different version of what transpired' (*The New York Times*). Nor does it mean turned out. It means emerged or leaked out.

Trigger off   Cliché.

Try and   Many people regard this as sloppy. 'Try to . . .' is correct.

U-turn   Much overused, particularly by political correspondents, some of whom remember Mrs Thatcher's famous 'you turn if you want to' speech. It should only be used for a sudden and complete reversal of policy.

Undergone   As in surgery. It's probably more natural to say 'had'.

Under consideration   Is officialese, much better expressed as 'being considered'. Likewise 'under preparation'. 'Under the circumstances' is better, as 'in this/that case'.

Under way   Used in scripts far too much; people don't use this phrase in normal conversation very often. 'An attempt is under way . . .', 'A search is under way . . .'. The simple active voice is usually better: 'They're trying to . . .', 'The police are searching . . .'.

Unique   By definition, the word cannot be qualified, as in 'quite unique' or 'totally unique' (although I would not quarrel with 'almost unique').

Utilise   Official-speak for 'use'.

Valued at   Worth. But take care. Damage cannot be worth anything. It may be estimated to cost quite a lot. Valuations of fire damage, stolen items or 'lost production' can be exaggerated. It is wise to attribute them.

Vehicle   A world seldom used in spoken English. Try to say what kind. 'Motor vehicle' is officialese.

Victim   Victims of AIDS or cancer victims are victims of insensitive journalism. People have AIDS or cancer. They are patients, not victims.

Virtually   It means 'in effect', not 'nearly'. It's now misused so widely in spoken English that it is virtually a lost cause, but good writers avoid this usage.

Vital   Much over-used.

Vowed   Promised/threatened/predicted/said.

Walkabout   When the Queen walked up to the crowds for the first time on a tour of Australia, 'went walkabout' was a very clever piece of journalism. Now it has become a rather tedious cliché. The British royals have a long-established policy of contacting people directly on nearly every visit. Elliot's guide says, 'Went walkabout smacks of the nursery'.

Walked free   (from court). Cliché.

Warders   No, they are prison officers.

Wed   As in 'Joan Collins to wed again' is journalese (unless you are deliberately deploying a North of England usage).

Well planned   If we report that robberies are 'daring' or 'well planned', it might seem to indicate approval or admiration. Better to say 'carefully planned'.

Which   Is often confused with 'that'. It's correct to use 'that' when the following words qualify the noun, rather than act as a subordinate clause, or take you on to a new idea. 'This is the car that was used in this carefully planned robbery'. 'This car, which was used in the robbery, had been stolen a week earlier.' 'This is the stolen car, which someone may have seen parked in this street.'

While   It means 'during the time that', and is also acceptable as 'although': 'While I can understand your position, I can't agree . . .'. But it should not be used to mean 'and' or 'whereas'. (It's nonsense to write, 'The Party Chairman opened the conference with a silent prayer while the Prime Minister delivered a stirring call for unity.')

Whose   Can be used with things as well as people. 'The tree whose branches were laden with apples . . .' is correct, and far better than 'The tree, the branches of which . . .'.

Widespread anxiety   A cliché which causes some programme editors mild concern.

World   As in 'the world of entertainment, or athletics, or business'; it is usually quite easy to drop the world.

Further reading

There are scores of books about the English language, writing and journalism, though surprisingly not all that many about writing for broadcast news and current affairs. Here is a selection of books and websites you might find most useful.

BROADCAST JOURNALISM AND BROADCASTING TECHNIQUES

Block, Mervin, *Writing Broadcast News*, Bonus Books Chicago, 1997 (American usage)

Boyd, Andrew, *Broadcast Journalism – Techniques of Radio and TV News*, Focal Press, 5th edition, 2000

Chantler, Paul and Harris, Sim, *Local Radio Journalism*, Focal Press, 1997

Chantler, Paul and Stewart, Peter, *Essential Radio Journalism*, Methuen Drama, 2009

Fleming, Carole, *The Radio Handbook*, Routledge, 3rd edition, 2009

Griffiths, Richard, *Videojournalism*, Focal Press, 1998

Holland, Patricia, *The Television Handbook*, Routledge, 2002

Hudson, Gary and Rowlands, Sarah, *The Broadcast Journalism Handbook*, Longman, 2nd edition, 2007

Marr, Andrew, *My Trade – A Short History of British Journalism*, Pan Books, 2005

Ray, Vin and Simpson, John, *The Television News Handbook*, Macmillan, 2003

Wilson, John, *Understanding Journalism*, Routledge, 1996

Yorke, Ivor, *Basic TV Reporting*, Focal Press, 2nd edition, 1997

THE DEVELOPMENT AND USE OF THE ENGLISH LANGUAGE

Amis, Kingsley, *The King's English*, HarperCollins, 1998

Bragg, Melvyn, *The Routes of English*, BBC Publications, 1999

Bryson, Bill, *Mother Tongue*, Penguin, 2009

Burchfield, R.W., *Fowler's Modern English Usage*, Oxford University Press, 2004

Burchfield, R.W., *The English Language*, Oxford University Press, revised 2006

Cochrane, James, *Between You and I: A Little Book of Bad English*, Icon Books, 2003 (revised edn 2005)

Crystal, David, *The Cambridge Encyclopedia of the English Language*, Cambridge University Press, 2nd edition, 2003

Fowler, H.W. and Fowler, F.G., *The King's English*, Oxford Language Classics, Oxford University Press, 2003

Gowers, Ernest, *The Complete Plain Words*, Penguin, 3rd edition, 2004

McCrum, Robert, MacNeil, Robert and Cran, William, *The Story of English*, Faber, 2002

Merriam-Webster's Collegiate Dictionary (American usage), Merriam Webster Publishing, Springfield, USA, 2004. www.m-w.com

Orwell, George, *Politics and the English Language* (in *Collected Essays*), Penguin, 2000

Oxford English Dictionary (2005) and *Concise Oxford Dictionary Revised* (2009), Oxford University Press. www.oed.com

Partridge, Eric, *Usage and Abusage: A Guide to Good English*, Penguin, 3rd edition, 2005

Wells, J.C., *Longman Pronunciation Dictionary*, Longman, 2008

GUIDES TO WRITING STYLE IN JOURNALISM AND OTHER REFERENCES

Allen, John, *The BBC News Styleguide*, BBC Training and Development, 2003. www.bbctraining.com/pdfs/newsstyleguide.pdf

Banks, David and Hanna, Mark, *McNae's Essential Law for Journalists*, Oxford University Press, 2009

BBC College of Journalism. www.bbc.co.uk/journalism/skills

BBC Editorial Guidelines. www.bbc.co.uk/editorialguidelines

Bryson, Bill, *Troublesome Words*, Penguin, 2009

Centre for Policy Studies, *Lexicon of Contemporary Newspeak*, CPS, 2008 (*The 2009 Lexicon: A Guide to Contemporary Newspeak* can be downloaded from www.cps.org.uk)

Crockford's Clerical Dictionary, Church House Publishing, 2010

The Economist Style Guide, Profile Books, 9th edn, 2009. www.economist.com/research/StyleGuide

Evans, Harold, *Essential English*, Pimlico, 2000

Fort, Tom, *A Pocket Guide to Radio Newswriting*, BBC Radio News, 1999

Granada plc, *ITV Cultural Diversity Guide*, 2003. email to request a copy: cultural-diversity@granadamedia.com

Hicks, Wynford, *English for Journalists*, Routledge, 3rd edition, 2006

Hicks, Wynford with Adams, Sally, Gilbert, Harriett and Holmes, Tim, *Writing for Journalists*, Routledge, 2nd edition, 2008

Keeble, Richard, *Ethics for Journalists*, Routledge, 2nd edition, 2008

Marsh, David and Hodsdon, Amelia, The *Guardian, Observer and guardian.co.uk style guide*, Guardian Books, 2010. www.guardian.co.uk/styleguide

Ministry of Justice (terminology for the judiciary). www.judiciary.gov.uk/about_judiciary/forms_of_address/index.htm

The New Oxford Dictionary for Writers and Editors, Oxford University Press, 2005

The Times Concise Atlas of the World, eleventh edition, Times Books, 2009

The Times Guide to English Style and Usage, Times Books, 1999

Waterhouse, Keith, *Waterhouse on Newspaper Style*, Penguin, 1993

Weber Shandwick Adamson, *Interactive Guide to the European Union*. www.webershandwick-eu.com/reports-and-guides/interactive-guides

Index